ROSELLINI

Immigrants' Son and Progressive Governor

ROSELLINI

Immigrants' Son and Progressive Governor

Payton Smith

University of Washington Press
Seattle and London

Library of Congress
Cataloging-in-Publication Data
Smith, Payton.
    Rosellini : immigrants' son and progressive
governor / Payton Smith.
        p.   cm.
    Includes index.
    ISBN 0-295-97595-4 (alk. paper)
    1. Rosellini, Albert D. (Albert Dean),
    1910–   . 2. Governors—Washington
    (State)—Biography.   3. Washington
    (State)—Politics and government—
    1951–   . I. Title.
    F895.22.R67S65   1997
    979.7'043'092—dc21
    [B]   96-40135
                                              CIP

∞The paper used in this publication meets the
minimum requirements of American National
Standard for Information Sciences—Permanence
of Paper for Printed Library Materials, ANSI
Z39.48-1984.

Contents

Acknowledgments   vii

Introduction   3

1. The Early Years   10
2. The State Senate
   and a Political Agenda   22
3. Legislative Priorities   33
4. Statewide Investigations   43
5. The First Campaign for Governor   58
6. Public Perceptions:
   A Politician Practicing Law   66
7. Langlie and Rosellini   74
8. Launching an Administration   97
9. Budget Reform   108
10. Institutional Reform   115
11. Higher Education   132
12. Economic Development   140
13. The Second Lake Washington Bridge   159
14. Taxes and the 1960 Campaign   175
15. Rosellini, Evans, and the 1964
    Campaign   195
16. The Campaigns of 1969 and 1972   212
17. Epilogue and Conclusion   227

Chronology   234

Notes   237

Index   259

Acknowledgments

A first-time author could not complete this kind of work without a great deal of assistance from a host of individuals. My acknowledgments and thanks, therefore, are owed to many friends, partners, acquaintances, and loved ones whose encouragement, ideas, research, and moral support shaped and guided this book. At every step I received support in ways I cannot state, nor can my thanks do justice to the people listed here. While I have tried to include everyone, I am sure I have overlooked someone because of my errant recordkeeping. My sincere apologies if that is the case.

First, I want to thank those friends of Governor Rosellini who generously contributed the funds necessary to assist my research efforts: Walter Straley, H. DeWayne Kreager, Richard D. Ford, Ancil H. Payne, Robert J. Block (died March 1996), Morrie and Joan Alhadeff (Morrie died March 1996), James R. Ellis, Bert McNae, Stanley D. Golub, Victor Rosellini, George Prescott, Gerald Grinstein, Robert J. Williams (died June 1995), George M. Haskett, Bernice Stern, Jack Gordon, and Andrew V. Smith. I am especially indebted to Walter Straley, Richard Ford, and DeWayne Kreager, who coordinated this fund-raising effort and also succeeded in obtaining matching gifts from U.S. West Communications and AT&T. I was gratified that all of these gifts and contributions qualified as matching funds for the University of washingion Press's National Endowment for the Humanities Challenge Grant, which was successfully met in 1991 and 1992. Walt Straley, in addition, not only quarterbacked the fund-raising effort but provided constructive suggestions upon reading an early draft of the manuscript.

Second, I want to thank all those individuals who provided critical information and insights about the personal and political life of Governor Rosellini as well as about the events chronicled in this biography. Each and every one of them was extremely cooperative, candid and forthcoming. They are (in alphabetical order): Ida Bachechi, Warren Bishop, Robert J. Block, Virginia Burnside, Dr. William Conte, Governor Daniel J. Evans, Edward Guthman, Louis Guzzo, George Haskett, Charles Hodde, Gerald A. Hoeck, Frank Keller, H. DeWayne Kreager, Herbert Legg, George Mack, John L. O'Brien, Dr. Charles E. Odegaard, Mrs. Ray Olson, Ancil H. Payne, Maryann E. Reynolds, B. J. Rhay, Ethel Rosellini, Evelyn (Mrs. Dean) Rosellini, Lynn Rosellini, Victor Rosellini, Shelby Scates, Henry Siedel, David Sprague, Scott Wallace, and David G. Wood. Warren Bishop, in particular, as Rosellini's chief of staff during the administration, provided an overview that was critical to my analysis of a number of issues. I want to pay a special tribute to my friend Bob Block, who passed away before this book was completed. His life, as well as his words of encouragement, was an inspiration that helped me through some times when I had doubts about completing the manuscript.

Third, I want to express my appreciation and thanks to the staff of the Washington State Archives, who never tired of my questions or need for assistance. They were excited by my topic and gave me all the help I needed—and more. Timothy Fredericks, Director of the Archives Oral History Project, early on guided me to the critical research materials I needed. Pat Hopkins, Chief Assistant Archivist, always exuded enthusiastic confidence in the project, and gave me the kind of assistance that ensured the completeness of my research. David W. Hastings, Kathleen Waugh, Faith Meek, and Dean and Mary Vanderhoof were also extremely helpful. In the latter stages, George Scott, after he became State Archivist, became a good friend and supporter of the book's completion.

Fourth, I need to mention the authors of a number of books and articles critical to my research and writing. Anyone who is interested in the historical events that shaped Governor Rosellini's political life would enjoy reading the respective works, cited in my end notes, of Ken Bellington, Norman Clark, Edward E. Carlson, David Nicandri, Murray Morgan, Eric Scigliano, and George Scott. I was fortunate enough to be able to talk to Ken Bellington, Norman Clark, David

Nicandri, and George Scott as my research and work progressed. Each of them offered helpful analytical comments. I would be remiss if I did not make special mention of George Scott's excellent Ph.D. thesis on Governor Arthur Langlie. His research and insights about the circumstances of the state's institutions in the late 1940s and early 1950s were invaluable as was his information concerning the 1952 and 1956 campaigns involving Langlie and Rosellini. My discussions in Chapters 5 and 7 were greatly assisted by his detailed work.

Fifth, I need to thank those whose research assistance was instrumental. Kathleen Waugh of the Archives staff was amazing in her analysis of the vast material concerning our state's institutions as well as the details of the 1963 coalition that controlled the legislative council. Elizabeth Smith, my daughter, spent many hours analyzing and describing the complex legislative events surrounding Governor Rosellini's approach to taxes and the fascinating circumstances of the crime hearings in 1951 and early 1952. Without her keen eye critical aspects of Governor Rosellini's administration and career would have been missing. Jan Creighton, at an early stage, recognized, in ways that I had overlooked, the importance of Governor Rosellini's heritage and background to his political career. Her research and guidance in this area were invaluable. Professor Dennis Willows of the University of Washington's Friday Harbor Laboratories read the chapter on the Second Lake Washington Bridge and gave much-needed insight and perspective. I also want to thank Paula Brady, Jennifer Knapp, Sharman Webb, and Marilyn Pleskoff for their typing and editorial assistance.

Sixth, I want to thank a number of my friends at the University of Washington Press as well as my partners at Davis Wright Tremaine for their support and encouragement. Donald R. Ellegood, Pat Soden, Naomi Pascal, Julidta Tarver, Robert Hutchins, and Cynthia Wilke of the University of Washington Press, were always supportive—even when it seemed like nothing was happening. Their enthusiasm for the book never waned and for that I am in their debt. A number of my law partners, Richard Derham, Michael Green, Edward N. Lange, Bradley Diggs, Keith Allred, Dennis McLean, P. Cameron DeVore, and Donna Peck-Gaines, encouraged me in ways they probably do not remember. Dick Derham, in particular, read drafts of chapters and gave me constructive suggestions that greatly improved my objectivity. Brad Diggs, as the managing partner of my firm, generously allowed me to take an unplanned sabbatical in the fall of 1995 so that I could complete the manuscript.

Seventh, I want to thank David G. Wood, Virginia Burnside, and Scott Wallace for allowing me unfettered access to their private collections of materials, newspaper clippings, and memorabilia concerning Governor Rosellini. Their collections were critical to my discussion of a number of events surrounding his campaigns in 1956, 1969, and 1972 and provided key information about Governor Rosellini as a candidate for office and the issues he addressed. Along the same lines I want to salute those family members, secretaries, and members of Governor Rosellini's staff when he was a lawyer and legislator who kept a complete clipping file of newspaper accounts of his activities from 1933 to 1952. Without these sources my analysis and study of Governor Rosellini's early life and legislative career would have been extremely difficult and perhaps impossible.

Last, but by no means least, I want to acknowledge the debt I owe to the two people who were ultimately responsible for the book. Governor Rosellini spent virtually hundreds of hours (or so it seemed) with me in going over events and circumstances. He was unfailingly honest and forthright regardless of the frank nature of my questions or my implied criticism, at times, of what I was hearing. He is a man who is humble to a fault (at least compared to other politicians I know) and I had to pry many details from him over countless lunches and meetings. Finally, I want to thank my wife, Patsy, whose outstanding editorial and organizational skills largely molded my comments, descriptions, and insights into a readable whole. Her ideas and suggestions were always on the mark and to the point. Without her talent and steady encouragement the book would never have happened.

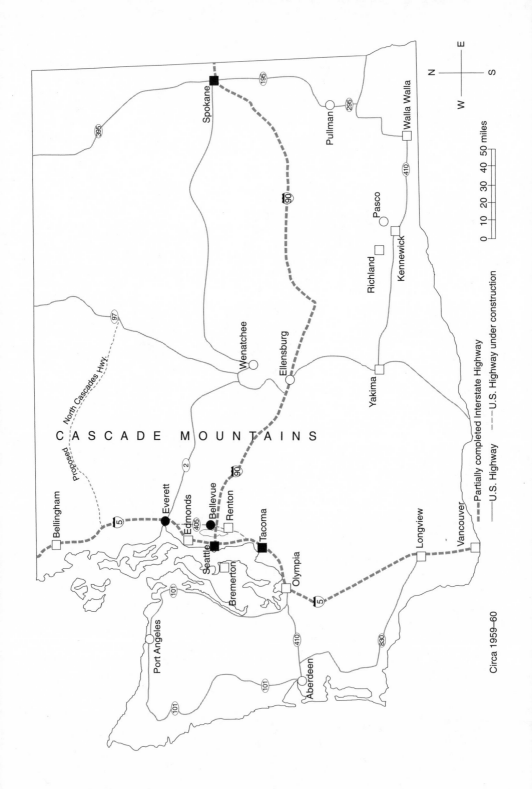

N
E
S
W

0 10 20 30 40 50 miles

Spokane

195

Pullman

295

Walla Walla

410

90

Pasco

Richland

Kennewick

395

97

North Cascades Hwy.

Proposed

Wenatchee

Ellensburg

Yakima

C A S C A D E   M O U N T A I N S

2

90

Bellingham

5

Everett

Edmonds

405

Bellevue

Renton

Seattle

Tacoma

Bremerton

Olympia

5

101

410

830

101

Longview

Vancouver

Port Angeles

Aberdeen

101

········ Partially completed Interstate Highway

——— U.S. Highway

- - - - - U.S. Highway under construction

Circa 1959–60

ROSELLINI

Immigrants' Son and Progressive Governor

"To be turned from one's course by men's opinions, by blame, and by misrepresentation shows a man unfit to hold an office."

Fabius Maximus

"A leader has to lead, or otherwise he has no business in politics."

Harry S. Truman

Introduction

This book covers Albert D. Rosellini's early life and his active career in politics. I have discussed the forces that shaped him as a politician and described Rosellini's political motivations and philosophy of government along with the key issues that were the major focus of his two terms as governor of the state of Washington.

Rosellini was an activist governor. He was attracted to issues where progress could be made and measured, and was less comfortable articulating a broad philosophy of government. Budget reform, economic development, transportation, higher education, and institutions were the core matters to which he devoted his talent and governmental know-how. Although a progressive, he was more practical than liberal, usually focusing on areas where his knowledge of state government and the political process could bring about almost immediate change. Consequently, I have chosen to limit the scope of the book accordingly, leaving out his work on the other issues such as civil rights, parks and conservation, fisheries, and agriculture. I believe that the issues that I discuss in depth are those in which Rosellini made a singular and perhaps unique contribution.

Rosellini was also unusually controversial throughout his career. Nearly every action by the man or his administration generated a partisan response, even beyond the norm for political life. In fact, discussions of Rosellini still elicit strong feelings, more than thirty years since he left public office. I have described in detail those examples which, in my opinion, best illustrate the polarized environment within which he operated. I am certain that both his admirers and his detractors will point out areas that should have been included. Nonetheless, I believe that this book provides an appropriately detailed and objective history of the man, his political life, and the actions of his administration. The evaluations and conclusions in the final chapter are strictly my own.

Rosellini's Cultural Background

As the early chapters took shape, I became aware that Rosellini's heritage as the son of Italian-Catholic immigrants not only molded his actions, but also shaped the attitudes and perceptions of the public and the press toward him in ways that were far beyond his, and perhaps their, control. Many readers in the late 1990s will not fully understand the prevailing attitudes and prejudices—in Washington and throughout the country—toward Italians during Rosellini's career in public office. Without some knowledge of these attitudes, however, it is impossible to appreciate the role they played in shaping Rosellini's professional and political life.

David L. Nicandri's book, *Italians in Washington State: Emigration, 1853–1924*, chronicles the flight to America of great numbers of poor and unemployed Italians. The agricultural depression and economic collapse of Italy (which began in the late 1880s and lasted for decades) produced a rising tide of immigrants who came to America to "survive." Locating first in the large cities of the East and Midwest, and crammed into slums run by exploitative *padroni* bosses, many of them migrated to the West. They worked as section hands, ditch-diggers, junk-collectors, and gardeners—whatever was hard and dirty. Most were men who worked long hours, gambled, drank, spoke little English, and saved their money so that they could send for their wives, families, and friends.[1]

This process fed on itself, encouraging more and more immigration. Bringing with them their language, their mores, their clannishness, and a suspicion of strangers, they settled into "little Italy" enclaves, where they were not absorbed into the rest of society. Even within these communities, the immigrants tended to settle among others from the same part of Italy. Compared with other European immigrants, the Italians were poorer and had by far the highest rate of illiteracy. This was particularly true when contrasted, as in Washington State, with the Scandinavian immigrant population who generally were educated and trained in a craft or skill. As a result, the Scandinavians rather quickly assimilated into the mainstream and became a part of the governing establishment.[2]

Another roadblock to assimilation was their attitude toward formal education. Most Italian immigrants viewed it as an elitist concept that deprived the family of labor and money. This attitude not only alienated them from middle-class society, but also greatly limited the upward mobility of Italian children. It consigned many, if not most, to "the skills of the hand," as contrasted with "skills of the intellect."[3] Surveys in 1913 and 1915 showed that more than 80 percent of Seattle's Italians were unskilled laborers. Less than 20 percent were running businesses, and there were only two Italian doctors and one lawyer in all of King County.[4]

The prejudice toward Italians was also fed by militant Protestants' fears of their Catholicism and alleged civil allegiance to the Pope. "Chianti, Catholicism and Crime" was the phrase often used as a stereotypical slur. Indeed, the national prejudice against Italians had grown to the point that immigration from Italy was severely restricted in 1920—when Albert Rosellini was already ten years old. In several parts of the country (although not in Washington State), Italians were lynched. Between 1874 and 1915, thirty-nine Italians died as a result of vigilante action.[5]

Washington State and King County's prejudice toward Italians mirrored attitudes of the country as a whole. Nellie Roe, in a 1915 thesis for the University of Washington social science department, detailed her sociological study of the "Italian Immigrant in Seattle." She described the Italians' dominant characteristics as "ignorance and optimism," and their homes as "poorly cared for, dirty dishes unwashed and everything in a state of confusion." Much of her thesis was devoted to the social deficiencies of the Italians and whether they could be helped without diluting the standards and ideals of the rest of the population. As she put it, "shall we sacrifice a few upward steps in our civilization in order to keep them along, or shall we forge ahead and leave them to slower unaided assimilation?"[6]

Other forces worked to alienate Italians, not only from middle–class society, but also from other laboring groups. Their closed societal ways led to unproven but constant rumors that they operated within a "black-hand" criminal society to protect themselves. Their religion and their willingness to work for lower wages caused labor unions to deny them membership and object to their employment by businesses. In the early 1900s, for example, Spokane made it city policy not to hire Catholics and Italians. The unions that did accept Italians, such as the United Mine Workers and the Industrial Workers of the World, tended to be militant, and Italians became further associated in the public mind with violence and anarchy. The nationwide wave of bombings that accompanied the post–World War I labor unrest and the country's fear of Bolshevism resulted in the conviction and execution of Italian-born anarchists Nicola Sacco and Bartolomeo Vanzetti in Massachusetts, where the anti-Italian prejudice of judge and jury was palpably clear. These executions confirmed most Italians' belief, at the time, that they could not expect justice under state or federal laws. The alienation of the Italian immigrant community was therefore more complete than for any other Caucasian group.[7]

Fear of the Italians' perceived propensity toward crime seemed to dominate society's view even as threats of radicalism faded. Eric Scigliano wrote in his study of the Italian community in Seattle that "no subject touches more raw nerves in any discussion of Italian-American life than crime, in particular organized crime." It was, as he illustrates, a fear that lingered long after assimilation had begun and the second and third generations were achieving relative affluence. The names of the mob bosses during Prohibition and the rise of the Mafia following its repeal merely reinforced public suspicion, particularly from 1930 through the 1950s, that Italians were connected to criminal activity.[8] It was also more openly expressed than were the prejudices against their religion and culture—which by the 1960s had become "politically incorrect."

Gerald A. Hoeck, a longtime Seattleite and public relations consultant to Senators Henry M. Jackson and Warren G. Magnuson, and, after 1956, to Rosellini, says that Seattle society's distrustful attitude toward Italians continued into the 1960s. "The establishment always wanted to keep them down in Garlic Gulch," was his way of describing it. Rosellini's successor, Dan Evans, confirmed that Rosellini's name alone often gave him "a bad rap." Certainly the religious issue did not disappear during Rosellini's public life. Hoeck vividly recalls Seattle *Argus* editor Phil Bailey, in 1959, describing John F. Kennedy as "the Catholic candidate for President," without ever giving his name.[9]

It is painful for many of us to go back in time and relive prejudices that now seem archaic. Yet as recently as 1972, otherwise enlightened political figures such as then Gov. Dan Evans and then Attorney General Slade Gorton grossly played on the public's worst fears of Italians in order to achieve their political objectives (see Chapter 16). Thus, I do not believe one can truly understand Governor Rosellini's life and career or his strengths and weaknesses as a political leader outside the societal context of the time. However, I do not mean to overstate the point. While the anti-Italian prejudices faced by Rosellini and others in Washington State were significant—and critically important to Rosellini's legislative and gubernatorial career—they were in general less intense than in other areas of the country. The fact that Albert was the first Italian governor west of the Mississippi is proof enough of that proposition. Nicandri, Scigliano, and others, such as Angelo Pellegrini, have rightfully pointed out that Washington's attitudes toward Italians, while mirroring those of the rest of the country, were more open and accepting than most.[10]

It is equally important to understand how these prejudices and his background shaped Rosellini's political actions and legal career. Typically, he grew up trusting few people who were not family or close friends. When he was a legislator, and later governor, his closest advisors were usually "family": his first cousins, Dr. Leo Rosellini and Victor Rosellini, and his distant relative, Hugh Rosellini. Even his statewide campaigns were tightly controlled by those close to him or his family—a fact that led to innuendo and suspicion by the Seattle *Times* and others. Albert's ethnicity and cultural heritage made him intensely loyal to clients and friends who, as Italians, operated liquor-related businesses that were "beyond the pale" to most society, especially the predominantly Protestant and prohibitionist middle class. Nicandri's book details the vast schism that separated Italian attitudes toward liquor (and gambling) from the prevailing views of the white, middle- class establishment in the 1920s through the 1950s.[11] As discussed in Chapter 1, prohibitionist fervor lingered for decades after the country's repeal of Prohibition in 1932. Albert Rosellini grew up in a culture which was puzzled by the larger society's obsessive dread of alcohol. His willingness to represent friends and other clients in alcohol-related endeavors was not surprising, nor could it be described as a "moral weakness" on his part, until political opponents with different cultural beliefs chose to use it to their advantage.

Charges of Corruption

While working on this book, I frequently encountered allegations and assumptions of personal and political corruption on the part of Rosellini. Whenever I could, I made it a point to track down the source. In three instances, I personally interviewed reporters who were reputed to have knowledge of these matters, and in each case I learned that there was no verification for any allegations of corruption on the part of Governor Rosellini.[12] I also probed as deeply as I could with many people who were close to Rosellini's administration but who no longer have ties to him or any personal need to hide such information. I am satisfied that had there been skeletons, I would have found them.

Finally, given Rosellini's high profile and controversial reputation, I believe that if evidence of corruption had been available, local officials or the United States attorney would have brought charges. Certainly the Seattle *Times* and Ross Cunningham would have rushed into print any such information. Hoeck vividly recalls hearing that the *Times* gave its reporters "a blank check" to try to prove corruption charges, but they could not do so.[13] After he left office, Rosellini continued to live and work in Seattle. He ran for office again in 1969 and in 1972. Every aspect of his life has been scrutinized. If there were any truth to the rumors, it would have surfaced. Consequently, I believe that Albert Rosellini's political life and administration must be judged on the basis of what we know and can prove, not on rumor and innuendo. That is what I have tried to do.

Chapter 1

The Early Years

Albert Dean Rosellini was twenty-three years old when he passed the Washington State bar examination in August 1933. Raised in an Italian-speaking home and never entirely at ease with English, he had completed a three-year joint BA-law degree at the University of Washington and graduated with honors. While Albert was growing up, his father, Giovanni, drifted in and out of a series of saloon and private-club businesses, and also served a year in prison. Albert worked at odd jobs throughout his school years to help support the family. Despite these obstacles, by the time of his graduation from law school Albert was a member of Tau Kappa Epsilon fraternity, an amateur boxer of passing note, and one of the most popular young bachelors in the Italian community.[1]

When Albert passed the bar examination, Giovanni threw a huge party to honor his son. One of Albert's clearest memories of his early life is that party, the toast in his honor made by his father, and the pride his family felt upon his becoming a lawyer. As the only son—loved and protected by his mother and sisters, and the major source of his father's pride—Albert was expected to do well in the name of the family. He had responded with hard work and determination, and had already risen above his family's working-class immigrant background. In many respects, however, the future state senator, governor, civic leader, and businessman would always be trying to live up to his father's pride and his family's expectations.

Family and Education

Albert Rosellini's father, Giovanni, was born in 1884 in the small Tuscan village of Chiesina, about thirty miles from Florence. In 1901, he immigrated to America. After working as a railroad section hand in Chicago, he migrated to Tacoma, Washington, and joined the Alaskan gold rush in 1904. Upon returning to the Tacoma area a year later, Giovanni renewed his friendship with another native of Chiesina, Pietro Pagni, owner of Pagni's Little Country Grocery—a hangout for Italian immigrants. Giovanni met Pietro's sister Annunziata during a visit home to Chiesina, and their courtship began.

Shortly after her brother brought her to America in 1905, Annunziata and Giovanni were married in Tacoma's St. Leo's Church. Over the next ten years, four children were born—Rena, Argie, Albert, and Ida. The Rosellini family was Roman Catholic, and the children were raised in that faith. Annunziata was religious and attended Mass regularly; Giovanni only on rare occasions. All four children were married in the Catholic tradition, and their spouses converted to that faith.

From the outset of his life, Albert was favored. As the only son, he was, according to his sister Ida, "the apple of his mother's eye" and "the source of his father's pride." For example, he had his own room, while his three sisters shared one. He could stay out late or spend weekends with friends, his sisters could not. But his sisters were close to Albert and protective of him. Annunziata was not one to push her son in any direction, although she did insist that he take violin lessons for several years. In stark contrast to many Italian families, his mother and father believed that it was important for Albert to get a college education. During the early thirties, Ida, who was two years younger, left school to work so that Albert could stay in college. Ida recalls that Albert always tried hard to please his family, especially his father.[2]

Both parents' had limited English and Annunziata insisted that her children speak Italian in the home. The future governor was never comfortable with public speaking in formal settings; in fact, years later he was tutored in public speaking by another Italian immigrant, Angelo Pellegrini. Angelo's parents and the Rosellinis were close friends. Pelle, as he later came to be called, and Albert met while Rosellini was in high school, and they became friends. As an English professor at the University of Washington, Pelle taught both Albert and his best friend, Hugh Rosellini, in speech classes. Indeed, for a time Hugh and Pelle were roommates.

Albert's close relationship with Hugh also went back to childhood. Hugh Rosellini's father, Primo, was not closely related to Giovanni, but the two were from the same town of Chiesina and immigrated to Tacoma at the same time. Hugh and Albert were raised together and were best friends from grade school. As Albert put it, they were "closer than brothers." They enrolled together at the University of Puget Sound in 1927, and Hugh followed Albert to UW in 1929 to complete his law degree.

Hugh was elected to the state house of representatives from Tacoma in 1938—the same year that Albert was elected to the senate. During the first six years of Rosellini's senate service, the two shared an apartment in Olympia during legislative sessions. In 1944 Hugh left the legislature to run unsuccessfully for prosecuting attorney of Pierce County. At Albert's urging, Governor Wallgren appointed Hugh to the superior court for Pierce County in 1945, where he served until his election to the state supreme court in 1954. Until he died on November 26, 1984, Hugh was Albert's closest advisor and confidant.[3]

Giovanni had also been joined in his new homeland by his brothers, Vittorio and Cecceo, and in 1907 the three brothers established Marconi Wine, Spirits, and Grocery Store on Sixteenth and Broadway in Tacoma. Vittorio soon married Fine Gasperetti, who, with her brother, owned and operated the Tuscano Restaurant across the street. Vittorio and Fine Rosellini's two sons, Victor and Leo, would both gain prominence—Victor as a restaurateur, and Leo as a surgeon. Fine and the Gasperetti family established the region's first well-known Italian restaurants.[4] After Vittorio died, Fine and her second husband opened the Roma Cafe, which was popular with Seattle's political crowd and lovers of Italian food. Fine's nephews founded Gasperetti's in Union Gap, Washington, later moving the restaurant to Yakima. In 1916, Giovanni lost his Tacoma saloon as a result of Prohibition, and the family moved to Seattle, where Giovanni entered the private-club business. His club, located on the second floor at the corner of Second Avenue and James Street, provided a vantage point for young Albert to watch World War I military parades as they marched down Second Avenue.

In a first-generation Italian-immigrant family, everyone worked hard. Albert's first job, at the age of seven or eight, was to get up early and light the furnace for two elderly women who lived down the street; by age nine he was carrying newspapers. During his grammar- and high-school years, Albert worked in a door factory, a meat market, and a pharmacy. Despite his workload and also playing sports, Albert graduated from high school in three years. Later he worked as a long-shoreman on the Tacoma waterfront. These work habits carried over into everything he did. As governor he worked sixty to eighty hours a week and was a tireless campaigner. Life was not always hard for the Rosellini family, however. Giovanni was an inveterate gambler, and he would frequently play siginetto all night for high stakes. When he was flush from gambling winnings, he loved to treat his family. On one such occasion in 1922, the entire family traveled to Italy to visit the parents' native village. Giovanni wanted to show off his family and to see his older sister, Erma, who had never visited the United States, and his brother Vittorio (father of Leo and Victor), who had moved his family back to Chiesina the previous year, using the money he had saved in America to buy several farms. In Italy, Albert observed the specter of totalitarian politics when he saw Black Shirts marching through the streets of several cities. Mussolini's rise to power soon prompted Vittorio to abandon his property and return to the United States.[5]

While Albert was a teenager, his father operated a private club located next door to the Tacoma gym where Jack Conners, Tacoma's best-known boxing manager, trained his fighters. While doing chores at his father's club, Albert met Conners. Taking the young Rosellini under his wing, Conners taught and trained him for several years and had him spar on occasion with two of his best Northwest prospects,

Eddie Roberts (a good welterweight) and Freddie Steele—who went on to become world champion middleweight in 1935, when he decisioned Gorilla Jones. A newspaper account of Albert's first year as a lawyer tells of his winning an amateur bout in San Francisco in 1928. Another reporter, in the Seattle *Post-Intelligencer (PI)*, quipped: "Like most boxers he quit the game to spend time before the bar—but in his case it was a different kind of bar."[6] Tacoma was a rabid fight town and for a short time Conners urged Rosellini to consider a professional boxing career—an idea immediately quashed by his parents.

Politics was rarely a subject of conversation in the Rosellini home, although Albert's mother did take him to hear President Woodrow Wilson speak in Tacoma. Albert also recalls discussions of Albert Smith's candidacy for president, primarily because Smith was Catholic. Although not strongly partisan, the Rosellinis distrusted President Herbert Hoover and the Republicans.

While Albert was still in high school, Giovanni was involved in an incident that had a profound effect on the family and on his son. In 1926, Giovanni and his friend Primo Rosellini (Hugh's father) had visited Tijuana. There they met Louie Grandi, who was connected with narcotics and bootlegging. While the details are not entirely clear, Rosellini recalls that his father became involved with Grandi. A year later, Giovanni and Primo were arrested and charged with trying to smuggle narcotics out of Mexico. The trauma of his father's arrest at the family home, the sensational headlines and the gossip at school, and the experience of visiting his father in the federal prison on McNeil Island made an indelible impression on the seventeen-year-old. Looking back on the incident sixty-five years later, Rosellini believed it may have motivated him to enter law school.

Giovanni severed all ties with Grandi after his imprisonment. Following his release in 1928, he helped run Angelo's Cafe at Sixth and Jackson until after the repeal of Prohibition, when he opened the Sideboard Tavern at First and Pike with the help of a friend. In the early 1940s, Giovanni added a dance hall above the tavern. During the war, the Sideboard was popular, featuring continuous music from two bands. After the war, Giovanni sold the tavern to Rena's husband, who turned it into a restaurant.

Times were often difficult for Giovanni's family in the late twenties. The Great Depression had started, and few of the Italian immigrants had work. At one point the Rosellinis—unable to pay rent—were evicted from their home. Rena, the oldest sister and the only member of the household who was employed, supported the family with her job at Lou Johnson Apparel.

In 1928 Albert enrolled in the University of Washington, and after a brief hiatus from school to work, he entered the university's BA law-degree program. Albert started law school when he was twenty years old. Many lasting friendships grew out of his university years. Perhaps the most noteworthy was with Harold Shefelman, newly appointed professor of legal ethics. Shefelman went on to become a prominent bond lawyer and one of the founders of the firm Roberts, Weter, and Shefelman. A lawyer and an outstanding civic leader who chaired numerous commissions and citizens committees in the 1950s and 1960s, he remained a mentor to Rosellini and advised him on many occasions. Although Rosellini does not recall his grades in law school, a clipping in the August 31, 1933, Seattle *PI* lists his membership in Phi Alpha Delta, the law honorary fraternity. Rosellini does remember having a part-time job as a meat cutter during law school; on Saturdays he worked twelve hours at Dan's Meat Market.

Rosellini first ventured into politics during the 1933 legislative session, while still in law school. He was dating the daughter of Ben Eide, a Puget Sound marine pilot, and the pilots were pushing legislation to establish a pilotage commission. Rosellini had worked part-time for Edward (Ned) Cochrane, a lawyer, and had been a campaign supporter when Cochrane ran for the state house of representatives as a Democrat in 1932. Ben Eide asked Rosellini to help lobby the pilotage commission bill through the house because of his relationship with Cochrane, who, though only a freshman, was the chair of the committee on harbors and waterways. The bill passed in 1935 and remains law to this day.[7]

Beginning Practice

Eighty-two applicants took the Washington State bar examination in the summer of 1933. Among the sixty who passed were Hugh and Albert Rosellini. Many of the other new lawyers would also become prominent in Washington State's legal community, including Daniel Allison, Byron Condon, Eli Ellis Dorsey, Stanberry Foster, John Franco, Elton P. Jones, Maurice Kadish, Wilbur J. Lawrence, John S. Lynch, Jr., Harold A. Pebbles, Patrick A. Geraghty, and Fred G. Clarke. Albert's first law office was in room 822 of the Northern Life Tower, where he shared quarters with Ned Cochrane and Harold J. Kuen. In one of his first cases, he was the court-appointed attorney for a former boxing opponent, who was eventually found guilty of burglary. The local newspapers relished the human-interest angle of this case— "Lawyer's First Client Negro He Whipped in Prize Fight," trumpeted the Seattle *Times*. The Tacoma *News Tribune* reported that: "Two young amateur boxers faced each other in a San Francisco ring one night five years ago. Now one of them, Albert D. Rosellini, the victor will step into a new arena with his foe, Miles Williams."[8] This was one of a number of colorful cases that Rosellini handled during the early years of his practice. The first to receive significant notoriety involved James Ashe, a literary agent accused of swindling wealthy women looking to him for advice on whether their manuscripts could be published. Rosellini was court-appointed defense counsel for Ashe, who by the time of the trial was indigent. One of the key witnesses was Ashe's former secretary, Ethel McNeil, who would later become Mrs. Albert D. Rosellini.

Ethel McNeil's mother, Erika Ahlen, had moved from Sweden to Seattle in 1906 or 1907, where she met and married an Irishman, John McNeil. John died in the influenza epidemic of 1918, when his daughter was six years old. Unable to afford college, Ethel was forced to get a job when she left high school in 1929. She had worked for Ashe prior to accepting a comparable stenographer's position in the King County purchasing office.

The "Literary Racket" case, as it was called, provided lurid daily headlines in the Seattle papers: "Widow says literary agent swindled her with prize as Lure," "Trial halts as couple embrace in Courtroom," "Pretty wife at Ashe's side in Fraud Trial." Ethel McNeil was a featured witness and the subject of several news stories. As Albert interviewed and worked with Ethel through the lengthy trial, eventual mistrial, and ultimate retrial, their relationship grew. They were married on June 1, 1937. After the ceremony in Our Lady of Mt. Virgin Church and a party at the Seattle Yacht Club, the couple spent the night in the Olympic Hotel and breakfasted at the Rosellini family home. That same day they took the train to San Francisco, where they boarded a cruise ship to New York by way of Cuba. The newlyweds paid a total of $125 each for the full cruise. From New York, they took the train to Detroit, where they picked up a Ford—their first car—and drove to Seattle.[9]

The Sunday-Closing Case

In the fall of 1934, just a year into his practice, Rosellini filed a lawsuit that had a lifelong impact on his legal and political career. The suit arose out of his first professional involvement with beer and liquor interests in King County. One of Rosellini's clients, another young Italian, Sarafin Lelli, had asked the young attorney to set up a corporation called S. Lelli Company, a beer distributorship. Their business relationship grew into a close friendship, and through Lelli, Rosellini met most of Seattle's tavern owners. Within a short time the Tavern Owners' Association was paying him a retainer, and Rosellini became known as a lawyer able to handle the licensing intricacies involved in operating taverns and bars. Rosellini's notoriety in the area was assured when, on September 1, 1934, he sought a temporary restraining order against the King County commissioners, the King County sheriff, and the King County prosecuting attorney directing them to fully enforce the county's Sunday "blue laws," which were being selectively applied to businesses serving liquor. The restraining order would shut down all sports contests, golf courses, ice-cream parlors, theaters, grocery stores, and billiard parlors that were operating on Sundays.[10]

Rosellini's main clients in the Sunday-closing case were Peter Desimone and J. L. Crawford. Peter Desimone was the son of the legendary Joe Desimone, who founded the Pike Place Market and donated land to Boeing for its first offices and buildings. Desimone owned and operated a tavern just outside Seattle's city limits, and Crawford owned the Red Wing, a dinner resort. The latter was a private club—private in the special sense of an era that allowed no public consumption of hard liquor. With public temperance strictly enforced, restaurants hid behind a "private club" label. Desimone and Crawford's lawsuit also had the support of the Beverage Dispensers' Association, made up of all owners of establishments licensed to sell beer. Also supporting the attack on Seattle and King County's liquor regulations were the 700 members of the King County Beer and Wine Vendors Association. Rosellini's legal maneuvers—highly publicized in the newspapers—forced King County officials to allow beer parlors and taverns to remain open on Sunday for several weeks while more current liquor control regulations were being enacted.[11]

From a 1990s perspective, it is hard to appreciate the social and political thicket faced by anyone involved with businesses that handled beer or liquor in the middle and late 1930s. Some background on Prohibition and its aftermath is necessary.[12] The passage of the Volstead Act in 1920 had not made America—or Washington State—completely dry. The measure permitted people to drink liquor that was already on hand and to make home-brew in private residences. Washington's proximity to a "wet" Canada, however, facilitated the free flow of alcoholic beverages for purchase as well. The public demand for alcohol and the difficulties of enforcing Prohibition laws left the state's law-enforcement officers unusually vulnerable to the generation of successful bootleggers who had adequate means to make payoffs. Many officers either were openly practicing a form of tolerance or were frankly corrupt. A young Seattle police lieutenant named Roy Olmstead became the acknowledged head of what the New York *Times* called "one of the most gigantic rumrunning conspiracies in the country." In 1923, the mayor of Seattle, along with his chief of police, described the Volstead Act as "the cause of more police delinquency than all other laws put together."[13]

Prior to Prohibition, the saloon and tavern owners had scoffed at Sunday-closing laws. They kept their establishments open twenty-four hours a day, seven days a week in the early 1900s, openly ignoring the law. Public fear of these conditions had led to the formation of the Anti-Saloon League in Washington, which helped pass the law bringing statewide prohibition to Washington in 1919. Reflecting this public fear is a statement made by the editor of the Seattle *Argus* in 1914:

> There are saloons in which fights are of nightly occurrence. There are saloons where drunks are "rolled." There are saloons where the man who gets his check cashed stands mighty little show of getting away with any of the coin. There are saloons where liquor is sold to boys. And against these saloons the prohibition law is aimed.[14]

The thirteen years of Prohibition did not change negative attitudes toward saloons and their supporters. The different religious and social positions between the "wets" and the "drys" that had led to Prohibition continued after it became law and long after Abolition. In 1931 and 1932, Washington State experienced another battle between the polarized factions over Initiative 61, which repealed the state's Prohibition statute.

Although the wets prevailed, it was acknowledged by a majority of Washingtonians that the old-type saloons should not return. Shortly after national repeal of the Volstead Act in 1933, however, visions of pre-Prohibition days began to appear in the minds of Washington's citizens—the result of the hiatus between repeal and the state's enactment of proper liquor regulations, a period that the *Argus* called "fifteen months of liquor wildcatting." In *The Dry Years*, Norman Clark describes the scene: "Roadhouses were wide-open everywhere, peopled generously with drunks and prostitutes. Bartenders served drunks, minors, and rowdies, and in most cases local police refused to take any responsibility for enforcing laws that did not exist."[15]

Seattle and the state were, therefore, especially polarized on the subject of alcohol in 1933 and 1934. State and local government needed to enact regulations that would control rampant drinking and still give citizens who chose to do so the right to drink. It was in this charged atmosphere that young Albert Rosellini filed the Sunday-closing suit.

When Prohibition was abolished, the Steele Act did not require Sunday closing; it merely authorized local authorities to make reasonable regulations. Seattle and King County were forced to rely on

"Sunday blue laws" from an earlier era in order to regulate drinking at all. These laws were widely enforced, but only as they applied to the sale of alcoholic beverages. Rosellini argued that, since officials were utilizing the 1909 statute to ban "drinking saloons," then the rest of the law—dealing with "noisy and boisterous sports" and "businesses employing labor," and excepting only "livery stables and garages" and "works of necessity and charity"—should also be enforced. Rosellini cited the fact that the King County commissioners had adopted no Sunday-closing regulations, and he also attacked the Seattle city ordinance, which mirrored the state law.[16] His intention was clear: make the old Sunday-closing law so onerous that it would be repealed, allowing his tavern- and club-owner clients to keep their businesses open on Sundays.

The lawsuit attracted a great deal of publicity. In the midst of the controversy, the newspapers tied Rosellini's handling of the suit to his candidacy for the legislature. He had filed that summer to run for the Democratic nomination for the state senate in the thirty-third legislative district. One article, describing the restraining order that allowed beer parlors to remain open on Sunday, reported that "Rosellini, who is running for the state senate, wanted the hearing postponed until after the election—and the restraining order continued in effect over another weekend."[17] Rosellini would admit later that "I may have timed the TRO lawsuit for political advantage, since it got a lot of ink."

When the state did reimpose regulatory controls—through the recommendation of the governor's advisory commission on alcohol—those regulations reflected a fear of the old-time saloon and a belief that "the sale and drinking of hard liquor in public places should be prohibited."[18] The conflict between temperance forces and those in favor of modernizing liquor laws, which continued for years, was political dynamite for any politician who attempted to seek a legislative solution. For example, the public sale of liquor by the drink was not permitted until 1948, when it was mandated by an initiative. The sale of liquor on Sunday did not occur until 1968, when another initiative vote abolished the Sunday Blue laws that had been the subject of Rosellini's 1934 suit. This cleared the way for the State Liquor Control Board to lift its ban on Sunday sales of alcohol. The negative attitude toward liquor in a political context lasted, in varying degrees, throughout Albert Rosellini's career in public life.

In the thirty-third district, however, Rosellini's involvement with liquor interests was neither politically damaging nor sensitive. In the Italian enclave known as "Garlic Gulch," a key part of his district, many—if not most—of the law-abiding Italians could see no sense in Prohibition or in laws related to liquor or gambling. The same was true for most of the other immigrant groups in the district. Rosellini's family and his friends in the Italian community, who accepted alcohol as a part of everyday life and often owned businesses which sold liquor, brought their legal problems to him. Consequently, the negative and long-term connotations of handling legal matters involving liquor were of little concern to the very young, brash, and inexperienced lawyer as he was building his practice.

The aspiring politician, however, had chosen to identify himself with an issue that offended the conservative establishment. The Sunday-closing case was the first of many times that Rosellini became embroiled in public controversy. This willingness to take on high-profile issues and turn them to his political advantage was a strategy that he would use many times during his career.

Chapter 2

The State Senate
and a Political
Agenda

Albert Rosellini was elected to the state senate in November 1938. His district—the thirty-third—started on Seattle's Mount Baker Ridge and ran south along Lake Washington into portions of Rainier Valley. Consisting primarily of working-class, first-generation Italians, Irish, Slavs, and Japanese, it also included an active Jewish population. It was tailor-made for the liberal son of an immigrant family with strong roots in the community and good personal contacts. The only reliable Republicans in the district were the homeowners scattered along Lake Washington's waterfront—a tiny minority among its approximately twenty thousand residents.[1]

Rosellini's district included the heart of "little Italy," served by the city's only Italian-language newspaper, La Gazetta Italiano. Its articles kept its three thousand subscribers in the Everett, Seattle, and Tacoma areas informed about the activities in the central Italian community. On several occasions, Rosellini and his political activities were featured, which helped the candidate gain volunteer support and financial contributions. Not surprisingly, La Gazetta also gave Rosellini its formal endorsement.[2]

Although Rosellini had little thought of political office when he began legal practice in September 1933, this had changed when he joined the Young Men's Democratic Club of King County. There he met Tiger Jim Murphy, the King County Democratic party chairman, and became acquainted with a number of other Democrats. In Rosellini's words, "It was an exciting time. There were a lot of colorful guys around like John Dore, Vic Meyers, and others who were running for office just to have something to do." The story of Seattle *PI* reporter Doug Welch talking Vic Meyers, a popular local band leader, into running for mayor "just to make it more interesting" is a Rosellini favorite. The story ends with Meyers filing for lieutenant governor—because it was the only filing fee he could afford—and winning.[3]

By summer 1934, intrigued by politics, Rosellini had identified the thirty-third district as one where his name and background would be advantageous. At the urging of a group of young New Deal Democrats, he filed for the state senate against his former mentor, Tiger Jim Murphy. At the time, he did not even live in the district, and he used the address of a young friend in order to qualify. Identifying himself with the liberal wing of the party, Albert "campaigned like a fool," and claims that he rang every doorbell in the district. An advertisement in the July 11, 1934, edition of the *PI* lists his campaign issues as the consolidation of counties, aid for the unemployed, old-age pensions, and reducing the costs of government.[4]

Murphy, a long-time incumbent, did not take Rosellini's candidacy seriously. Because the Democrats were divided between conservatives and New Deal liberals, however, the young challenger came within eighty votes of winning. Rosellini was aided by the publicity he had received as the lawyer attacking the Sunday blue laws. The close race encouraged Rosellini, and he remained active in the party. More important, he caught the attention of the Democratic candidate for King County prosecutor, Warren G. Magnuson. When "Maggie" won the primary by a large margin, he asked Rosellini to join his campaign and also offered him a job as a deputy prosecutor if he (Magnuson) won the general election. After Magnuson's overwhelming victory, Rosellini joined the prosecutor's staff in January 1935, along with Paul Coughlin, Jack Shermer, and Lloyd Shorett.[5]

At that time, deputy prosecutors could also represent private clients if no conflict was created. They were also *expected* to be activists in community and political organizations. These aspects of his new position served Rosellini well—both financially and politically. Newspaper accounts from the mid-1930s reveal that Rosellini was a frequent speaker at meetings of the Sons of Italy, the Maple Leaf Club, and numerous Democratic Club affairs. The Seattle *Star* referred to Rosellini as a "popular young leader in Seattle's Italian colony."[6]

By 1938, Rosellini was a lawyer-politician with experience, exposure, and excellent contacts. He could hold political office and still retain his position as a deputy prosecutor by taking a leave of absence while serving in the legislature. Rosellini had used the four years since his first race to build a strong base of support in the thirty-third district. He had developed critical liaisons to the Jewish and Irish populations of the district, while solidifying support in the Italian community.

The major issue facing the thirty-third district, and the rest of Washington State, was the fight over Franklin Roosevelt's New Deal. The liberal programs of Roosevelt's administration were opposed vigorously not only by Republicans, but also by the conservative wing of the Democratic party. In 1938, the district Democratic Club was unmistakably liberal, and Rosellini had been much more active in the club than other potential candidates for the state senate. Tiger Jim Murphy, the incumbent, had died, and the King County commissioners had appointed W. N. Miller as his replacement. Miller, of Slavic descent, lacked strong organizational ties in the district. Rosellini received key liberal endorsements over more conservative Democratic candidates, such as John O'Brien, Henry Callahan, and the incumbent Miller. Winning the primary over five other candidates, Rosellini faced Paul Green, an insurance broker, in the general election. Rosellini describes the campaign as bitter and divisive. He recalls that his parish priest, Father Caramello, expressed concern over the vitriolic nature of the debate between the New Deal and the old guard. In a Depression-era landslide, Rosellini received more that 65 percent of the votes.[7]

Rosellini had just turned twenty-nine when he arrived in Olympia as the youngest member of the senate. He had no staff or secretary. However, he did have two patronage positions which he was free to fill, and he brought with him Angelo Cappellitti and Carlos Scarengi, both of whom had worked on his campaign. These men welcomed the stipend of five dollars a day—a large sum in 1939. They proved to be valuable assets—greeting and entertaining constituents as well as communicating with other senators. Ethel Rosselini, expecting the couple's first child, stayed in Seattle. John Michael was born on May 21, followed by Janey Katherine (Campbell) on October 9, 1941; Sue Ann (Stiller) on May 18, 1943; Lynn Christine on May 23, 1945; and Albert Dean, Jr., on February 19, 1951. During those years when the children were young, Ethel spent little time in Olympia, preferring not to disrupt the household with frequent absences. Albert shared an apartment with Hugh Rosellini, who had been elected to the state house of representatives that same year. This living arrangement continued until Hugh left the legislature in 1944.[8]

Rosellini was one of six freshmen senators that year. Among the other newly elected legislators in 1939 were Representative Julia Butler (better known in later years as Julia Butler Hansen), who served for many year as chair of the highway and bridges committee, and Senators Michael Gallagher, Wilbur "Web" Hallauer, and William Gissberg.[9] This group became close friends and political allies who later provided critical assistance to Rosellini and his administration.

The Democrats had a substantial majority in the 1939 state senate, but they were divided into two factions—the conservatives and the liberal New Dealers. In 1939 the senate did not elect its own leadership; the governor by tradition appointed the senate leaders. Gov. Clarence Martin, although a Democrat, was a conservative banker from eastern Washington who naturally looked to the conservative wing of his party for leadership. He appointed Sen. Joseph Drumheller from Spokane as majority leader and Sen. Earl Maxwell from Renton as his assistant. Although they constituted a clear majority, the liberal Democrats in the senate had no leadership or power.[10]

Although the economic pressures of the Great Depression had eased somewhat in response to New Deal programs, state government was still focused on Depression issues when Rosellini entered the senate, and most senators, including Rosellini and even Drumheller and Maxwell, had similar positions. However, it was a mundane and innocuous piece of Depression-type legislation that first set Rosellini apart from that conservative leadership, and ultimately led him to seek greater power on the political scene.[11]

Approached by the macaroni and candy industry associations, Rosellini sponsored legislation aimed at regulating pricing practices. In the middle of the 1939 session, while Rosellini's macaroni and candy bill was moving through the senate with little controversy, Drumheller and Maxwell sponsored—with the governor's backing—a bill seeking to restrict both the right to form public utility districts (PUDs) and the right of existing PUDs to build transmission lines to carry the power they generated.[12] Few legislative issues have raised the kind of purely partisan ideological differences that surrounded public versus private power measures from the late 1920s until the mid-1970s. The public-power movement, which in Washington state had originated in the middle 1920s with the support of the Washington State Grange and representatives of Local No. 46 of the Electrical Workers Union, was vehemently opposed by the state's major private-power companies. Although there had been municipal utilities in Seattle and Tacoma for several years, the creation of *statewide* public-power ownership began in 1930, when Initiative 1 passed by a narrow margin after the legislature had refused to enact similar legislation. The initiative, which permitted the establishment of PUDs that would own and operate dams and other power-generation facilities, spawned several more initiatives—some designed to weaken public power and others designed to strengthen it—and many legislative attempts to restrict or expand PUD operations. Throughout the 1930s and 1940s, the battle over public power continued, as more counties sought to form PUDs and private power interests fought back.[13]

Drumheller and Maxwell's 1939 legislation was opposed by the Grange, organized labor, and most Democrats. The senate leadership concentrated on the freshmen senators as the Democrats most likely to change their position. Frank McLaughlin of Puget Sound Power and Light "wined and dined" Rosellini and other freshmen. Standing firm, Rosellini voted against the bill, and it was defeated easily. However, neither Drumheller nor Maxwell was generous in defeat; according to Rosellini, "all hell broke loose." His patronage was stripped from him, and Cappellitti and Scarengi were sent home. A few days later, the macaroni and candy bill was killed in committee. For the rest of the

1939 session, Rosellini was isolated from the Democratic leadership. It was the only time Rosellini would be blackballed during his legislative career.[14]

Senate Leadership

During that session, Rosellini had become acquainted with Les Hunt, a political writer for the liberal Seattle *Star*, who had observed the factionalization of the senate Democrats—especially over its leadership. Hunt suggested to Rosellini that the senate should elect its own leaders rather than having the governor appoint them. Intrigued by this idea, Rosellini spent the next two years working behind the scenes to organize the senate. He also kept in close touch with business associations—such as the grocers, gasoline dealers, and druggists—that had backed the regulatory laws killed by the conservatives. These groups assisted in Rosellini's efforts to reorganize the senate and supported liberal senators seeking leadership reform. Years later, their statewide organizations provided support for Rosellini's gubernatorial races.[15]

Rosellini's efforts on behalf of these groups went beyond his role as a legislator, however. In 1940, as a deputy prosecutor, he tried a case against a gasoline dealer accused of selling gas below cost on behalf of a national chain. Fair-trade laws were popular among state legislatures during the Depression, although they were ultimately ruled unconstitutional by the United States Supreme Court in 1975. The major supporters of Washington's fair-trade act (also called the "Loss-Leader Act") were the "mom and pop" stores throughout the state, who feared that national stores buying in large volume and selling below cost would drive them out of business.[16]

Between sessions, Rosellini worked to develop the strength of his local district Democratic organization. Under his leadership, the Thirty-Third District Democratic Club became one of the strongest in the state. Its annual Italian banquet was the political event of King County—raising between $1,500 and $2,000 annually—and enabled the thirty-third district to help other senate candidates and to contribute money to various Democratic groups.[17]

By November 1940, Rosellini's efforts to organize the senate were beginning to succeed. As he describes the situation, "I was getting more and more active and developing a real taste for politics and how the legislature worked. . . . I kept working on the leadership issue behind the scenes with members of the senate—but neither Maxwell nor Drumheller suspected." That same year, Clarence Martin ran for an unprecedented third term as governor. He was defeated in the primary by C. C. Dill—a former United States senator and one of the "grand old men" of the public-power movement. As a senator, Dill was a major proponent of Grand Coulee Dam, whose construction in eastern Washington began in 1934.[18]

Although Dill lost a close race to Mayor Arthur B. Langlie of Seattle, the 1941 legislature was again heavily Democratic. Dill's defeat worked to Rosellini's advantage in his push for leadership reform. With no incumbent governor to assist them, Maxwell and Drumheller were outmanned by the liberals, and Rosellini opposed them openly. Immediately after the legislature convened, Rosellini called for a caucus of the Democratic senators and moved that they follow the federal pattern and elect their own leadership. The motion passed, and Rosellini was elected majority leader.[19]

The 1940 election of Arthur B. Langlie brought to power the man whose policies and leadership Rosellini would oppose for the rest of his legislative career. Rosellini's first partisan act as majority leader was a motion to delay the certification of Langlie's election pending an investigation into alleged voter fraud in several western Washington counties. The election had been extremely close, with Dill and Langlie separated by fewer than 6,000 votes. There had been a huge voter turnout because of Franklin Roosevelt's third-term race against Wendell Wilkie. In Washington, 784,268 votes were cast for president and 777,844 for governor. Wilkie lost by 140,022 votes, but Langlie won by 5,816. Given Dill's popularity, the discrepancy between the two races raised suspicions among some Democrats. Press accounts contained numerous allegations of improper vote-counting in Pacific and Grays Harbor counties, and Rosellini believed those allegations to be true.* However, after a few days of heated debate, Rosellini's motion was defeated in both houses.[20]

*Rosellini still believed that in 1996.

The 1941 legislature convened as the country was on the threshold of war. Even in 1939, Washington's shipyards and logging industry had begun to prepare for the coming of World War II. By 1941, depression-era issues were no longer in the forefront. Boeing was emerging from its infancy and rapidly expanding production. Seattle's shipyards were operating at high levels.

Rosellini played a leading role in one of the early controversial measures generated by the rising war effort. During the 1941 session, at the request of several women's organizations, he introduced "equal pay for women" legislation. Boeing and most other businesses opposed the measure, which was the subject of heated hearings. Langlie declined to take a position, and the bill was defeated.[21]

Many legislative concerns in 1941, however, still centered around the lingering problems created by the Great Depression. The most important measures sponsored by the new majority leader were designed to relieve the hardships caused by economic stagnation. For example, Rosellini introduced a bill that provided Social Security benefits to physically disabled people who had not qualified for work benefits. Rosellini proposed doubling the cigarette tax (to one-tenth of 1 percent) and distributing the revenues to "the school, college and general fund" and also to a "disability fund for the handicapped." At the same time, he was urging the Democrats to support a measure that would allow a popular vote on a proposed income tax.[22]

Fair-trade laws also received Rosellini's attention during the 1941 session. He proposed amendments, supported by State Attorney General Smith Troy, that added teeth to the act's enforcement. The floor fight between Rosellini and Joe Drumheller over this measure had a far different outcome than Rosellini's political exile in 1939. Despite opposition from conservatives and "big business," the Rosellini amendments passed.[23]

Establishing a Political Agenda

At the age of thirty-one, Rosellini emerged from the 1941 session as the unquestioned leader of the senate and a widely recognized Democratic spokesman. His charisma and leadership skills were obvious. He got along well with his political colleagues, and they trusted him.

However, it was not yet clear which issues Rosellini would adopt as his own.

The advent of World War II brought new challenges. In contrast to the experience of the Japanese living in the Seattle area, the Rosellini family was never the target of overt discrimination because of its Italian heritage. However, according to Rosellini, all of Seattle's Italians felt a deep-seated sense of anxiety and remorse over the actions of Mussolini and his fascist government, and they responded by enlisting in great numbers and becoming very active in war-bond drives. In June 1942, a *PI* article with the headline "People of Italian Blood Top War Bond Buying" featured three prominent Seattle residents of Italian descent. One of the three was State Senator Rosellini, who responded to Mussolini's statement that "Democracy is a putrefying corpse" by saying that democracy "is alive and on the march and will make a corpse out of the whole fascist regime . . . there is no compromise possible with fascism." Actual enlistment, however, was not an option for Rosellini, who was by then thirty-two, with two children and neither military nor specific business skills.[24]

The war changed the situation in the 1943 legislature. Instead of dealing with Social Security and old-age pensions, the legislature debated veterans' voting rights, civil defense, and war-related emergency concerns. The equal-pay bill, reintroduced by Rosellini and his cosponsor, attracted the largest public hearing ever held by Washington's legislature, as female workers and their supporters packed the house chamber and galleries. This time the bill passed the legislature almost unanimously and was signed by Governor Langlie.[25]

Although the 1943 session was drenched in patriotic fervor, it was not devoid of partisan maneuvers and political conflict, even when dealing with war-related agendas. This was intensified by the quasi-conservative coalition between eastern Washington Democratic senators and the Republicans. While not a formal alliance, this conservative bloc often joined forces, with the aid of Governor Langlie, to block legislation proposed by the Democratic majority. For example, the Democrats were determined to work for the enactment of Initiative 12, a controversial measure that would allow PUDs to join together to condemn properties of private-power companies.

Enough signatures were obtained, primarily by the powerful Washington State Grange, to present the initiative to the legislature. Supported by most Democrats—and a number of Republicans from public-power counties—the initiative passed the legislature. However, private-power backers promptly filed Referendum 25, which sought to repeal the new law and obtained enough signatures to place the referendum on the 1944 general-election ballot. The referendum passed by a margin of 373,051 to 297,191.[26]

Another partisan matter was Governor Langlie's proposal to create a state forestry board to take over the management of state timberlands. The bill stripped the land commissioner—a position then held by popular Democrat Jack Taylor—of most of his power. In the senate, the conservative coalition of Democrats and Republicans supported Langlie's proposal. Rosellini led the opposition to the bill, which passed the senate but eventually died in the house, where liberal Democrats had a majority.[27]

During the 1943 session, Rosellini also introduced legislation to create a medical and dental school at the University of Washington. Rosellini had been interested in medical affairs for a number of years. In 1939 he had been appointed to the board of trustees of Harborview Medical Center and Hospital; by 1941, he was the board's president. His cousin Leo had served as an intern, a resident, and later chief of staff at Harborview. In the late 1930s, Leo, Dr. Alfred Strauss, and others began to press for the establishment of a medical school. A statute passed in 1903 had empowered the University of Washington to include a medical school in its curriculum, and a 1937 statute gave that university exclusive jurisdiction for a medical school in the state. Working closely with Leo and university administrators, Rosellini introduced a bill to establish medical and dental schools. The measure, which was opposed by the Langlie administration for fiscal reasons, as well as by local dentists and their association, failed to pass the senate during that session.[28]

Langlie's refusal to support measures to fund adequate services was a constant aggravation to Rosellini as a legislative leader. The conservative coalition in the senate, strengthened by Langlie's administration, had prevented the passage of all significant Democratic measures. Rosellini and other Democratic leaders were determined to defeat Langlie in the 1944 election. Quoted widely in the press as calling Langlie a "do-nothing governor," Rosellini was spurred in his efforts by Langlie's opposition to the medical school legislation and to most social service measures. The problem was to find a viable and attractive candidate, a strong figure who would not create a divisive primary race, to oppose the incumbent governor. Rosellini and a group of Democratic leaders met with U.S. Sen. Mon C. Wallgren and urged him to run for governor. Moderately liberal, Wallgren was also a good friend of Sen. Harry S. Truman, who was rising quickly to national prominence. According to Rosellini, Wallgren was the ideal candidate, since his national prominence would eliminate serious primary opposition. His position on social issues also countered Langlie's record of relative inactivity. In addition, Wallgren's defeat of Langlie in 1944 helped return substantial Democratic majorities to both houses of the legislature.[29]

Chapter 3

Legislative Priorities

In the 1945 legislative session, Rosellini began to emerge as a statewide political force. He was the leader of the senate, and the liberal wing of his party had working majorities in both houses of the legislature. Governor Wallgren was a friend and ally, and Rosellini's major political foe, Arthur B. Langlie, was absent from the scene. Rosellini's supporters organized the senate committees so that the conservative Democrats could not block the programs proposed by the liberal majority. In only his fourth legislative session, and his second term as a senator, Rosellini was already moving toward the governor's chair.[1]

At the beginning of the session, Rosellini and fellow senator Donald Black moved quickly to reintroduce the bill to establish medical and dental schools at the University of Washington. The measure quickly gained support, and Governor Wallgren voiced his approval. However, it became evident that, because of the wartime shortage of materials, construction of the school buildings and hospital would need to be postponed. The university agreed to use existing facilities for the first two years of instruction. The bill carried an appropriation of $450,000 for operation during the upcoming biennium, with $3.75 million provided for the construction of a medical-dental school building and a hospital once materials and labor became available. Rosellini was part of a group of senators who persuaded Wallgren to appropriate the construction money as part of a special group of Class-A post-war projects.[2] Rosellini moved the medical-dental school legislation through both houses of the legislature and onto the governor's desk for signing in less than two months. It remained one of his proudest accomplishments. In subsequent legislative sessions, whenever funds were needed for the medical and dental schools, Rosellini was usually the sponsor of such appropriations.[3]

It was another event, however, and the legislative activities that surrounded it for the next six years, that marked Rosellini's emergence as the senate's dominant political figure. A few days after the 1945 legislative session opened, a sixteen-year-old boy, John Emberg, was tortured and killed in the King County jail. He was being held in the adult section of the jail on minor juvenile charges. William G. Long, juvenile court judge in King County, had jurisdiction over Emberg. The Seattle newspapers and many prominent citizens called for an investigation into the conditions of the jail as well as the adequacy of facilities for juveniles. In the midst of the controversy, Judge Long called Rosellini and asked for his help. The two had become acquainted when Rosellini had handled juvenile cases as a deputy prosecuting attorney, and Judge Long had stayed in touch with Rosellini after he became a state senator.[4]

As a deputy prosecutor, Rosellini had been aware of the lack of proper facilities for the detention of juveniles. In 1941, he had sponsored an unsuccessful proposal to reform juvenile laws and improve rehabilitation facilities. In his plea to Rosellini following the Emberg incident, Long described the lack of juvenile facilities in King County and the terrible condition of juvenile facilities throughout the state. He explained that King County had no funds to help with the crisis, and that money was not being spent in other counties that did have the funds. When the National Probation Association, at Long's request, had reviewed King County's facilities, it condemned the county's handling of juveniles and its use of adult jail facilities to hold young offenders.[5]

In response to Judge Long's urging and the public outcry, Rosellini acted. He and Rep. Harry J. Martin, also of Seattle, prepared a joint

senate-house resolution proposing that a seven-person interim committee study and report on the conditions in "institutions of confinement" for juveniles.

Other circumstances soon added to the urgency of the situation.
When King County Prosecutor Lloyd Shorett tried to obtain emergency funds from the county to deal with the problem, he learned
that state law prevented county commissioners from releasing emergency funds for improvement of facilities. Rosellini introduced additional legislation which required counties to provide separate quarters
for juvenile offenders. This legislation permitted the commissioners
no discretion and required immediate action, enabling Washington's
counties to invoke emergency powers to appropriate funds.[6]

Considerable remorse and guilt on the part of legislators was
behind the rush to correct the conditions exposed by Emberg's death.
Rep. John L. O'Brien, Rosellini's fellow legislator from the thirty-third
district, reminded the house of the earlier study and recommendations
made by an interim committee on penal institutions, and the failure
of the 1943 legislature to heed its findings. The gruesome details of
Emberg's death finally exposed the drastic nature of the crisis. The
Seattle newspapers also described acts of sexual perversion forced on
young boys, roaming gangs of juveniles preying on smaller boys, and
cases of torture—all taking place in Washington's juvenile-detention
facilities.[7]

The legislation requiring action by the county commissioners was
quickly passed. The Rosellini-Martin investigation proposal passed
also, and the senators unanimously added an amendment requiring
the appointed commission to begin its work at once so that the legislature might receive a preliminary report during the current session.
Rosellini was named chair of the joint committee; instead of the original $10,000, the appropriation to cover the cost of the investigation
was raised to $25,000.[8]

The hearings, which began in Seattle on April 13, 1945, revealed
that the facilities used to house juvenile offenders were, in Rosellini's
word, "horrible." This was true of every county that the committee
visited. In King County, no new facilities had been built in years, and
little had been spent to maintain existing ones. (Adult jails, where

juveniles were often placed because of overcrowding in youth facilities, were even worse.) The report on the Kitsap County juvenile detention home was typical. Rosellini's committee discovered (1) that children were routinely housed with prostitutes; (2) that juvenile offenders picked up in Bremerton were held overnight with adults in the city jail—the "likely locale for another Emberg case"; (3) that children with contagious diseases were being housed with healthy children; and (4) that as many as twenty-five children were being quartered in a space designed for twelve.[9]

Initially, the committee suggested remedial measures that would drastically change every aspect of the current law—such as establishing a new department that would handle detention, and creating a series of new courts with juvenile jurisdiction. Although the committee had broad support from advisory groups interested in the juvenile issue, three powerful groups opposed the substance of these initial proposals—the Washington State Bar Association, the Superior Court Judges Association, and the State Association of County Commissioners. Constitutional concerns raised by these groups, as well as political events, played a critical role in altering the committee's final recommendations. The 1946 election was a national and statewide Republican landslide, resulting in a much more conservative legislature. Rosellini was the only Democrat on the committee who was reelected. Harry Zent, a Republican committee member from Spokane, was also reelected, but he had not been active. Lacking support for drastic reform, Rosellini's committee proposed legislation which only modified the existing juvenile law, and made rehabilitation and prevention of delinquency, not punishment, the primary purpose of juvenile detention.[10]

The 1947 state senate was organized by a coalition of twenty-three Republicans and the eight conservative Democrats who had been "frozen out" in the 1945 session, giving the group a two-thirds majority. The liberal Democrats, led by Rosellini and Earl Coe of Klickitat, were often called the "futile fifteen." Their proposals were blocked by the solid Republican majority in the house and the conservative coalition in the senate. The conservative Democrats made no secret of their wish to repay the liberals for the way they had been treated in the 1945 session. As the *PI* reported: "Revenge was sweet for eight conservative Democratic senators but infuriating to a minority bloc of 15 other Democrats." Rosellini expressed the collective feeling of the liberals: "The way the Republican organization has tentatively set up matters such as committee appointments, seating arrangements and patronage is the most selfish and unfair to any minority group that has ever been proposed in the history of the state." With conservatives controlling the agenda, the youth protection act did not make it out of committee.[11]

Although the juvenile measure was killed, Rosellini's activities as chair of the interim committee had altered his political focus and given him a statewide forum for the first time. The investigations also gave him firsthand knowledge of the substandard conditions in the state's institutions. From that point on, Rosellini was known as a legislator with extensive knowledge of, and intense interest in, Washington's institutions. He was automatically a member of any group dealing with institutional affairs. The refusal of the Republican-controlled legislature even to consider the juvenile measure ultimately worked to the advantage of Rosellini and his party in other ways as well.[12]

Between sessions Rosellini attacked the record of the 1947 legislature on juvenile reform. His leadership of the juvenile commission provided him with opportunities to speak throughout the state on this and other liberal issues. Even though the commission's proposals had been ignored, chairing the statewide hearings on conditions at Washington's juvenile facilities had provided Rosellini with experience which he would later use to great advantage (see chapter 4).[13]

The 1948 election, although a victory for Truman nationally, returned Governor Langlie to the statehouse in Olympia. It also gave control of the state senate to the Republicans. In the house, however, the Democrats had a majority, and Charles W. Hodde of Colville was named as speaker. Rosellini was named minority leader of the upper chamber once again. With Republicans in control of the senate and Langlie as governor, few Democratic measures received serious consideration. Even though the Juvenile Protection bill was reintroduced with bipartisan support and passed the house, its fate was sealed. An article by Rosellini in the Rainier *Reporter* explained:

"Although the [juvenile protection] bill was passed by the house by a unanimous vote, and is sponsored jointly by Republican and Democratic representatives, the word has come up from Governor Langlie that the bill should be killed in the senate." Langlie got his wish. So complete was the stalemate that in February 1949, Stub Nelson reported in the *PI*, as of the thirtieth day of the session, lawmakers had not passed a single major measure.[14]

The 1949 session was not a total loss for Rosellini, however. Since Democrats controlled the house, they were assured of a majority of members on the influential legislative council. Created during the 1947 session, the legislative council's purpose was to study areas of state government between sessions and to recommend needed legislation. As originally envisioned, the council would meet year-round, whereas the legislature met only for a sixty-day regular session every other year. The council had the power of subpoena, as well as other powers held by the legislature itself, and it was assisted by a full-time staff which included attorneys and government experts. Since the house speaker appointed eleven members and the president of the senate appointed only ten, the Democrats were assured of control. Rosellini and two other Democratic senators appointed to the council by Lt. Gov. Vic Meyers joined the eight Democratic council members from the house and assumed chairmanships of all the council's interim committees.[15]

Council chair Hodde appointed Rosellini to the standing committee on state and local government. At Rosellini's insistence, a subcommittee was appointed, with Rosellini as chair, to continue investigations of the juvenile justice system. The scope of the hearings held by Rosellini's subcommittee went far beyond reform of the juvenile justice system. Ironically, the Langlie administration itself precipitated events which put Rosellini in charge of an investigation into all state institutions. During the first half of 1950, conditions at the Monroe Reformatory had deteriorated, and the director of institutions, Harold Van Eaton, brought in an expert from out of state—Kenyon J. Scudder, superintendent of the California State Institution for Men at Chino—to investigate and report on the situation at Monroe. Langlie refused to release Scudder's findings, although they were widely discussed in the legislature.[16]

Rep. Reuben Knoblauch of Sumner, head of the house interim committee on institutions, called for an immediate investigation of the situation at Monroe and requested a copy of the report. Stating that "Langlie had not only vetoed the interim committee appropriation of $8,000 but refused to give it any money from his emergency fund," Knoblauch accused the governor of ignoring his legislative committee, and reported that Langlie "told us members of the interim committee [we] were a bunch of snoopers." Rosellini asked the legislative council—by then he was the vice-chair—to authorize his subcommittee to carry on joint hearings with Knoblach's committee. Since the legislative council had its own funds, the investigation could proceed. Thereafter, the two groups acted together on all matters relating to institutions.[17]

Following an inspection of the reformatory, the joint committee issued reports of deplorable conditions at Monroe. The committee emphasized the need for more money, asserting that "there is great need at the reformatory for increased vocational training, education, guidance, and rehabilitation programs. And further that there exist inadequate facilities for segregation of inmates as to age, seriousness and type of crime." The report identified the only solution to the problems at Monroe and other state institutions as "the passage of the twenty-million dollar bond issue to be voted upon in the November general election, and more adequate appropriations by the legislature." The committee's investigation in September 1950 uncovered neglect and inadequate staffing at the Rainier State School for mentally deficient children, and staffing problems were also discovered at the Grand Mound Training School for girls.[18]

Rosellini had stated that political patronage hiring was to blame for many problems at the various juvenile facilities—more so, at times, than a lack of funding. Continuing that concept, he proposed legislation to establish a six-person commission to run all state institutions. His proposal would also require the commission to set up a merit system. (Although the commission format was not enacted, a merit system was adopted after Rosellini became governor.)[19]

In 1950, the Democrats and Rosellini also supported efforts to qualify Initiative 175, which would establish a state Department of

Youth Protection and create politically independent boards designed
to protect juveniles. An editorial in the always conservative Yakima
Herald questioned the intent of the initiative:

> Because of the measure's ancestry . . . we believe a searching study of
> the proposal is in order. . . . The granddaddy of the present proposal was
> drafted by a 1945 legislative interim committee which included four
> persons named by the Canwell Committee* as Communists. Two of those
> four were Thomas C. Rabbitt . . . and William J. Pennock. . . . Rabbitt
> and Pennock are perhaps better known as Washington Pension Union
> leaders who helped engineer Initiative 172, the welfare scheme that is
> now breaking the state.

The editorial concluded by expressing concern that the current initiative " be the camel's nose under the tent wall; that it [would] open the
way for its father, the Rosellini bill, and its grandfather, the Pennock-
Rabbitt concoction," and by asserting that these measures would "set
up a state agency which not only would take over the state training
school but also would absorb the county detention homes and the
county juvenile departments." In the face of partisan pressure, the
initiative failed to get enough signatures to qualify for the ballot.[20]

The 1950 general election returned Democratic majorities to both
houses of the legislature. Rosellini sensed that the highly publicized
needs of the juvenile institutions would cause the legislature to act
quickly. He introduced legislation calling for a permanent youth council and youth service department to promote and coordinate state and
local programs and services in the field of delinquency prevention. The
proposal did not request either a separate court system for juveniles
or the removal of juvenile sentencing from county jurisdiction, a
compromise which neutralized the most powerful opposition to the
earlier version.[21]

Passage of the compromise legislation was soon jeopardized, however. At informal meetings of Democratic legislators, eight conservative senators, led by Jack Rogers of Bremerton, formed a rump group

---

*The Canwell Committee was Washington's legislative verson of the notorious
anti-Communist House UnAmerican Activities Committee.

of so-called dissidents, highly critical of Rosellini, who announced their intention to elect one of their group as president pro tem of the senate. Rogers claimed that "Senator Rosellini now labels himself a moderate, while in previous sessions he was the leader of the left-wing faction." Most of the dissidents—Dave Cowen, Spokane; Stanton Ganders, Bickleton; James Keefe, Spokane; Rod Lindsay, Spokane; Ed Riley, Seattle; Jack Rogers, Bremerton; Howard Roup, Asotin; and Ted Schroeder, Puyallup—had been part of the coalition with senate Republicans in the 1947 session. Stub Nelson of the *PI* presented the other Democrats' response: "The moderates said it was not a case of leaving the party, but 'continuing as we always have.' They pointed out that they always have been against the Rabbitts and Pennocks and against screwball legislation." In the Seattle *Times*, Ross Cunningham provided another version, closer to that of the Yakima *Herald*: "The senate differences are based on clashing ideologies as well as personalities. Senators Schroeder, Jack Rogers, David C. Cowen and Howard Roup often have been aligned in past sessions against the Rosellini faction," adding that "the rupture became pronounced in 1945, when the group Rosellini now heads collaborated with advocates of the Communist party line." The Yakima *Herald* and Cunningham were indulging in the anti-Communist rhetoric of the time, rather than reporting established fact. Although legislators such as Pennock and Rabbit were ultraliberal by 1951 standards, they had not changed their actual positions from those of a standard, aggressive New Deal Democrat of the late '30s to middle '40s. Rosellini said more than forty years later that there was never any proof that they had belonged to any Communist group. The Rogers-Schroeder group didn't go along and was threatened with reprisal from the Democratic organization.[22]

Although the conservative faction backed away from forming an official coalition, and Rosellini was elected majority leader, the eight dissidents collaborated with Republicans to appoint conservatives—including themselves—to key chairmanships, forming what Rosellini referred to as "the gas-pipe coalition," referring to the fact that two of the dissidents were on the board of directors of a gas company seeking a franchise in the state. Since this group opposed substantial portions of the youth protection act, Rosellini was concerned about its future.[23]

Nevertheless, the Youth Protection Act did finally pass in the 1951 session. Various forces that had been divided on how to handle the problem came together in support of the measure cosponsored by Rosellini and Tom Hall, a Republican from Skamania County. Langlie, who had appointed his own committee on youth, gave the measure his full support after his committee proposed changes similar to those contained in the Rosellini-Hall measure. Those changes included: the creation of a division of children and youth services with jurisdiction over all institutions where juveniles are given custodial care; the designation of the Chehalis and Grand Mound training schools as "maximum security" institutions; the establishment of a statewide system of "minimum security" institutions; the establishment of a diagnostic service which would be available on request to any juvenile court; the creation of a post-institutional placement program; the authorization for two or more counties to join in establishing juvenile detention quarters if needed; the creation of special facilities in public institutions for juveniles needing treatment for emotional disturbances; and the creation of a permanent council on children and youth.[24]

Once these proposals were made public, the two legislators worked closely with Langlie's committee in the final drafting process. Langlie's support guaranteed the act's passage. The only substantive difference between the youth committee's plan and Rosellini's original proposals was the removal of temporary custody situations from the jurisdiction of superior court judges. On February 8, 1951, the senate passed the Youth Protection Act by a unanimous vote. The enactment of this legislation was an arduous process, and many groups—as well as general public sentiment—helped to bring it to fruition. Without question, however, Rosellini was the guiding force who kept the measure alive and moving. There was little about the issue that could translate into immediate political gain or support for a state senator from Seattle. Yet, between 1945 and 1951, Rosellini demonstrated a dogged and abiding concern for and consistently devoted his energies to improving Washington's juvenile institutions. Only after he was elected governor was he able to fully accomplish that objective.

Chapter 4

Statewide Investigations

When the 1951 legislature convened, Rosellini had served as state senator for thirteen years. It was the midpoint of Langlie's second term as governor. The Youth Protection Act, passed during that session, had been Rosellini's major legislative focus for more than six years. In the course of the measure's erratic road to acceptance, Rosellini had broadened his interest to include all state institutions. His legislative council subcommittee on juvenile delinquency had in effect preempted the senate's committee on state institutions during the joint hearings held in 1949 and 1950. During the 1951 session, two other statewide investigations were set in motion that ultimately shifted Rosellini's focus to the governor's office.[1]

The "Little Hoover" Committee

Neither the 1949 nor the 1951 legislature managed to pass appropriations and budget bills during the regular session. Even after passage of revenue bills that technically allowed the legislatures to adjourn, the legislators were called back to Olympia for extraordinary special sessions in the summers of 1950 and 1951 to deal with constitutional limitations on state indebtedness. In the summer of 1951, the state was forced to issue warrants to meet payroll and other financial obligations for more than a week as a result of a lawsuit challenging the budget bill from the regular session. Langlie called another special session, which passed revenue measures sufficient to restore government operations.[2]

This crisis was precipitated by the conservative coalition in the senate, which during the 1951 session had introduced a budget that curtailed spending and eliminated the need for new taxes. Although neither Langlie nor the regular Democrats approved of the coalition's proposed cuts for education and other services, they were unable to achieve a consensus on new taxes that could pass both chambers. The conservative senators were proposing the elimination of programs in education that had been in place for years—for example, kindergarten, nurseries, school buses, and health protection for the common schools. A Democratic member of the coalition, Sen. Jack Rogers, explained the rationale: "There has been a lot of talk about frills in education. Just what are frills? And what should parents pay for? This may be an old fashioned thought, but several committee members thought the parents should pay for their children's lunches and get them back and forth to school."

Failure of the senate and house to agree on these and other cuts proposed by the coalition led Roderick Lindsay, chair of the senate appropriations committee, to lock up all appropriations measures in committee by way of a response.[3]

The underlying reason for this maneuvering was the stringent state restriction on local school levies, a longtime political battleground. As Ross Cunningham pointed out in the Seattle *Times*, "Foreseeing financial difficulties in future years, school forces have renewed their drive to have the restrictions of the 40-mill-tax limitations relaxed so they may vote more money on local levels more easily. Their measures to accomplish this have been bottled up by the defenders of the 40-mill-tax limitation." Attempts by Langlie to force higher property tax assessments were also unsuccessful. These conflicts were not new, and they lay at the heart of the 1951 legislature's inability to pass a budget.[4]

Forty years later, Rosellini described the situation during the late days of the 1951 legislature: "The real problem was that no majority in the legislature had come to realize the tremendous pressure on services that the end of the war and the growth in the state was creating." Without a governor capable of leading his own party to that recognition as the situation was developing, state funding was limited to fringe or nuisance taxes and increasing pressure on savings and budget cuts. Another reason for the impasse was the Democrats' opposition to Langlie's proposed tax solutions, even when he tried to assert leadership. In both the 1949 and 1951 sessions, Rosellini and the Democrats opposed as regressive and punitive the flat income tax that Langlie proposed to fund additional services. The liberal Democrats themselves were often divided on the issue. In 1949 a liberal bloc in the house had tried to support such a tax as a first step toward a graduated net income tax. Rosellini filibustered against it in the senate, which passed the bill anyway. It was rejected by house Republicans when the Democrats raised the exemption level from $1,000 to $5,000. In both sessions, Rosellini and the other Democrats also opposed any increase in the sales tax or its extension to other services.[5]

At one point Langlie suggested a 4 percent corporate income tax—over the objections of most of his own party and many of his supporters—but it received little serious consideration once the senate coalition voiced its opposition. Langlie's administration also proposed, in the 1951 session, a measure allowing counties to levy a 1 percent excise tax on real-estate sales. Since the bill also permitted the legislature to allocate the funds statewide—regardless of the county where the monies were raised—it got nowhere. Neither of Langlie's proposals seems to have been serious, since they lacked support from his own party.[6]

Both sides, therefore, were content to play politics, accuse the other of insincerity, and try to use nuisance taxes or budget cuts to prevent deficit spending. Rosellini himself opposed new taxes on the grounds that any increase should be based on a more thorough study of the state's needs—a position that was used against him later when he was accusing Langlie of neglecting institutions and other services.[7]

Despite the partisan bickering over revenue and budgets in the 1949 and 1951 sessions, even the Democrats recognized that Langlie had tried to act responsibly in connection with the tax issues. Following the special revenue session in 1950, Rosellini exempted Langlie from his statements that the Republicans had been "insincere all the way through on revenue legislation." In the special session of August

1951, Rosellini and other Democratic leaders worked harmoniously with the governor in attempts to arrive at a package of minor taxes which would be acceptable to all the factions.[8]

Langlie's revenue proposals drew substantial criticism from his own party, however. The Seattle *Times* reported a move by prominent party members to draft King County Prosecutor Charles O. Carroll to run against Langlie in the primary. Many Republicans believed Langlie should have cut state services more in the 1951–53 biennium, rather than trying to increase revenues. Arguing against any tax increase, the Republican-dominated state conference on state finances urged a 5 percent across-the-board cut by all state agencies, a proposal supported by Rosellini. Langlie accused these critics of "lack of knowledge of the requirements of state government and a lack of courage to take the responsibilities for effects of reductions." Six years later, Governor Rosellini directed all state agencies (except institutions) to cut 15 percent of their budgets during the 1957–59 biennium in order to reduce deficits, while at the same time he increased funds for institutions and education.[9]

Faced with a continuing shortage of funds and the inability to pass revenue measures in 1949 and 1951, the legislative council placed a high priority on studies of state government. Rosellini asked to chair the eight-member subcommittee responsible for those studies. Believing that "the state could benefit from studies patterned after those of the so-called 'Hoover Commission' which recommended beneficial changes in the federal government," Rosellini saw a need to "explore the means by which state expenditures could be limited to the 'lowest amount' consistent with efficient performance of essential services, to eliminate overlapping functions, and consolidate similar services where feasible."[10]

As a result, the legislative council proposed the establishment of an advisory committee, made up of thirty representatives of business, labor, school, farm, and church organizations, to work with the legislature. The committee's job was to study the operations of state government and its services and recommend to the legislative council changes that would promote efficiencies, eliminate duplications, and, they hoped, save money.[11]

It is difficult to tell whether this idea actually originated with Rosellini and the legislative council. Just five days after their plan was made public, Governor Langlie announced that he was setting up his own commission—the Washington State Committee on State Finance, to be made up of chambers of commerce and representatives of business and industry—to make a similar study. The newspapers lampooned the proliferation of advisory groups. In the *Times* Ross Cunningham commented, "A skeptic might remark that the first thing needed is a commission to simplify the commissions studying the simplification of state government." Rosellini and Langlie engaged in a debate of sorts over whose study was begun first, but they quickly agreed that they should cooperate in their examination of state government.[12]

Harold Shefelman, Rosellini's former law school professor, agreed to chair the citizens' committee. The first meeting was in October 1951, with only Shefelman and a few proposed members. Shortly thereafter, the rest of the members were appointed jointly by Langlie and the council. Additionally, four legislators from the council, two governor's representatives, and representatives of the state's elected officials sat on the committee as nonvoting members. Called by the press and others the "Little Hoover" committee, the citizens' group had been formed because of political pressures to cut costs, not from any public outcry for basic restructuring. Indeed, the compromise nature of its appointment by both the governor and the council meant that its mandate was murky at best.[13]

Regardless, under Shefelman's leadership and with a staff of three full-time aides, the committee and its six subcommittees held numerous meetings with state government officials and department heads, together with experts from within and outside government. Despite the relatively short time available and limited staff, the committee presented a report at the beginning of the 1953 legislative session, which recommended substantial changes—many of which would require constitutional amendments. It recommended abolishing the elective offices of state superintendent of public instruction, commissioner of lands, and insurance commissioner, and establishing a civil service system for state employees. It also recommended a far-reaching reorganization of all the state's budget and accounting functions. Neither

Langlie nor the legislature was prepared to accept many of these proposals. While several specific suggestions—including a state civil service system—were introduced through proposed legislation, none was passed, and no further reports were submitted.[14]

The importance of the Little Hoover committee for Rosellini was twofold. First, it identified him for the first time as a political leader on a par with Langlie. Second, it gave Rosellini prominence as an expert on state government and its operations.

The Crime Committee

The second statewide investigation that followed the 1951 session involved law enforcement and organized crime. Even before the formation of the Little Hoover commission, Rosellini had had several meetings with U.S. Sen. Estes Kefauver of Tennessee. At the time, Kefauver's Senate Crime Committee was probing into activities of organized crime and holding hearings in various parts of the country. Kefauver was prominently mentioned as a possible Democratic presidential candidate to succeed Truman in 1952. At meetings with state legislators around the country, Kefauver suggested that the crime problem was not limited to heavily populated states.[15]

Rosellini felt that his legislative council subcommittee could investigate whether organized crime was operating in the state, determine its impact on state government, and recommend legislation. Realizing that a preliminary investigation was needed in order to justify such a study in Washington, Rosellini obtained legislative council funds to hire an independent investigator. Through Attorney General Pat Brown of California, he identified Tom Judge, who had worked with Brown's office on a similar problem in California. Judge made a quiet preliminary investigation, reporting directly to Rosellini. He found evidence of organized crime operating in several Washington cities and of payoffs and other types of gratuities being received by public officials and law enforcement people. Rosellini presented these findings to his subcommittee, and they decided to hold hearings in a number of the cities identified by Judge, whose role was made public before the hearings began. The subcommittee retained George Kahin of Seattle as counsel, and armed with subpoena power, rapidly moved toward hearings.[16]

At the outset, Rosellini reiterated that the committee's mission was purely fact-finding and designed to identify needed legislative reforms. The committee had no power to arrest, prosecute, or incarcerate. Yet the hearings rapidly took on the appearance of a grand jury rather than a fact-finding study by a legislative group. "State Crime Probe Due Here Oct. 12" was the headline in the Vancouver paper the week before hearings began in that city. The proceedings became a media bonanza for the newspapers, radio stations, and the embryonic television industry. KING-TV was the only television station in the Northwest at that time, and program director Lee Schulman set up a program to interview the committee following its first week of hearings. Called "Crime Report," the half-hour program aired at 10:00 p.m.—immediately following "Husky Hi-Lites" and before the "Fight of the Week." Advertisements in the *PI* urged people to "hear the Rosellini Committee's hearings on VICE AND CRIME" every day there were hearings. Local radio stations carried the hearings live, and highlights were aired each evening, with Stub Nelson of the *PI* offering commentary for both radio and television broadcasts.[17]

Some of the early interviews with Rosellini fueled the circus-like atmosphere. Immediately prior to the Vancouver hearing, he told the press: "I know you are interested in news, and it is not news here that there is gambling going on, that lotteries have been running openly, that bookmaking has flourished, protected by some sort of license." The report continued: " 'As far as I can tell,' judged Rosellini, the mild tone of his voice unchanged, 'all these things have been going on with the full knowledge and acquiescence of the city officials.' " Dramatic confrontations between Rosellini and counsel representing some of the witnesses provided further grist for the media mill. Rosellini and his crime committee quickly became household names. The nature of the hearings and the publicity surrounding them had detractors, however, and Rosellini was often accused of political opportunism.[18]

Initially, the legislative council had allotted $15,000 to carry out the investigation, and the subcommittee ultimately required another

$15,000 to finish its work. Before the money ran out, public hearings were held in Vancouver, Tacoma, Aberdeen, and Seattle. Because of lack of funds and time, private hearings were held in many other cities, including Spokane, Yakima, Pasco, Kennewick, Richland, and Port Angeles.[19]

Rosellini was openly defensive about the decision to hold public hearings, saying that the policy was adopted "reluctantly and after much consideration." It was, however, a tactic that Kefauver and Brown had used effectively. As Rosellini admitted, "such hearings and inquiries are the most vicious sort because they lack established procedures and legislative bodies can write their own rules." The committee tried to pattern its hearings on the Kefauver model, and avoid the excesses of the infamous House Committee on Un-American Activities or, closer to home, the Canwell Committee of the Washington State legislature.[20]

This was not always easy to do. Some of the witnesses, particularly government officials who were asked to comment on the tolerance of gambling, prostitution, or other unlawful activities, accused the crime committee and Rosellini of violating constitutional rights and engaging in "McCarthy-type tactics." The prosecuting attorney in Clark County, for example, said the hearings were "condoning rumors" and "aiding and abetting in the violation of a man's sacred right of privacy." The most frequent complaint was that the committee sensationalized what was already known and allowed witnesses to discuss things that could not be proved.[21]

In most cities, the committee conducted a "preliminary survey" to collect pertinent information. Committee members—in some cases Rosellini himself—would set up office hours in a public building and gather relevant information from local residents. The committee was not interested solely in exposing problems in law enforcement; it also wanted to know what *did* work in law enforcement practices throughout Washington.[22]

The first hearings began in Vancouver on October 12, 1951. They were particularly unpopular locally because Vancouver had traditionally been an "open" city. Rosellini recalls Las Vegas–run high-stakes bingo games, not connected with any charity, houses of prostitution operating under the tolerance of public officials, and the like. The hearings were played down by the Vancouver press, but the Tacoma *News Tribune* found that "the most shocking thing about the findings at Vancouver of the 'Little Kefauver committee' . . . is the complacency of the city administration and the police department at conditions as revealed in testimony before the legislators." The National Guard was used to serve subpoenas, and the hearings were highlighted by the refusals of some witnesses to testify. Although Rosellini ruled that the witnesses were in contempt of the legislature, no one was ever prosecuted for refusing to give testimony. A number of citizens did testify freely, including the mayor, who readily admitted that a horse-book operation and bingo games had been licensed and running for years. He also said the city used the tax revenues from these sources to meet the services demanded by its citizens. When asked about his open tolerance policy, the county prosecutor, R. DeWitt Jones, called the committee to task for engaging in "McCarthyisms."[23]

Four decades later, this appears to be fairly tame stuff. Gambling and lotteries are now universal—with the state operating the largest lottery of all twice a week. But in 1951 these hearings were the first investigation into the tolerance policies by law enforcement officials toward non-alcohol-related vice. Clark County Prosecutor Jones said, in concluding his testimony, "if the City undertakes by city ordinance to license these places and thereby creates a veil of legality, I'm not going to act as a Reformer." Clark County Sheriff, Clarence McKay, highlighted the dilemma when he said "you can't license these establishments with one hand and slap them with the other."[24]

The investigation in Vancouver revealed the extent to which some cities openly condoned and benefited from otherwise illegal operations and activities. Not surprisingly, other communities were not anxious to have hearings in their area. The Tacoma *News Tribune* noted that "we should not preen our feathers with too righteous an air because of the tarnish on Vancouver's reputation since there is nothing to prevent either Sen. Albert Rosellini's group or its federal counterpart from moving to Tacoma and pawing over our soiled linens." Tacoma, fittingly, was the next venue for public hearings, scheduled to open November 26 at the state armory. More than twenty-five witnesses were subpoenaed. Rosellini's statements to the press were more precise and detailed than was the case prior to the Vancouver hearings: "[The] committee primarily is concerned with prostitution, police pay-offs, gambling, book-making, and, though it will consume a smaller portion of the time, narcotics."[25]

By this time, KING-TV recognized the public interest in the hearings and requested the right to broadcast them live. Several legislators protested the plan, including Rep. Gordon Brown of Tacoma, who wrote to Rosellini and to Hodde and complained that televising the proceedings would be "an infringement of personal rights" of a witness.

The Tacoma hearings more than lived up to expectations. The star witness was a madam who testified about payoffs to policemen for protection. A widow of a gambler who had shot himself over his debts asked for a new law to protect those with the "disease of gambling." In response to a request from Lee Schulman at KING, the hearings were held from 10:00 a.m. to 12:30 p.m. and from 1:30 to 4:00 p.m. to coincide with broadcast scheduling. Years later, Rosellini recalled that it was sometimes necessary to juggle witnesses in order to fit testimony into a television time format.[26]

The public could not get enough. "Spectators at the Armory love it. They come early, stay late and won't give up their seats at recess," wrote Sam Angeloff in the *PI* under the headline "Tacoma Drops Everything to See Big Probe." One witness, Tacoma Public Safety Commissioner James Kerr, demanded equal time. When he learned that his testimony would not be televised, he said, "This is unfair to me. I should have the same treatment as those who attacked me." His request was granted, and he appeared on television. According to Angeloff, the hearings drew the largest viewing audience—estimated at more than 450,000—since television arrived in the Pacific Northwest. Tacoma merchants complained that holiday business was lost because of the hearings.[27]

One witness noted Rosellini's past association with liquor-license clients. Tony Zatkovich, a former Tacoma police chief, was asked if he had ever paid for drinks at Ann Thompson's Place, a local bottle club. After an evasive answer or two, he was asked why he did not arrest the owners if they were selling liquor illegally. Zatkovich snapped, "Maybe Mr. Rosellini can explain the operation of bottle clubs better than I can." According to the *PI*, "Rosellini leaped to his feet pounding his gavel and stormed: 'We are not going to tolerate impertinent answers. . . . Is that understood?'" Another witness referred to "a widespread belief that the hearing was a political thing."[28]

Witnesses at subsequent hearings would be more direct in their accusations of political opportunism on Rosellini's part. Before one hearing, Rosellini announced that children under eighteen would be excluded, and he urged parents to keep their children away from television sets—because the proceedings were "apt to become pretty lurid today." Whether he was actually fearful of lurid content and not promoting greater public interest is difficult to decide. Rosellini certainly knew that the hearings were helping his name familiarity, and he was never shy about publicity.[29]

The crime committee uncovered many allegations of corruption within the Tacoma law enforcement community. Rev. Harold B. Long and several other witnesses called for a grand jury investigation because of the conflicting testimony. While he admits that the hearings failed to prove actual payoffs to government officials, Rosellini points out that Tacoma's form of government changed as a result of the hearings. The same thing happened in Vancouver, where an appointed city manager form of government was adopted within a year or two of the hearings.[30]

The next hearings were scheduled in Aberdeen. Apparently alarmed by the nature of the televised proceedings, one of the proposed witnesses, police captain John Gillespie, sought a court order to bar the committee from holding hearings in Aberdeen. Filing suit in Thurston County, the officer obtained a temporary restraining order on the basis that the committee was looking into matters outside its mandate since its primary focus was on local law enforcement and city ordinances as opposed to any state regulatory statutes. In his ruling, Judge Charles T. Wright held that "the investigation of county and city matters is not one of the powers granted to the committee." Before responding to Judge Wright's order to show cause, however, the committee was granted a temporary writ of prohibition by the state supreme court, which removed Wright's injunction. Rosellini announced that the hearings into local law enforcement issues would be postponed until the high court issued a final ruling on the committee's right to investigate city and county matters.[31]

While waiting for that ruling, the committee proceeded with hearings in both Aberdeen and Seattle, limiting inquiries to state matters. The state supreme court, by a five-to-four majority, eventually upheld the crime committee's right to probe into local and city matters, reasoning that "municipal corporations, cities and counties are regarded as subordinate subdivisions of state government." The Seattle hearing had its share of dramatic moments. The committee became embroiled in the angry aftermath of the city's recent mayoral campaign. This outcome was not surprising, since unsuccessful candidate Allan Pomeroy had made the city's tolerance policy an issue and had challenged incumbent William Devin to join in his request to hold hearings in Seattle. Police Chief Eastman and Mayor William Devin, when called to testify, clashed with Rosellini and defended tolerance of a certain level of gambling. Devin charged that the hearings were "purely political" and, in an obvious reference to Rosellini, asked the committee to investigate "tie-ups with liquor" and inform the public as to whether any legislator represented bottle clubs or speakeasies.[32]

Rosellini responded that Devin was the one engaging in "smears and innuendoes," and accused Devin and Eastman of "defying" state laws when they openly permitted cardroom gambling. Telegraphing, perhaps, his intention to run for governor later that year, Rosellini said that Devin was being used as a cat's paw by Langlie when he made his charges. Indeed, Devin's references to bottle clubs is strange in view of the passage of Initiative 148 four years earlier, which rendered them obsolete. His use of the term "speakeasy" is instructive of the lingering effect of Prohibition and the ease with which some people linked liquor to crime.[33]

In addition to Devin, other Republicans used the occasion to attack Rosellini's motivation. Sparks flew when Rosellini ousted from the hearings a fellow state senator, present as counsel for a witness. As William Goodloe's client finished her testimony, the Republican senator stated his desire to "forsake [his] role as an attorney and make certain remarks as a state senator." Despite Rosellini's request that they be put in writing, Goodloe asked whether Rosellini was running for governor. Rosellini interrupted Goodloe, stating that he had answered that question in press interviews, and that he intended to continue to serve as a state senator. Goodloe persisted with his questioning, which turned into a speech, and, after several warnings, was escorted from the hearings by a state patrolman. This was the most dramatic example of such charges. But the issue of Rosellini's political opportunism permeated the Seattle hearings. By the spring of 1952, there had been several articles mentioning Rosellini as a possible candidate for various political offices. A Seattle *Times* editorial asserted that staging the hearings for television "should dispose of any argument over whether the star characters in the drama were politically motivated.[34]

It is true that the hearings happened to coincide with the emergence of television as a statewide medium for the first time. The fact that the hearings were carried live on television does not establish that they were politically motivated. The coverage occurred because the subject matter caught the attention of Lee Schulman at KING, and Rosellini had nothing to do with Schulman's decision. However, once the decision was made, only an extremely naive politician would have turned down the opportunity to shape the hearings accordingly. Rosellini was neither naive nor lacking in ambition. The *Times*'s accusation of "political motivation" rings hollow, since Rosellini's investigations fit into a pattern of commonplace political activity— nationally and in Washington State. Today the accusation of political staging would be implausible. Perhaps more bothersome to the *Times* and Republicans such as Devin and Goodloe was the fact that Rosellini and the committee were probing areas of illegality which Rosellini, in their eyes at least, had himself ignored or tried to liberalize.[35]

Without question, Rosellini's actions as chair were motivated at least in part by political considerations. For example, a series of seven articles about the investigation, "Crime in Washington State," written by Rosellini, was syndicated in weekly newspapers throughout the state. Designed to explain the committee's workings to "all sectors of the public" and produced at no cost to the state, the series broadened Rosellini's statewide exposure.[36]

Rosellini also used his visits to various Washington cities in the course of carrying out the committee's work as opportunities to address local groups. In an address to the Omak Chamber of Commerce, Rosellini spoke about the intentions, methods, and results of the probe. While in Pasco, he spoke to the Chamber of Commerce about both the ongoing hearings and the possibility that he might run for governor in the approaching election. In Ellensburg, he commented that criticism of his committee had come from two sources—the underworld, and officials whose "toes have been stepped on." Addressing Kennewick's Chamber of Commerce, Rosellini sounded like a gubernatorial candidate when he took the opportunity to express his intention to push for highway construction in the area—although he also discussed the investigation.[37]

The crime hearings formally ended on June 20, 1952, when the committee had exhausted its funds. However, Rosellini visited Bremerton, Everett, and Bellingham and held private meetings with governmental officials before closing down the committee's activities. By that time, either Rosellini or his committee, or both, had visited almost every city of any size in the state. The report remained to be written, and committee member Milton R. Loney of Walla Walla County stated that the committee would retain full authority to subpoena witnesses and records as needed in order to write that report.[38]

Yet, despite the thorough report filed with the legislature for the 1953 session, no legislation resulted from the committee's activities. In fact, the committee's subpoena power was removed. Rosellini explained that the legislature felt that he had run away with the committee, and his decision to file for governor within a week of the committee's close of business strongly reinforced that feeling. The fact that the committee was looking into areas where the state had no power (e.g., to file charges or to bring indictments) exacerbated a sense that the hearings were mostly for show and reinforced the criticism that all they had accomplished was to give certain cities an undeserved bad name.[39]

A further complicating feature was the lawsuit over the committee's power and the narrow decision by which the hearings were allowed to proceed. Public statements by Rosellini, and to a lesser extent other committee members, also soured the process in retrospect at least, since they pointed to the presence of vice and crime when the committee lacked the ability to cause law enforcement to act. In an address in Spokane, Rosellini told the Exchange Club, "Racketeers routed from the east by crime-investigating committees are attempting to invade [Washington]." Disagreeing with many law enforcement officers that "Washington is the cleanest state in the Union," Rosellini said, "Crime lords are looking for a place to light and have tried to gain a foothold here." He did admit, however, that the primary purpose of his committee was to provide "tools for the local law enforcement agencies to cope with criminals and to prevent corruption in government at all levels."[40]

What had begun as a legislative investigation with legitimate, though slightly grandiose, intentions, ended with little to show for its efforts—except for the extraordinary publicity received by its chair. Even though two of the cities visited by the committee changed their form of government, it is not clear whether the hearings were the primary catalyst. Certainly they helped, but the overall opinion of the committee's work does not seem to have been enhanced by these results. Thus, one is left with the actions of the legislature itself as the ultimate assessment of the hearings and its chair. The decision to withdraw subpoena power and to withhold further funding con-clusively reveals the extent of the legislature's disapproval. To be fair to Rosellini, however, the hearings were held at the urging of Senator Kefauver and mirrored similar efforts in a number of other states. Some other legislator no doubt would have initiated the investigation had Rosellini not done so.

Chapter 5

The First Campaign
for Governor

The crime commission ended its work the last week of June 1952. One week later, five Democrats filed for the office of governor—House Speaker Charles Hodde, State Treasurer Tom Martin, Congressman Hugh Mitchell of Seattle, Charles Ralls, a Seattle lawyer who was a former national commander of the Veterans of Foreign Wars, and State Sen. Albert D. Rosellini. The odds-on favorite was Mitchell, who had announced his intention to run, with considerable backing from the party, in late March. Charles Hodde, the fifteen-year legislator and five-time Speaker, was also a formidable candidate because of support from the Grange and education forces.[1]

As the crime probe drew to a close, it seemed clear to everyone that Rosellini was planning to run for governor, but today he says that he decided at the last minute. His decision was a surprise to his closest friends and supporters, although some of them—including Michael Gallagher and Earl Coe—had suggested that he enter the governor's race. In early 1952, he had considered running for mayor of Seattle. William Devin, the conservative incumbent, had not decided about running for reelection, and many Democrats felt he was vulnerable because he had held the position for more than ten years. The *PI* listed Rosellini as a possible candidate, along with Alan Pomeroy, a

Seattle lawyer who had narrowly lost to Devin in 1948. Rosellini had also given some consideration to running for Congress, but he was too busy with the crime committee to do or think of anything else until summer.[2]

In interviews years later, Rosellini said he filed in 1952 because he feared that Hugh Mitchell could not beat Langlie. Initially, Mitchell had wanted to run for the U.S. Senate against incumbent Harry P. Cain—who had defeated him in 1946 but had not performed well in office. Mitchell decided to challenge Langlie only after Warren Magnuson, the key to large financial contributions, endorsed Everett Congressman Henry M. ("Scoop") Jackson over Mitchell for the Senate. Rosellini believed that Congressman Mitchell was too closely tied to the liberal wing of the national party and that that would hurt him in Washington State. Everyone expected a national sweep by Eisenhower. He would carry Langlie with him unless the Democrats waged a campaign that focused strictly on state issues, where Langlie was vulnerable. Rosellini and many other Democrats doubted that Mitchell had the background in state politics that would be required to exploit that weakness.[3]

Rosellini's 1952 Campaign

Rosellini's campaign was slow getting started. Most of the regular party people had been preempted by Mitchell and Hodde. As a result, Rosellini's campaign staff and volunteers were largely family and close friends. In responding to questions he told Ross Cunningham that "I am acting as my own campaign manager and I am financing most of my own campaign." In fact, most of his funds came from a $40,000 loan from the National Bank of Commerce that Rosellini's father arranged and cosigned. (It took Rosellini more than two years to retire the debt following his unsuccessful campaign. His primary race four years later was largely financed by a similar loan.) Contrary to a belief held by his opponents and the newspapers, who thought Rosellini's campaign was well-financed from outside sources, his work on the crime committee had made it difficult to raise money from groups such as the Tavern Owners' Association. For example, his tight budget would not cover the cost of radio or television advertising.[4]

Opening his campaign, Rosellini paraphrased Franklin D. Roosevelt in declaring that the state had for too long "been at the mercy of a few economic royalists who dictate their policies to the present governor." He said his filing was a response to petitions, urging him to run, signed by more than 25,000 people, and by the "thousands of letters and telephone calls" he had received. Listing his qualifications, he stressed his years in the state senate, his work for improvements in the juvenile justice system, his legislative leadership in establishing the University of Washington Medical School, his efforts to reorganize state government, and his "recent service to the people against underworld crime and corruption."[5]

During the summer Rosellini and his family traveled throughout Washington, visiting county Democratic picnics and appearing in parades. He would speak from the back of a truck wherever he could find an audience. His main attraction was the presence of Jack Rivers, a fairly well-known country singer. At every stop Rosellini would work the streets, visit the union halls, and drop by the local radio stations and newspapers hoping for an interview. He was often isolated at formal Democratic gatherings in the more populated urban centers. At the King County picnic, for example, Rosellini felt that his motorcade had been prevented from entering the grounds so that he could not make a good showing.[6]

Rosellini's campaign was grass roots in every sense of the term. Taking full advantage of his immigrant heritage, his campaign was populist in its appeal and played to his strengths as a legislator. It contained no hint of the elitist liberal aura that surrounded Mitchell, yet sounded themes even more liberal than the typical ADA programs. Tying in his experience as chair of the crime hearings, which had been open to the public, he called for open government, elimination of waste and inefficiency in government, elimination of the sales tax on food, state support of industrial growth, better management of state law enforcement, rehabilitation of mental and penal institutions, implementation of the Youth Protection Act he had recently sponsored, better schools, comprehensive planning of new highways and bridges, and a more enlightened policy on Washington's wildlife and water resources. His campaign material also highlighted his fourteen years as a legislator, the leadership he had provided in the state's treatment of juveniles, establishing the university's medical school, and his chairing of the "Little Hoover" committee and the state crime committee.[7]

Rosellini, like all the candidates, made sweeping statements in an attempt to distinguish himself from the others. A number of these claims were challenged. For example, Hodde and Langlie pointed out that Harold Shefelman, not Rosellini, was the actual chair of the Little Hoover commission. All the candidates took issue with claims that anyone had a monopoly on "reorganization and efficiency of state government." For example, Langlie was vigorously attacked for his claim that he was responsible for the 1950 bond issue to build schools and institutional buildings when he had opposed this matter in 1949. The same was true of his claim regarding highways.[8]

It was another Rosellini position, however, that generated the most controversy. That was his call for eliminating the sales tax on food. Hodde claimed that this was a promise no governor could keep. Cunningham and the *Times* also took up the issue and implied that the position was designed solely to get votes. This was bolstered in the *Times*'s view by Hodde's assertion that Rosellini had never pushed such an exemption in the legislature. In fact, for years the Democratic party had supported a platform calling for less regressive taxes and the elimination of the sales tax on food. Rosellini had voted for such proposals on many occasions.[9]

It is difficult to gauge what it was about Rosellini's position on the sales tax on food that rendered him more expedient than the other candidates on the issue of cutting taxes. Perhaps it was his focus on a single tax that families could identify and quantify. Perhaps it was because his proposal had such popular appeal. Perhaps it was his naivete of approach, which did not hide behind typical political generalities. Nonetheless, the issue caused other candidates and the political writers—the *Times*'s Cunningham, in particular—to react strongly.[10]

Rosellini and Mitchell

Despite Rosellini's hard work and organization, in the first week of August, the *PI* questioned whether he would actually mount a full-fledged campaign. Most of the state's newspapers and political pundits felt that Mitchell was leading the group and that Martin and Hodde were keeping close. Bringing up the rear were Rosellini and Ralls.[11]

Rosellini's response to this ranking demonstrated his combative political style and personality. Hurt by lack of support from his own party and angry over the favoritism shown to Mitchell and Hodde by party regulars, he attacked both men. "As for the little giant from the East Side, he knows a lot about farming, but it takes more experience than that for governor," was his comment about his friend, Charlie Hodde, a man of small physical stature. His attack on Mitchell was more damaging. Playing on the anti-Communist hysteria that was dominating United States politics, he accused Mitchell of being a "left-winger" (a euphemism for a Communist sympathizer). Charging that Mitchell was "controlled by the Americans for Democratic Action," he went on to describe the ADA as a "small minority (leftist) group trying to take over the Democratic party" for their own personal gain.[12]

Rosellini's labeling Mitchell as a left-winger drew an angry rebuttal from the ADA. James B. Wilson, chair of the Seattle chapter, issued the statement: "Mr. Rosellini is discrediting only himself with his irresponsible attacks on the A.D.A. We refer him to President Truman's recent address to the national A.D.A. convention in which the President highly praised A.D.A. for its service to liberal causes." Going on, he said, "We cannot think that Mr. Rosellini is personally ignorant of the facts regarding the A.D.A. He solicited their support in Spokane last May, and he has attended A.D.A. meetings in Seattle."* Wilson's closing included a telling misconception: "Apparently those forces who are paying the bills for Mr. Rosellini's heavily financed bid for control of state government are insisting that he use any method, however unethical, to try to salvage their investment in him."[13]

---

*The ADA was founded in 1945 by liberal members of the Democratic Party in an effort to distance the party from the Communist Party while influencing Truman's administration to become more progressive. Its original founders (among them, Eleanor Roosevelt, Sens. Paul Douglas and Herbert Lehman, Leon Henderson, and Hubert Humphrey) were the first actually to bar Communists from membership, and they also sought to oppose Henry Wallace's Progressive Citizens of America organization, which was dominated by members of the Communist

The bitter tone of the Rosellini-Mitchell battle continued through the primary. While they were only two of the players and other issues were discussed, there was little question among Mitchell supporters that Rosellini was providing Langlie and the Republicans with a potent issue for the final election. Many later blamed him for Mitchell's ultimate defeat. Whereas primary races often help the opposition party in the final, Ancil Payne, former regional director of the ADA and manager of the 1952 Mitchell campaign, recalls that Rosellini's attacks were particularly damaging because Langlie was able to use them to great effect in the general election, stating that "even the Democratic leader of the senate" says Mitchell is a left-winger, and so forth. In truth, however, Mitchell would probably have lost in any event. Immediately after the primary, Langlie launched an attack against Mitchell that was far more deadly than Rosellini's. Realizing his own vulnerabilities on state issues, Langlie and his major supporters, the *Times* and *PI*, relied almost exclusively on anti-Communist hysteria, smears, and innuendoes in the campaign against Mitchell.[14]

Other forces were clearly at work in the fight between Rosellini and Mitchell. Both the national political parties were fighting the backlash created by McCarthyism. On the Republican side, the "America First" (or "Pro America") faction was endorsing candidates believed to be true-blue anti-Communist. In the Democratic party, the schism between the ADA and party regulars had surfaced at the national convention, which finally chose Adlai Stevenson as its (and Truman's) nominee, although it is well-documented that Truman endorsed Stevenson only after an exhaustive search for another candidate. This division carried over into a number of Washington's primary election campaigns. The state was still in thrall to the scare tactics of Rep. Albert Canwell and his "unAmerican activities" legislative committee. Canwell's investigations and hearings, the most controversial of which led to the dismissal of three University of Washington faculty members in the late 1940s, continued through

---

party. The group provided an organization for liberal, reform Democrats that they hoped would be free from attack by the anti-Communist zealots. (Interview, Ancil Payne, Nov. 2, 1995; *PI*, Aug. 19, 1952.)

September 1952, when several local Communists were arrested. There was a natural tendency for local Democratic officeholders to distance themselves. Many partisan Democrats also found the ADA's defense of the professors during the Canwell hearings difficult to accept.[15]

In early August, Ross Cunningham detailed numerous anti-Communist attacks against candidates who were receiving ADA support. Several weeks prior to Rosellini's statements about Mitchell, Charles Ralls had pointed out that Mitchell and the ADA had refused to endorse Truman's possible candidacy for another term in 1950, and said: "In their last national convention they [the ADA] went on record as being neither Democrat or Republican. . . . I believe in the basic principles of the Democratic Party and I do not want it sabotaged by a bunch of impractical dreamers." The liberals supporting Mitchell should have anticipated much of the regular party's discomfort with his candidacy.[16]

On September 9, 1952, Mitchell won the Democratic nomination by a narrow margin over Rosellini, with the other three candidates trailing far behind. If nothing else, the campaign proved that Rosellini could run an effective statewide race against a well-organized opponent who was better financed. Equally important, his excellent showing meant any future candidacy would be taken seriously by the groups who traditionally supported Democratic candidates. The close finish also made Rosellini wonder what might have been the outcome had he started sooner and been better prepared. Contrary to the predictions of a number of his political friends, neither his Italian ancestry nor his Catholicism had been used against him, at least directly. Equally important to Rosellini personally was the fact that no one raised the issue of his father's imprisonment for narcotics smuggling—a concern for Rosellini throughout his career, although it never became a political issue. Finally, the close race convinced him that he could run again for the office and win.[17]

The 1952 primary also had long-lasting negative results for Rosellini. Even though he campaigned for Mitchell in the general election, his relationship with the Mitchell forces, and with some party regulars, was irreparably damaged. The fact that Rosellini had been a leader of the New Deal, liberal Democrats undoubtedly contributed to the liberals' sense of betrayal when he attacked Mitchell and the ADA. It may also be true that Rosellini was the major object of the liberals' anger because he came so close to winning. Many believed that he had sacrificed Mitchell for his own benefit. The liberal, intellectual wing of the state and national party never forgave Rosellini for his campaign against Mitchell. Rosellini believes this was one reason that the liberals and the Kennedy forces were unwilling to offer either personal or financial support in his 1960 race against Lloyd Andrews or in his 1964 bid for a third term.[18] The Mitchell massacre also prevented Rosellini from obtaining the liberals' respect and enthusiasm when his leadership achieved legislative victories on liberal issues and produced far-sighted changes in the delivery of social and human services.

The harshest result of the 1952 primary, however, had nothing to do with the Democrats or the opponents against whom Rosellini campaigned. Rather, it was the antagonistic reaction of the Seattle *Times* and Ross Cunningham. In an editorial printed the Sunday before the primary election, the *Times* assessed the various candidates and their campaigns. After first stating its support for Langlie, the *Times* endorsed Hodde as the most desirable of the five opponents. The editors went on to say: "We believe that the least desirable of the Democratic gubernatorial candidates is Albert D. Rosellini. He has waged an utterly irresponsible campaign. We wonder if many voters will be gullible enough to be taken in by Rosellini's tactics." This assessment stung Rosellini, who felt that it was an unfair and undeserved personal attack. He believed, however, that it was driven as much by fear for Langlie's reelection as it was by any notion that his campaign was dishonest or irresponsible. That editorial started a feud with the *Times* and Cunningham that lasted throughout Rosellini's political career.[19]

Chapter 6

Public Perceptions:
A Politician
Practicing Law

The Seattle *Times*'s criticism of Rosellini in the 1952 primary, as well as his fellow legislators' reaction to Rosellini's handling of the crime committee cannot be viewed in too narrow a context. It was not merely the *Times* or political opponents attacking Rosellini or questioning whether, for example, the crime hearings were motivated by sheer opportunism.

Early in his career, Rosellini demonstrated a shrewd sense of the political value derived from publicity. Rosellini, the lawyer, represented numerous clients in the liquor and tavern business—a class of clientele held in low public esteem in the years following repeal of Prohibition. As a legislator he continued those relationships and involved himself, frequently, in the politically volatile process surrounding alcohol regulations. At times—for example, with the Sunday-closing case—he had demonstrated an eagerness to tweak the mainstream establishment if it would bring publicity or notoriety. Thus, it was not only his background and heritage that attracted and made him loyal to clients, friends, and businesses most mainstream society condemned. Rosellini was also more direct than most in making his political ties help his law practice.

Finally, as outlined in the introduction, his name alone raised lingering suspicions of ties to crime, liquor, and Catholicism. At the very least, his Italian name connoted someone who did not "belong" culturally and who did not operate within establishment limits. Thus, even before the crime hearings began, and long before the 1956 primary, Rosellini had a negative image in the eyes of a large part of the press and the public, quite apart from the attacks by his political opponents. Some elaboration on the roots of that perception is necessary.

From the day he opened an office, Rosellini's law practice was successful. As one of Seattle's first Italian attorneys, he attracted a number of clients from his family's friends and the rest of the Italian community. Even after he joined the prosecutor's office in early 1935, Rosellini maintained a private practice on a reduced scale. By the time he opened a full-time law office with Lloyd Shorett in the summer of 1941, the country was preparing for war. The shortage of lawyers and the notoriety he had gained as a public figure provided Rosellini with an ample clientele. The nature of his practice and his activities as a politician, however, led directly to public perceptions that would become a liability when Rosellini sought statewide office. Rosellini knew this. H. DeWayne Kreager remembers that during his interview for the position of director of economic development in 1957, Rosellini said the business establishment viewed him as "nothing but a Chinatown lawyer."

Liquor Licensing and Bottle Clubs

Rosellini's representation of Lelli and the Tavern Owners' Association in the 1934 Sunday-closing suit not only made him notorious, but also made him one of the few legal experts in the state on the licensing and regulating of businesses that sold alcohol. The frequent modification of these regulations by the state and local authorities following the repeal of Prohibition made his expertise all the more valuable. In 1934 Rosellini had also helped to license and incorporate a number of "bottle clubs"—private clubs where the members could bring their own liquor. He said he originated the idea of bottle clubs so that blue-collar people would have a place to socialize. Although Rosellini pointed out that the clubs were regulated and licensed under the same laws as were the Rainier Club and the Seattle Tennis Club, the conservative middle class tended to view them as little different from the old-style saloons—places that encouraged licentious drinking. Even Rosellini admitted that "I am sure some of these people skirted the law a bit."[1]

Given the tenor of the time, Rosellini's club- and tavern-owner clients were controversial. However, he never considered the work he did for these clients to be sordid or questionable, since the clubs were chartered by the state and, after 1934, all liquor establishments were heavily regulated. Also, these cases first came up during the Depression, and young lawyers did not turn down business. Still another factor was Rosellini's desire to help his or his family's friends if he could. In this he was typically Italian. Nor did he change his practice or sever his connections with these clients after his political position made association with these kinds of businesses a liability. Indeed, he did substantial work on behalf of the Tavern Owners' Association and other alcohol-related businesses up to the time he became governor.[2]

Public and Legislative Activities

In late 1941 Russell Fluent, a county commissioner who had been a deputy prosecutor with Rosellini, appointed him to the county hospital board which supervised Harborview and Georgetown. Both hospitals were struggling to maintain their viability because of the Depression and the impending war, and Fluent believed that it would be helpful to have a hospital trustee who had a voice in the legislature. While Rosellini felt his service on the board would provide greater prestige in the community (and perhaps it did), it also gave rise to several instances of unfavorable public controversy. At the very outset, his appointment was challenged by a political foe of Fluent on the grounds that Rosellini was not yet thirty-five years old (he was thirty-one). Although the suit was thrown out, it was indicative of the political climate faced by Rosellini in his first experience on a public-interest board. Later events proved that Rosellini was relatively insensitive to the political ramifications of his position.[3]

In August 1945, Rosellini was chair of the board when it requested the resignation of hospital administrator, Dr. A. J. Hockett. Stating that Hockett was guilty of "inefficiency and mismanagement," the board charged that he had failed to apply for an adequate number of doctors' deferments, had sold penicillin to a private Seattle dealer, had improperly purchased supplies, and had jeopardized Harborview's reputation and existence as a teaching hospital. Hockett did not go quietly, however, and responded to the improper-purchasing charge by stating that one order to a Tennessee firm had been placed at the request of Senator Rosellini and Lt. Gov. Vic Meyers. Hockett told the press that he had lost his job because of the "political" operation of Harborview. While it turned out that the order placed with the Tennessee firm had been withdrawn and the monies repaid two years earlier at Rosellini's insistence, Rosellini had in fact introduced the firm's representative to Hockett as a favor to Vic Meyers.[4]

Just as Hockett's discharge was gaining notoriety, another controversy arose. The newspapers reported allegations that a shakedown attempt had been made in connection with choosing an architect for the hospital's $3 million new wing. After several weeks of sensational headlines, both Hockett's charges and the shakedown allegations proved to be unfounded. In fact, Rosellini's name had never been connected to the shakedown allegations. Still, his willingness to help political friends like Vic Meyers had placed Rosellini in a position where any charges that had an aura of substance made news. After the headlines faded, the public was no doubt left with the impression that Rosellini was part of an unsavory political situation—even though he was re-elected chair of the board and appears to have served with distinction.[5]

Legislative Politics

The nature of Rosellini's law practice and the fact that he was advocating for his clients while also holding political office inevitably led to partisan accusations and insinuations. Several examples from the 1940s are illustrative.

While addressing a League of Women Voters group on the need for reform of the juvenile justice system in January 1946, Rosellini was verbally attacked by a thirty-third district constituent, Mrs. Aubrey Ramm, for helping to obtain a license for a tavern situated within 500 feet of a grade school. Referring to a character-reference letter that Rosellini had written on behalf of the owner, Ramm said, "I don't think Senators should be able to apply for tavern licenses." By no coincidence, within the next few days the *PI* published letters from Ramm, repeating her charges and also pointing out that Senator Rosellini was on the state payroll as a deputy attorney general. In one week, with one well-publicized letter, Ramm drew Rosellini into a controversy that attracted negative publicity for several months.[6]

Even though Ramm's letter took liberties with the facts concerning Rosellini's participation in the tavern controversy, and implied that Rosellini's actions as a special deputy attorney general were improper when they were not, she succeeded in raising ethical questions that were difficult to counter on a public level.

The tavern controversy, which received a great deal of attention in the press, involved the transfer of a tavern location due to the destruction of a building. The business was owned by John Fornaciari, a family friend from Rosellini's district. All Rosellini had done was to submit a character-reference letter on the young man's behalf— a procedural requirement that had nothing to do with location or license-application issues. Ramm's assertions, however, as opposed to the facts, dominated the news stories.[7]

The Ramm reference to Rosellini's employment as an assistant attorney general drew attention to the senator's participation in a practice which was coming under public scrutiny. For years governors had hired legislators to work in various departments of state government between sessions. The influence this gave the governor was obvious, and by 1946 the practice was heavily criticized, even though there was no legal prohibition against it. Similarly, there was no prohibition against a legislator holding a position as an assistant attorney general (just as there had been no bar to a deputy prosecutor having a private practice). When Rosellini and Shorett left the prosecutor's office in 1941, Attorney General Smith Troy asked both of them to act as part-time attorney generals. Not only was it good politics for Troy, since Rosellini was already a senate leader, but it enabled him to remedy a wartime shortage of lawyers for his Seattle office. By 1945 Troy had released Rosellini from his position, as part of a plan to expand the Seattle office with full-time lawyers and also, no doubt, to avoid future political squabbles over legislators on the state payroll.[8]

The letters from Ramm suggested that Rosellini was unethical, or at least that his actions were improper. This was not the case.

Yet the atmosphere surrounding liquor laws and the postwar attitudes about legislators on government payrolls made Rosellini vulnerable to her attack.

Another incident later in 1946 reveals Rosellini's public image among business-oriented establishment groups. The Seattle Municipal League, a nonpartisan group that rated candidates for public office, gave Rosellini a favorable rating prior to the 1946 primary. The league described him as "Capable; Democratic floor leader; adroit politician." However, prior to the general election, the league changed its rating. The description of Rosellini read: " . . . cunning politician; sincerity questioned."[9] Rosellini attributes the Municipal League's attack to politics and to the league's clear preference for conservative candidates. Even if Rosellini's evaluation is true, however, his reputation was undoubtedly affected by the negative public image created by the controversies surrounding the King County hospital board and the allegations of Stella Ramm.

Wallgren, Liquor Investigations, and Rosellini's Law Practice

Gov. Mon Wallgren took office in 1945 determined to liberalize the state's liquor laws, which he believed to be archaic and detrimental to the hotel and restaurant industry. Pointing out that most western states allowed the public sale of liquor by the drink, the governor introduced an executive request bill to that effect. The bill did not even emerge from committee, but Wallgren's action did succeed in arousing anew the passions of the Washington State Temperance Association. Several initiatives were filed by both the wets and the drys. One sought to ban liquor sales altogether except in state stores. Although no initiatives passed, the battles resulted in allegations concerning the operation and licensing of private clubs, bars, and taverns. In turn, the 1947 legislature decided to hold hearings concerning such businesses. Initially, the hearings sought to discover whether the private clubs were in fact nonprofit, as required by law. Rather quickly, however, they were dominated by allegations of political influence in the licensing process.[10]

As would be the case in another legislative investigation into Liquor Control Board policies during Rosellini's administration, the

real story was the headlines generated, not the result of the committee's inquiry. The committee failed to uncover either a link between
Wallgren and licensing or anything else casting doubt on the liquor
board's neutrality. No legislative changes were recommended.[11]

An unfortunate spinoff of the hearings for Rosellini was a group of
articles by Robert Cummings of the *PI*. The first focused on Rosellini's
law practice and detailed that he, while a member of the senate
committee probing private clubs, had actually incorporated many of
these clubs—more than any other lawyer in the state. Cummings
juxtaposed the story with testimony from the hearings that lawyers
were paid "high fees" for representing clubs for political purposes, and
with the fact that several clubs incorporated by Rosellini had been
raided for bootlegging.[12]

The second article, published a year later in 1949, resurrected
the tavern-location incident raised by Stella Ramm in 1946. Entitled
"How They Vote Hinges on Where They Are," Cummings's article
accused Rosellini and others of voting one way in committee and
another on the floor on a bill, pushed by the state PTA, requiring
that taverns be located at least 500 feet from any church or school
(a follow-up to the situation identified by Stella Ramm). According
to Cummings, Rosellini changed his vote to please the gallery packed
with PTA members. Outraged by this story, which he claimed was
"absolutely false," Rosellini got into a fist fight with Cummings and
knocked him down. This incident could scarcely have added luster to
Rosellini's reputation as a public figure.[13]

The Ramm letters, the liquor committee investigations, Cummings' articles, and Rosellini's legal representation of clubs and liquor
licensees raise numerous questions. Why was Rosellini on the liquor
investigation committee? Did he recognize the possibility of conflict
between his legislative position on various liquor measures and his
law practice? At the time, did Rosellini care about the reputation
that would be created by his connection with liquor measures and
controversies? Did he realize the probability that this reputation would
stay with him throughout his career? Did he, as a legislator, ever give it
a thought? Rosellini is the first to admit that politicians were cautious
about votes on liquor, yet he always seemed to involve himself—as a

legislator and as an attorney—in liquor issues. Whenever he did so, as illustrated above, his actions were likely to create controversy and, at times, lurid headlines. It is fair to say that newspapers in the 1940s and 1950s were as prone as they are in the 1990s to play up politically divisive issues. This was certainly true as the state slowly developed more liberal attitudes toward alcohol and its public usage. Rosellini and Italians generally were consistently bemused by mainstream society's puritanical approach to alcohol. For them, it was "no big deal," and liquor was always part of "the good life." Rosellini's morally neutral and seemingly naive approach was not shared by the public at large or by the establishment press.[14]

As a consequence, Rosellini was accused of improper ties to liquor interests throughout his public career. While such accusations were never substantiated, they colored the public perception of his political leadership. Rosellini was not likely to be respected by those citizens who felt that politicians connected to liquor interests were tainted or were acting in areas fraught with corruption and dishonesty. Even though he was also advocating for issues that were much more crucial to the state's welfare, such as education, reform of the juvenile justice system, improvement of state institutions, or a medical school, this did not translate into public popularity or recognition as a socially responsible legislator. As Rosellini gained political maturity and became known statewide for his work on issues of substance, his image and reputation changed very slowly, if at all. His legal and political ties to liquor interests, as well as his refusal to separate himself from them, made him particularly vulnerable to innuendo and distrust.

Chapter 7

Langlie and
Rosellini

Hugh Mitchell lost to Governor Langlie by more than 57,000 votes (510,675 to 567,822) in the general election of 1952. General Eisenhower overwhelmed Governor Stevenson—winning all but two states—and carried Washington State by more than 75,000 votes. Eisenhower's popularity benefited not only Langlie, but Emmett Anderson as lieutenant governor, Don Eastvold as attorney general, license director Charles Mayberry as secretary of state, and eighty-one-year-old Democratic auditor Otto A. Case (persuaded by the Republicans to run against progressive Jack Taylor, the incumbent) as land commissioner. The Republicans also gained control of both houses of the state legislature for the first time since 1931. Thus, the legislature was more conservative than in the 1951 session. Just as critical for Rosellini (who was elected senate minority leader), all but one of the coalition Democratic senators who had voted as a bloc with the Republicans were reelected (Ted Schroeder was defeated in the primary.)[1] For Rosellini this meant that the 1953 session would be controlled by the Republicans.

However, this actually worked to his advantage. Even had the legislature been less conservative, Rosellini was determined to "keep his head down" during the 1953 and 1955 sessions. Assuming reelection to his senate seat in 1954, Rosellini would be able to concentrate, during the two years following the 1955 session, on the governor's race. Thus, he wanted to avoid any controversy that would carry over after the sessions in 1953 and 1955. Three other factors also influenced his final decision to run.[2]

First, even in the early days of the 1953 session, Rosellini was convinced that Governor Langlie would not run for reelection. Langlie appeared disinterested and even more aloof than usual. His whole-hearted alliance with the national Eisenhower movement had drained his enthusiasm for state issues, and his third-term bid had come about almost by default. During the 1951 session, Langlie had said he would "either run again, back another man of his choice, or defer to any Republican who could win." It was only after eastern Washington GOP leaders took him literally and began to develop an alternative candidate that Langlie became committed to the 1952 campaign.[3]

Name familiarity was a second factor that influenced Rosellini's decision to run. In 1950, Rosellini's closest friend and Pierce County superior court judge, Hugh Rosellini, had run for a seat on the Washington State Supreme Court against Judge Frederick Hamley and had been defeated by a wide margin. Senator Rosellini had been involved in Hugh's decision to run and had provided much of the organizational support for that statewide campaign. In 1954, after Albert's favorable showing in the 1952 Democratic primary, Hugh decided to run again for a supreme court position. Both Rosellinis felt that a victory for Hugh would augur well for Albert's second campaign for governor. Hugh Rosellini's defeat of Richard Ott (who was elected to the court one year later, in 1955) helped to crystallize Albert Rosellini's determination to run in 1956. There had been a Rosellini on a statewide ballot in each of the general elections since 1950. Hugh's victory and Albert's strong showing in 1952 seem to indicate that the voters had become accustomed to the Rosellini name and accepted it.[4]

The most critical factor leading to Rosellini's decision to run in 1956, however, involved conditions in the state's institutions. Twelve years of political infighting finally erupted in August 1953, and assured that institutions would be a major campaign issue for Rosellini in 1956—and one on which the Republicans rightly or wrongly would be on the defensive.

Langlie and State Institutions

From 1941 until the end of his third term in 1956, Governor Langlie constantly struggled with the troublesome problem of the state's institutions. In his political biography of Langlie, George Scott outlines the governor's infrequent and abortive attempts to improve conditions in institutions, and observes: "The turmoil in these refuges and the Governor's tenacious attempts to improve them best describe the strengths and limitations of his administrative methods."[5]

During the postwar years, the state institutions "regressed under the scourges of inflation and the spoils system." The year 1949 provides four telling examples. First, the state society for mental hygiene found that the mentally ill were surviving on $1.60 a day and that overcrowding and understaffing had reached unbearable proportions. This confirmed the findings of the legislative council's subcommittee on institutions following the 1945 and 1947 sessions (see pp. 35–39). The 1944–48 administration of Democratic Gov. Mon Wallgren had done almost nothing to improve the situation.[6]

Second, Langlie ordered H. D. VanEaton, director of state institutions, to return 10 percent of the 1949–51 appropriation for institutions—despite VanEaton's warnings that most of the funds would have to come from operations. Langlie also ignored VanEaton's requests for merit pay, facilities for the segregation of hardened criminals, and the evolution of the training schools and reformatories from custodial care to "education and true reformation."[7]

Third, in 1949 Langlie had resisted legislation to set up a separate Department of Youth Protection (similar to other Rosellini proposals), and had ordered it stalled in the senate.[8]

Fourth, Langlie fired the founding director of the Rainier School for the Retarded, who had campaigned for Wallgren in 1948, and the resulting furor brought renewed attempts to reform the system and to limit the power of the governor to appoint heads of such institutions. Led by Judge William Long, the State Federation of Women's Clubs, and the state PTA, Initiative 175 was placed on the ballot in 1950. This measure, which sought to implement some features of Rosellini's proposed juvenile and youth protection act, was narrowly defeated.[9]

In 1951, Rosellini's youth protection act finally passed (see pp. 40–42), which resulted in upgrading and modernizing the state's major juvenile facilities during 1953 and 1954. This was not the case, however, with the state's adult penal facilities or with the institutions for the mentally retarded.[10]

Langlie was traveling abroad on the morning of August 21, 1953, when a riot broke out at the Monroe men's reformatory. In the ensuing several hours one inmate was killed and three wounded in a melee in which more than three hundred prisoners took part. They set fire to the machine shop, garage, and powerhouse—causing $1.5 million in damage. Rosellini, as ranking Democrat on the interim committee on institutions, joined the chairman, Tacoma Republican Neil Hoff, in demanding a full investigation. Both urged Langlie to return from Europe to handle the crisis, but Langlie chose to leave the administration in the hands of Lt. Gov. Emmett Anderson.[11]

The hearings opened less than two weeks later, on September 2, 1953. Contrary to the wishes of the administration and Director VanEaton, Hoff determined to hold the hearings on-site at Monroe. The testimony revealed morale problems, as well as dissension among personnel and severe disciplinary breakdowns. The latter were evident during the committee's visit to one of the cell blocks, as the inmates cut loose with yells and catcalls, and tossed trays, paper, fruit, and other objects in their path. The assistant superintendent, J. L. Brady, criticized the "informer" or "stool-pigeon" techniques used by the captain of the guards. Capt. Dwight Smith stated that inmates, not guards or staff, ran the disciplinary system. There were charges that the sale of drugs and liquor was rampant among prisoners and guards; the committee also heard stories of guards borrowing money from inmates. Two officers testified that certain inmates were allowed to roam free and that the administration had no contingency plan in place to deal with a riot in the recreation yard, where the riot had started.[12]

Testimony by Paul Squire, the superintendent, and others revealed infighting and conflict among staff as to disciplinary policies and procedures. It confirmed drug-trafficking and alcohol use among inmates, negligence in following prison security procedures, and abortive attempts to terminate an insubordinate deputy superintendent. Finally,

Squire's testimony demonstrated a lack of control over the inmates, who intruded themselves into the disciplining of other inmates. The hearings also revealed that Monroe was receiving an overflow of hardened criminals from the penitentiary at Walla Walla. Indicative of the problems was the fact that another minor riot occurred on September 6, after the inmates learned of the dismissal of the assistant superintendent, Brady. Squire denied that the firing was the cause of the new disturbance—saying it was the result of ringleaders of the August riot being held in "deadlock," but others said that it was directly related.[13]

According to press accounts, Rosellini was the major questioner during the hearings. Distrustful of the prison administration, he suggested that the committee call inmates as witnesses. Hoff allowed Rosellini considerable leeway in examining the inmates—although he cautioned the senator at several points about going too far. It is likely that the more sordid conditions would never have surfaced without inmate testimony. For example, the pervasive selling of drugs and alcohol, as well as gambling, were first mentioned by the inmates themselves.[14]

Following the hearings, Rosellini maintained his focus on the administration, demanding urgent and immediate action from Anderson, and saying that the committee had "uncovered evidence of such vicious and undermining things as narcotics, whiskey and gambling in the reformatory." Though Rosellini's statements were partisan and inflammatory, even Hoff's report agreed with his basic conclusions.[15]

The subcommittee recommended a number of legislative and executive reforms: (1) change the law to give the superintendent more latitude to hire and fire his own people—the current law left this solely to the director of institutions; (2) change the law to make eighteen, not sixteen, the minimum age of inmates at Monroe; (3) establish a pre-sentence system (like the one used in federal courts) to enable a judge to determine whether a man belonged in Monroe rather than Walla Walla or elsewhere; (4) streamline the penal code and laws regarding sentencing, parole, and the nature of commitments. Later the subcommittee added other recommendations dealing with walkaways from honor camps, stiffer punishment for employees dealing in contraband, providing released prisoners enough money to carry them through the first month, and "separation of tough inmates." These recommendations mirrored, in most respects, positions Rosellini had espoused during earlier sessions of the legislature (particularly with regard to juveniles), as well as in his 1952 primary campaign.[16]

As a Republican, Hoff found himself in a delicate political situation. In an attempt to neutralize the subcommittee report's political consequences for Langlie, Hoff pointed out that the judiciary and the legislature were also in part responsible for the problems at the state's institutions. While that may have been true as a technical matter, Rosellini was more accurate in his assessment that the executive branch had failed to provide the leadership necessary to prevent such conditions from developing. Langlie's own people had warned him, in 1950, that discussions of rehabilitation at Monroe were useless as long as educational and vocational programs were minimal or nonexistent and as long as 275 inmates out of a population of 600 had nothing at all to do except serve time. Norman S. Hayner of the University of Washington, appointed to the parole board by Langlie in 1952, pointed out that there was no professionally trained person on the staff at Walla Walla—a prison housing 1,600 men. After the riots, Squire had told VanEaton and Langlie that "many guards at Monroe (and other institutions) are retired policemen, crippled loggers, ex-farmers, and men who are 'resting between jobs.' . . . Who could expect otherwise with the starting salary at $242 a month."[17]

In a commentary at a crime prevention conference in Seattle late in 1953, the supervisor of classification and parole at Monroe said that the cause of the August 20 riot was the inmates having assumed control by default from the prison administration. When management tried to regain control, those inmates who were in positions of trust and power brought about the unrest which led to the riots. Many years of underfunding, and the consequent lack of money to pay guards adequately, was a major contributor to the problem.[18]

Compounding Langlie's problems, prisoners rioted at Walla Walla on the evening of September 8, 1953, just as the interim committee was releasing its preliminary report on Monroe. Eight hundred rioters— half the inmates—withstood three volleys of tear gas and set fires that destroyed the metals plant and over one million 1954 license plates. Damage was estimated at more than $450,000. Ironically, the riot followed, by one day, an article in the Spokane *Chronicle* that said the Monroe situation would not repeat itself at the state penitentiary. Deputy Warden Al Remboldt could not explain the outbreak, as the inmates had made no demands.[19]

The Walla Walla riot—coming immediately after the hearings in Monroe—led to new calls for legislative investigations. These calls came, however, not from Rosellini, but from the three conservative legislators who represented Walla Walla's legislative district. By now the administration and Republican leadership had developed a "bunker mentality." Speaker Mort Frayn, a Langlie ally, tried to prevent the hearings and ordered Hoff to leave Walla Walla, but backed down when Hoff publicly declared his intention to proceed. Sensing the political vulnerability of the administration's position, Rosellini referred to "basic trouble in the management of all the institutions," and demanded a "complete study and public hearings."[20]

Predictably, the debate over hearings became increasingly political. On September 16, the state Democratic chair, Don Abel, sent Hoff a telegram urging that hearings go forward and also criticizing the administration. The telegram, with obvious input from Rosellini, concluded by drawing a parallel between Langlie's continued absence (he was by then in New York but not returning to the state for several days) and the neglect of state institutions by his administration.[21]

Hoff accused Abel of making a "purely political play," adding that the legislature, controlled for twenty years by Democrats, was equally to blame. Crediting Langlie with the integrity to "air the problems," he defended the governor's "first . . . vacation in years." He concluded by stating that the matter would be handled "without bringing partisan politics into the picture." Within a day or two, however, Hoff announced that hearings would be held at the Walla Walla facility. The committee planned to invite judges, prosecuting attorneys, law enforcement personnel, and even fire chiefs to express their views on Washington's statutes governing criminal incarceration.[22]

By September 21, Langlie had returned to the state, and he announced that his administration would make an immediate study of the riots at Monroe and Walla Walla, and would take action to correct any deficiencies in the penal institutions. Once again, Langlie would find little relief in reports from his own people. On September 26, Hayner stated that faulty administration had precipitated the riots. He also found a chronically substandard, untrained, and largely overage officer corps "rendered ineffective by factionalism." Hayner elaborated on his earlier warnings (see p. 79) and called for a separate Department of Corrections, diagnostic centers for adults, additional minimum security facilities, and expansion of parole and probation services.[23]

By mid-October, opposition to hearings at Walla Walla had vanished, and Hoff announced that the investigation would begin on November 13. Eight inmates were called as witnesses. A majority criticized the state board of prison terms and paroles, complaining that the board often interviewed incoming men for less than two minutes before pronouncing sentence. They said that parole conditions made normal life impossible for a released inmate, and they substantiated earlier reports that released men were given inadequate resources to enable them to find or keep a job. They reported problems of homosexuality and charged that little effort was made to segregate sexual predators and psychopaths within the prison. There was disagreement among the inmates as to the extent of illicit liquor and narcotics sales, although several told of guards trafficking in contraband and drugs.[24]

Warden John Cranor testified on the second day. Under intense questioning—mostly by Rosellini and Democratic senator Howard Bargreen—Cranor said that his officer-training program was handicapped by lack of personnel and that he had developed no riot plan, even though the staff had warned him several days in advance that trouble was brewing. He identified serious problems with the prison hospital, among them the lack of a full-time physician. According to Cranor, he was unable to provide a full-time chaplain on the funds available, even though one was required by state law. Despite his loyalty to VanEaton and Langlie, Cranor's testimony bore dramatic witness to the sorry conditions at the prison. Hoff, in relieving him from his oath, complimented him on his frankness as a witness. The final witness was Dr. Henry Ness, parole board chairman, who defended the board's role and tried to answer the many criticisms made by inmate witnesses.[25]

At the conclusion of the four-day hearing, the committee issued a preliminary report, stating that conditions at Walla Walla were so critical that immediate changes were needed. Hoff asserted that most of the trouble stemmed from lack of finances, adding that constant personnel changes—from department director to guards—had made administration difficult. Rosellini, as part of the report team, declared: "Conditions are so bad that I fear if something isn't done immediately there is going to be a bursting of tensions brewing within the penitentiary." He stated that certain situations should be rectified before the 1955 legislative session, and blamed the prison and parole board for much of the trouble.[26]

In his part of the report, VanEaton blamed inadequate funding for the situation at Walla Walla; he said that operations had been substandard for so many years that this condition had come to be considered normal. Langlie was stung by the report, but less than a week later he hired Fred R. Dickson, a California penologist, to superintend penal and custodial institutions, and left VanEaton in charge of purchasing—a division of responsibilities that had been recommended by the Little Hoover committee.[27]

Dickson's hiring brought some relief measures. Following his recommendations, Langlie used an executive proclamation to place all institutional employees under "merit" procedures on June 1, 1954. Earlier, in March, a new $1.5 million minimum-security structure had been opened outside the penitentiary courtyard. Yet the situation at Walla Walla had not eased in the six months since the hearings. Dickson cautioned Langlie that much remained to be done. In July 1954, the inmates staged a hunger strike and three days of passive resistance, which were called off only after the prisoners made numerous demands on Dickson. Frustrated by continued inadequate funding, in late 1954 Dickson announced his resignation to become head of the California men's prison at Chino—although he promised Langlie that he would stay through the 1955 legislative session.[28]

Dickson's short tenure bore witness to Langlie's inability to improve his management team and his failure to provide the means of procuring competent personnel at support levels. Langlie was merely reaping the seeds he had sown in the 1953 budget for institutions. VanEaton had apprised the governor of the effects the severe cuts would cause. The impact of the budget, passed over vehement Democratic objections, was decimating. Work weeks remained at fifty to fifty-two hours. The division of children and youth was eliminated (despite legislative approval in 1951), as were a diagnostic center, a forestry camp, a new boys' school at Chehalis, staff assistants, all merit-pay increases, an accredited teaching staff in vocational subjects at Monroe and Walla Walla, and all capital outlays. Indeed, Langlie's 1953 legislative program for institutions had gutted the juvenile justice reforms sought by Rosellini. Langlie's desperate attempt to shore things up the next year was a case, according to Scott, of "using the left hand to give back what the right had taken away after the damage was done."[29]

The drastic cuts included the parole board, resulting in the release of four parole officers and pushing caseloads to 160 per officer, despite Hayner's strenuous requests for seven more officers. Hayner then had to plead for emergency funds as the "difference between an adequate department . . . and a parole and probation system that will be virtually unable to cope with its assignments." Despite his testimony at Walla Walla, Henry Ness admitted to Hoff that without more officers to do the critical pre-sentencing investigations, the scanty information available to the board could easily lead to inequitable sentencing. This had been the one complaint voiced by all inmates who testified in the 1953 hearings.[30]

The parole board's troubles were compounded by Dr. Ness himself, a minister given to sermonizing and attempting to intimidate hostile interviewees. Ness felt threatened by the activities of Hayner, who sought to bring professionalism and training to the board, and who had described Ness as an "aggressive and individualistic" prima donna whose insecurity made him generous only in "domination." Yet Langlie had reappointed Ness as chairman in 1953. During the Walla Walla hearings, Rosellini's questioning had revealed that the former Assembly of God minister's doctorate was taken by correspondence from a Los Angeles Baptist seminary.[31]

The 1955 legislature convened with the situation at Walla Walla still seething. By then, Langlie had hired Dr. Thomas A. Harris, former chief of naval psychiatric services, to replace Dickson. Professor Clarence Shrag, chief corrections officer on leave from the University of Washington, issued warnings of dangerous conditions that could be harbingers of another disturbance. The unprofessional attitude of the parole board and its effect on inmate and staff morale continued unabated. On July 5, four inmates seized nine hostages, including the associate warden, and took over the central control room of the prison for twenty-six hours. The situation was brought under control only after numerous inmate demands were met. The one demand that Harris refused was that Langlie himself come to the facility and participate in the negotiations.[32]

In the heat of the takeover situation, Langlie agreed to Harris's request for a segregation unit; however, three months later, he apparently had second thoughts, and simply said, "We do need some facilities for our state institutions—there's no question about it, but it's going to take time to work the problem out." Though he remained publicly loyal to Langlie at the time, Harris later confided to Rosellini his frustration at the governor's lack of support. Following the 1955 riot, Rosellini repeated his charge that this riot, like the ones at Monroe and Walla Walla in 1953, was "primarily due to the shortsighted neglect of these institutions by Governor Langlie and his administration" and was caused by "unsanitary, degrading and unhumanitarian conditions."[33]

Whereas sufficient blame could be assessed all around—the administration, the legislature, the state bureaucracy, and the press itself as the public watchdog—one fact was undeniable: six years after Langlie's return to the governor's mansion, conditions at Walla Walla and other state penal and mental institutions were in a sorry state and still deteriorating. Shrag reported to Langlie in 1955 that in the previous year inmates at Walla Walla were computing release dates, handling confidential records, and operating locking devices. In 1955 the penitentiary continued to be dominated by a group of "con bosses," who successfully resisted civilian control.[34]

Vittorio, Cecceo, and Giovanni Rosellini (left to right) in 1908. This photo was taken when ADR's father, Giovanni, and his two brothers operated Marconi Wine, Spirits and Grocery at 16th and Broadway, Tacoma.

ADR, with parents and
sisters Rena (left) and
Argie, 1910.

ADR, age 7, in the
family home, 1917.

Giovanni and Annunziata, with Argie, Ida, Albert, and Rena in front of their Tacoma home, 1514 South G Street, in 1924.

A 1930 Varsity Ball photograph, University of Washington.

Wedding photograph, Albert D. Rosellini and Ethel McNeil, June 1, 1937, Our Lady of Mt. Virgin Church, Seattle.

ADR as Chairman of the Washington State Crime
Committee, with members, October 1951.

Democratic caucus, Washington State Senate, 1950.

The Rosellini Rose emblem, featured in all campaigns since early in the primary campaign of 1956.

(Left to right) ADR, Representative Mort Frayn, and Virginia Burnside prior to a taping of the television program "Question before the House," 1955. The program aired each Sunday during the 1955 legislative session, as Frayn and ADR discussed key issues, with Burnside acting as moderator. The program was a springboard for ADR to gain statewide prominence.

Illinois Governor Adlai Stevenson and ADR during
Rosellini's 1956 campaign for governor.

Top: The Rosellini family, November 1956, following ADR's election as governor. From left to right: Albert Jr., John, Sue Ann, ADR, Lynn, Janey, and Ethel.

Bottom: The Inaugural Ball, January 16, 1957, at the National Guard Armory in Olympia. Ethel and ADR in receiving line.

House Speaker John L. O'Brien, ADR, and Seattle businessman Leo Weisfield (left to right) visit Israeli Prime Minister David Ben Gurion in March 1958 on the occasion of the 10th anniversary of the founding of Israel.

ADR is greeted by townspeople of Chiesina, Italy, the birthplace of his father Giovanni and uncles Vittorio and Cecceo, in March 1958. Also shown in background is John L. O'Brien.

Ethel and ADR, Speaker John L. O'Brien and his wife Mary, and Leo Weisfield and his wife Sara, in an audience with Pope Pius XII, March 1958.

Scott Wallace (far left), a candidate for county commissioner in 1958, is shown with President Harry Truman, County Commissioner Ed Munro, and Senator Warren "Maggie" Magnuson at a Jefferson-Jackson Day dinner on September 4, 1958. Wallace and Munro became the majority commissioners responsible for helping fund the Evergreen Point Bridge.

ADR and Dr. Charles Odegaard, president of the
University of Washington, May 12, 1961, at the
University's Governor's Day ceremony, along with
Adjutant General George Haskett, head of the Wash-
ington National Guard, center.

Henry Seidel, budget director and administrative
assistant to Commissioner Scott Wallace, at a
planning meeting concerning the financing of the
Evergreen Point Bridge, August 1959.

Ross Cunningham, 1958. Cunningham, for many years editor and columnist for the *Seattle Times*, was a frequent critic and foe of ADR. Photo courtesy of *The Seattle Times*.

Governor Arthur B. Langlie in 1952. Photo courtesy of *The Seattle Times*.

Charles W. Hodde, Speaker of the House of Representatives, 1949 and 1951; primary opponent of ADR in 1952; Rosellini confidant and troubleshooter during his administration. Photo courtesy of *The Seattle Times*.

Lt. Governor Emmett Anderson, the 1956 Republican candidate for governor against ADR. Photo courtesy of *The Seattle Times*.

State Superintendent of Education Lloyd Andrews, 1960. Andrews, a former state senator from Spokane, was the Republican nominee for governor in 1960. In 1964 he ran against Senator Henry M. Jackson. Photo courtesy of *The Seattle Times*.

President Dwight D. Eisenhower, ADR, and Secretary of State John Foster Dulles, October 20, 1958, at the opening of the Colombo Conference in Seattle.

ADR and staff in spring 1959, during his first term. On far left is Warren Bishop, chief of staff and budget director. Also shown is Ed Henry (second from left) and counsel Max Nicolai, on the governor's immediate right.

1960 campaign photo of ADR with his daughters:
(left to right) Lynn, Janey, and Sue Ann.

Aerial photo, 1950, showing Seattle and the eastside prior to the construction of the second Lake Washington bridge at Evergreen Point. The photo is courtesy of Bert McNae, an eastside developer whose dream became a reality with the completion of the Evergreen Point Bridge in 1963.

Senator Henry Jackson, Democratic nominee John F. Kennedy and his wife Jacqueline, and ADR, September 7, 1960, during Kennedy's campaign visit to Seattle.

Eddie Carlson at the podium, with state senator
Michael Gallagher, ADR, Ethel, and Robert Rose,
head of Commerce and Economic Development, at
Century 21 World's Fair in Seattle, April 15, 1962.

ADR's campaign photo in 1964.

Elvis Presley visits with ADR, Albert Jr., Ethel, and Sue Ann at the Seattle World's Fair, May 1962.

Justice Hugh Rosellini, Dr. Leo Rosellini, ADR, and Victor Rosellini in photo taken for *Seattle Times* article, "The Four Rosellinis," published on October 29, 1978. Photo courtesy of *The Seattle Times*.

Four governors—Dixy Lee Ray, ADR, John Spellman, and Daniel Evans—July 1983.

Official ceremony, August 26, 1988, naming the Evergreen Point Bridge "The Albert D. Rosellini Bridge." ADR, second from left, is shown with former Governor Dixy Lee Ray.

ADR in 1993.

ADR and President William Clinton on November 19, 1993, during the APEC Ministers Conference in Seattle. Photo courtesy of Ed Kane, *Freelance Graphics*.

By late 1955 Rosellini had also discovered that the three state mental hospitals had lost their accreditation by the American Psychiatric Association. On October 29, 1955, he stated that Washington should "hang its head in shame" at the hospitals' overcrowded buildings, inadequate personnel, lack of preventive treatment and followup care, and the fact that "emotionally disturbed children were placed in the same ward as psychotic adults."[35]

Langlie did try, in 1955 and 1956, to address many of these problems. Harris split the Department of Institutions into the divisions of mental health, adult corrections, children and youth, and veterans homes. In his report in September 1955, Harris pointed out that "the criminally insane were segregated into a new building at Eastern, a reclassification plan developed and new management found for Walla Walla, and Monroe entered into an agreement to augment staff with the University's School of Social Work students." Langlie and Harris also improved the clinics and mental health centers within the system.[36]

But good intentions in 1955 and 1956 were unable to overcome the years of neglect and budget cuts. In 1953 mental health expenditures of $2.20 per day per capita put Washington last in the West. Yet, in the fall of 1955, when facing a request for increased allocations for mental patients, Langlie told the *Times* that there was "no basis for seriously considering it." A survey by the Western Interstate Commission for Higher Education, in mid-1956 at the close of the Langlie administration, ranked Washington institutions from unconscionable to mediocre—"compared to those of the rest of the Western states." According to the survey, the mental hospitals needed three times as many psychiatrists, four times the number of social workers, twelve times as many nurses. During 1956, Langlie did retain Dr. Karl Menninger as a "personal consultant." After a "cursory inspection," Menninger stated that Washington institutions were much above average, and "among the best in the country." According to George Scott, this surprising result may have been due to the inordinate amount of time that Menninger spent in Langlie's company rather than in the field. Ratings of Langlie's management of institutions by a federal inspection in 1955 ranged from excellent in one or two cases to "bordering on malfeasance."[37]

It was not until Harris arrived that significant attempts to address these problems began. These efforts came at the end of Langlie's twelve years as governor, and then only after public attention was focused on the problem. Although later commentators identified lack of funding from Democratic legislatures as the root cause of these problems (see p. 102), the truth remains that these were conservative legislatures, dominated by a coalition of Republicans and Democrats who were more conservative than Langlie. The governor knew, of course, that his budget proposals were likely to face additional cuts by this group. In 1951, for example, the Langlie figures for institutions were cut by more than $645,000. The governor's own proposals were only 10 percent higher than those for the previous biennium—despite a 13 percent increase in institutional population. For Langlie, state institutions were a stepchild, subject to budget-cutting on a par with other areas, and worthy of attention only when public events required. Langlie's biographer acknowledges his neglect of institutions in the following summary:

> Langlie fulfilled his duty to keep Harris' achievements from being lost by presenting an ambitious institutional budget to the 1957 legislature. It was an overdue recognition that the forgotten men in institutions would remain in the forefront until professional pay levels were added to job security. It was Langlie's successor who finally forced institutions out of the twilight zone.[38]

Rosellini's 1956 Campaign

By early 1955 Rosellini had begun to prepare for the 1956 gubernatorial campaign. Throughout the fall of 1955 and into the spring of 1956, in talks throughout the state, he urged the agenda for institutions that he had been refining since 1941. During the 1955 session he lined up broad party backing, determined that this time no other candidate would preempt the Democratic party regulars. Rosellini quickly obtained support from state senators Ed Munro, Mike Gallagher, and Francis Pearson. (Pearson was a close friend and political ally from Port

Angeles.) Along with Victor, Leo, and Hugh Rosellini, they formed the inner circle that made early strategy decisions. Under the aegis of Pearson and Gallagher, Democratic legislators in both the house and the senate signed petitions asking Rosellini to run for governor. Other key advisors in the early stages of the campaign were Dr. Frank James, Pierce County coroner, and fellow senators Jess Sapp, Bob Grieve, Bill Gissberg, Howard Bargreen, and Marie Tisch.[39]

Perhaps the most important early supporter, however, was Virginia Burnside from Seattle. Burnside had been active in the League of Women Voters in the early 1950s, and had met Rosellini when he had offered to help the league in its efforts to place a state presidential primary on the 1954 ballot. An experienced publicist, Burnside had done all the public relations work for the league's proposed initiative. In 1955, Burnside helped create a weekly League of Women Voters television program that dealt with the legislature's activities. It featured Rosellini and Mort Frayn—the Democratic leader of the senate and the ranking Republican in the House—who were joined by a guest for a discussion of legislative issues. Burnside acted as the moderator. Called "Question Before the House," it aired on Sunday morning originating from Seattle one week and from Spokane the next. The program provided Rosellini with valuable experience in discussing issues in a public setting and gave him additional exposure to the public at large. "Question Before the House" avoided controversial, partisan matters and focused on economic growth and trade issues. According to Rosellini, his participation on this program further developed his ideas about the need for a vigorous Department of Commerce and Economic Development, which became a critical part of his later campaign.[40]

Virginia Burnside also helped with many of his early campaign speeches. According to Rosellini, she deserved much of the credit for his success in the 1956 race. She was largely responsible for deciding which issues to stress in his election effort. Early on, she saw the potential appeal of the emerging crisis at the state's institutions. It was her idea to make a film concerning the terrible conditions at state institutions. Obtaining permission through Rosellini's contacts with Dr. Harris, Burnside and a cameraman visited all but one of the state's penal, mental, and juvenile facilities before Langlie finally heard about the project and denied further visits. The resulting film became the centerpiece of Rosellini's campaign. The ongoing emergency at Walla Walla had maintained the broadbased appeal of this issue. Rosellini financed the film as part of his campaign and paid all the costs.[41]

Virginia Burnside was the first person with public relations and communications skills to believe strongly in Rosellini's ability to win. A gifted writer, she helped transform his candidacy into a well-organized, sophisticated media and communications campaign—in marked contrast to 1952.

Two other candidates had filed for the Democratic nomination: State Sen. Roderick Lindsay from Spokane and Secretary of State Earl Coe. Neither Lindsay, an ultraconservative senator who had sided with Republicans in the legislature, nor Coe, also a former senator, had any substantial backing from the party. Lindsay was considered a non-candidate because of his ardent support of anti-union "right-to-work" laws in a heavily unionized state, and Coe had filed at the last minute after funds and volunteers were committed to Rosellini.[42]

From the outset, Rosellini was determined to campaign against Langlie and issues concerning his administration and pay little if any attention to his primary opponents. With no candidate from the national scene, such as Mitchell in 1952, the campaign would also be free from the anti-Communist, anti-McCarthy, and anti-Truman-crony factors which could sway state voters one way or the other. Albert Canwell was gearing up for another run for the at-large congressional seat held by Don Magnuson. The anti-Communist movement, though its strength was waning, was dying a slow death. However, by 1956, the Republicans had held power for four years and could no longer blame recent world events on the Democratic party or its national leadership.[43]

By early 1956 it was apparent that Langlie would run against Warren Magnuson for the United States Senate. Even earlier, in 1954, Ross Cunningham had reported that Langlie could be persuaded to run against Magnuson "if he thought there was a chance of winning," and Langlie finally declared himself a candidate in May 1956. As a practical matter, by that late date there was no other viable choice and the national administration was anxious, if not desperate, to have a strong candidate oppose Magnuson. The Seattle *Times* wrote a glowing editorial, calling Langlie "a good soldier in the Eisenhower wing of the Republican party," and "a national figure and national fighter for the things in which he believes." Magnuson had assumed that Langlie would be his opponent all along, and was preparing for a hard-hitting and messy campaign. The Eisenhower administration was determined to assist Langlie in any way possible. He was the keynote speaker at the national convention and received other national attention and support.[44]

The Magnuson-Langlie race worked in Rosellini's favor for several reasons. First, it gave the liberals a rallying point and diverted them from running their own candidate for governor. Second, it focused most of the Republican party's efforts on the Senate race, where Langlie was a decided underdog. While the ultraconservatives in the state often fought with him—particularly after the Taft-Eisenhower contest—Langlie had been the admitted leader and conscience of the party for sixteen years. A majority of the state's newspapers and business leaders concentrated their efforts on his cause. This was particularly true of those business leaders who were anxious to pass Initiative 198, a "right-to-work" proposal that sought to restrict the right of unions to organize and represent workers. Langlie's statewide organization of party volunteers was also the strongest. Its near-obsessive concentration on the Senate race was devastating to possible Republican gubernatorial candidates. Langlie's decision had also opened the field and eliminated the possibility of having to run against an entrenched incumbent. Third, Langlie had not tried to groom a successor; indeed, his indecision about whom to support and, in the end, his personal animosity toward Attorney General Don Eastvold, the most viable possibility, played directly into Rosellini's hands, and helped assure that the Langlie record would remain the focus of the campaign.[45]

Rosellini's formal campaign began in April 1956 with a rally at the Norselander Hall in Seattle. By that date Rosellini had visited every county in the state and had working organizations in most. His association with Maggie promised a unified front once the primary was over. However, raising money was a constant struggle. Many of the

usual sources of funds for liberal Democrats were backing Magnuson—
who was raising a war chest of more than $600,000. Again, Rosellini
and his father had contributed more than $40,000 through a loan,
and they signed a note for the $60,000 deficit that had been created
by the end of the campaign. The labor movement did raise some
funds because of Rosellini's active opposition to Initiative 198. He
received almost no support from business, except for the grocers' and
druggists' associations—longtime supporters that had helped in all his
campaigns. The Italian community, with Ben DiJulio as organizer,
played an important role in raising funds. Rosellini's organization
also raised money through grass-roots efforts, such as the "Rosellini
Membership" card, which cost a dollar and was sold at all party
gatherings.[46]

The Rosellini "rose" also made its first appearance in the 1956
campaign. Though not a fund-raiser as such, it became a signature
of all Rosellini's campaigns. Its origins dated to the summer of 1955,
when Rosellini was addressing a Democratic party group in Tacoma.
Mrs. Albert Tisch, a Democratic activist, asked whether he spelled his
name "Rosellini" or "Rossellini." The latter spelling was that of the
infamous movie director, Roberto Rossellini, who was involved at the
time in a highly publicized extramarital affair with Ingrid Bergman.
Rosellini explained the difference in spelling (and pronunciation),
and told her that the first syllable of his name was pronounced "Rose."
Mrs. Tisch proceeded to organize a women's group that hand-made
thousands of small lapel roses, which were handed out as campaign
emblems. In subsequent campaigns, many other groups joined in the
effort, and the "Governor Rosellini rose" was the most familiar of all
his campaign symbols.*[47]

Whereas the actual campaign did not start until spring 1956,
Rosellini had not stopped attacking the Langlie record since the day

---

*In 1961 the American Rose Society officially recognized the "Governor Rosellini
Rose"—a hardy red rose—which is still cultivated and sold. One rumor that still
circulates is that Rosellini changed his name (and its pronunciation) in 1960 to
take advantage of the University of Washington's first trip to the Rose Bowl. Not
true. (ADR interview, Dec. 18, 1995.)

he lost the primary four years earlier. During 1953, 1954, and 1955, he had maintained a steady criticism of Langlie's policies. As the campaign got underway, Rosellini returned once more to a number of themes he had used in 1952. His campaign highlighted eight basic points: (1) his sponsorship, advocacy for, and successful passage of the state's Youth Protection Act; (2) his successful passage of legislation establishing the medical and dental schools and a teaching hospital at the University of Washington; (3) his work as chair of the senate crime investigating committee and his efforts to fight organized crime; (4) his eighteen years of legislative experience dealing with state administrative problems; (5) his plan to create a Department of Commerce and Economic Development to bring business to the state; (6) his unequivocal opposition to the "right-to-work" Initiative 198; (7) his opposition to ratable reductions in the state's lien law applicable to senior citizens; (8) the need to improve and modernize the state's penal and mental health facilities for both adults and juveniles.[48]

Promising a "bright, booming future against another horse-and-buggy administration," Rosellini asked citizens to help restore confidence to state government. As in 1952, his opponents were quick to point out instances where Rosellini was taking credit for matters on which he had been only a part of the puzzle or had equivocated in his support. He was accused of saying one thing in eastern Washington and another in Seattle—on items such as the 40-mill-limit or passage of an income tax. His position against new taxes while advocating new and improved services was seen as demagogic. Rosellini was also criticized for lamenting Langlie's lack of a long-range tax bill while ignoring his own "no" votes on every attempt by the administration to address taxes on a long-term basis. Rosellini called Langlie inept and inefficient for allowing the state budget to go from $32 million in the black to $40 million in the red, calling the situation "unconscionable." In its defense of the Langlie record, the *Times* cast Rosellini as a "narrow partisan" for his failure to acknowledge that Langlie "had served the state well during his tenure in Olympia."[49]

Rosellini's critics were muted during the primary because of the strange nature of the Republican contest. Since mid-1955, Lt. Gov. Emmett Anderson and Attorney General Don Eastvold had been locked in a battle for the GOP nomination. Anderson, a rather colorless individual, was known primarily because he had been Exalted Ruler of the Elks—a fraternal organization that wielded considerable power from the 1940s on into the 1960s. Swept into the office of lieutenant governor by the 1952 Eisenhower landslide (he ran far ahead of Langlie), Anderson was totally inexperienced and not well connected with Langlie's administration. Eastvold was eloquent and charismatic and throughout most of 1955 was seemingly the favorite of everyone—including Langlie.[50]

Eastvold's campaign was based on a relatively liberal platform. School funding was given top priority, and Eastvold openly stated that the sales tax would have to be raised or an income tax implemented to meet the need for services. Of all the candidates in 1956, he was the only one who faced the revenue issue with candor and honesty. However, his personal life and what some saw as a willingness to take liberties with the truth in his campaign tactics proved to be his undoing. He was a heavy drinker and a womanizer, characteristics that ultimately offended the straitlaced Langlie. In the late summer of 1955, Langlie discovered that Eastvold, who was married, was having an affair with a secretary in Langlie's office. At that point, Langlie turned on Eastvold and was determined, according to Ross Cunningham, to "kill his chances of being elected governor."[51] Eastvold's anger over Langlie's open opposition had a major impact on both the primary and the general election. In late August 1956, Eastvold issued a detailed report, from the perspective of a Republican insider, in which he attacked a number of Langlie departments for "their failures." He listed six ways the tax commission "could materially improve," and said that he planned to "fire a substantial majority of Langlie's appointees" because more than 90 percent had "outlived their usefulness." This open feud provided ammunition to Rosellini and the Democrats. The primary campaign drew to a close with Anderson and Eastvold pounding one another so vehemently that George Kinnear, the Republican state chairman, warned them the party might not be able to survive their careless statements. Anderson won the primary by a two-to-one margin. Having won the victory by casting himself as Langlie's logical successor, he was stuck with defending the Langlie record.

According to Rosellini, Eastvold was so bitter after the primary that he provided Rosellini with information about Anderson's campaign strategy. Meanwhile, Rosellini easily won the Democratic primary, polling some 72,000 votes to Coe's 39,000. Lindsay was a poor third, with slightly more than 10,000 votes.[52]

The general election began with Anderson on the defensive; Rosellini's campaign even organized a "Republicans for Rosellini" drive. Attacking Anderson for his "extreme conservatism" on tax reform, Initiative 198, and public power, Rosellini also pointed out his opponent's lack of experience in dealing with state matters.[53]

Despite the fact that Rosellini campaigned primarily against Langlie's record and Langlie was also a statewide candidate, the two men crossed paths only once. At the little town of Winthrop, the two sat side by side at a nonpartisan rally. Rosellini ignored Anderson and tore into the Langlie record. Under that administration, he said, the state had suffered from "neglect" and a "do-nothing" approach. Schools were ignored and institutions were literally crumbling down around the inmates. Langlie abandoned his own race for the moment and defended himself. "I do not believe Senator Rosellini has been a good senator," he said. "In my judgment he has been a poor one for the simple reason he is one of those public officials who vote for spending measures and is against all taxes." Retorting, Rosellini said he hoped that the state would not have to endure "four more years of Langlie calling the signals through a handpicked puppet." This exchange turned out to be the final personal confrontation between two men who had been political opponents for more than sixteen years. The "new-versus-old" and "modern-versus-outdated" contrast between the two pointed to the inevitable result. Langlie's energy was spent, and his administration invited attack. It was a situation that would be repeated eight years later—only in reverse—when Rosellini faced the challenge presented by Dan Evans and his "Blueprint for Progress."[54]

In the last few days before the 1956 general election, the Republicans mounted a personal attack on Rosellini and his record. Literature began to appear (without attribution to any source), which pointed out how many Catholics were on the ballot and implied that Catholics were trying to take over. By inference this same literature sought to tie Rosellini to gambling, liquor interests, and even organized crime. In a letter to all the Republican county chairmen, a Seattle lawyer and Republican leader, Willard J. Wright, accused Rosellini of duping the voters as to his record. Wright listed numerous examples: (1) In 1939, Rosellini voted for Senate Bill 237, which would have licensed gambling within 800 feet of a school, church, or playground; (2) that same year, he introduced a bill to repeal the law which makes it a felony to sell liquor to a minor; (3) in 1941, he voted for a measure which would have permitted the sale of liquor in parks and beach resorts; (4) in 1945, Rosellini voted to remove the tax on liquor sales; and (5) in 1947, he voted against a bill to increase the taxes on pinball and slot machines. The clear inference of Wright's letter was that Rosellini's election would mean more gambling and more bars and taverns.[55]

The nature of the attack caught Rosellini by surprise. With barely a week before the final election, the question was whether the allegations could be refuted effectively. A few days later, in an advertisement paid for by the Rosellini campaign, sixteen state senators labeled Wright's charges as "a despicable type of campaigning—where you cite a vote and name a bill by number and then describe it as something it is not." They pointed out that the 1939 vote was not a bill to license gambling within 800 feet of a school or church, but to permit the operation of games such as bingo at state fairs, with suitable restrictions. Similarly, the 1945 vote was not to remove the tax on liquor sales, but to provide that a temporary wartime liquor tax should expire six months after the end of the war. The senators said these and other distortions were a cover-up by Anderson "to hide his own lack of a voting record" and "to divert attention from [his] lobbying efforts over the years on behalf of fraternal organizations to permit slot machines in private clubs."[56]

Rosellini saw these attacks as little more than an affirmation of his isolation from the establishment. On a larger scale, these last-minute tactics reaffirmed the negative image Rosellini had with these groups. He was upset by the deliberate distortions of his record, the personal nature of the attacks, and the anonymous attempt to bring his Italian heritage and religion into the race. Even though he felt he was leading, the *Times* and Ross Cunningham were calling the race a toss-up. Worse still, the *Times* continued to imply that his campaign and candidacy were tainted. In its final editorial in support of Anderson, the *Times* stated that "an era of clean, sound and progressive" government could be lost by Rosellini's election. Damning by their comparison, the editors pointed out that during the previous eight years there had not been a breath of scandal concerning the governor himself or his department heads. They went on to say that a vote for Anderson would preserve that rare integrity. Even on the issue of institutions, the *Times* leveled a charge that Rosellini's "concern for the patients in state custodial and other institutions was whetted considerably when he decided to run for governor." For a few moments, which stretched into several days, Rosellini envisioned his chances slipping away.[57]

In a television appearance, Rosellini responded to his critics in a speech prepared by Virginia Burnside: "People told me that because I am of Italian descent, and because I am of humble origin, that I should save my time. Somehow I couldn't quite believe that. I could not believe that the American people, living in a land dedicated to the principles of equality for all, would deny me that right. . . . I was warned that prejudice and bigotry would defeat me—that the special interests who have control of the present administration would spare nothing—no trick, no deceit, no fraud, to defeat me." He pointed out that the opposition had distorted his record, which, he continued, "has made me realize that maybe a man of humble immigrant parents cannot win a race like this. . . . I firmly believe that the American people are bigger than their prejudice; that they can rise above the efforts to play on ignorance and misinformation, that they can help me reaffirm my faith in the greatness of the country in which we live."[58]

The speech was grandiose and had perhaps exaggerated the nature of the attacks. Yet it accurately reflected Rosellini's deepest fears and beliefs. In the early days of his campaign, Mike Gallagher and others had told him that someone of his background would never be elected governor. In 1956 there had never been a governor west of the Mississippi who was Catholic, Italian, or a first-generation immigrant. He knew that his speech was awkward and too often betrayed his humble origins. He had, of course, frequently been accused of improper ties to liquor or gambling interests. He had never achieved the kind of confidence that made him comfortable with the establishment forces who were at the center of political power in Seattle and Olympia throughout the 1940s, 1950s, and even into the 1960s.

Despite Rosellini's last-minute concerns, a fortuitous combination of factors—a lame-duck administration with no viable successor, a weak opponent, a strong campaign by Maggie, intense labor interest in defeating Initiative 198, the public perception that the state's institutions were in total disarray, and Rosellini's own effective statewide effort—proved to be decisive. In the final election, Rosellini won by almost 100,000 votes.

Chapter 8

Launching an Administration

Rosellini's election was a mandate for change and modernization in state government. For at least eight years—if not longer—the state had been struggling with the tensions created by the depression, the war, and the recognition that state government under the old priorities was unable to provide proper services. The mushrooming school population and the return of the veterans from World War II had shown that tax support of schools was often inadequate. Pressures on higher education facilities necessitated expansion and additional funding.

The legislative battles between conservatives and liberals and the formation of coalitions in 1951 and 1953 were symptomatic of these strains (see chapters 3 and 4). The property-based tax system, which had been implemented in the late 1880s, was not adaptable to the state's needs. Revenue shortages had many drastic consequences— among the most prominent, the failure to provide adequate penal and mental-health facilities. Increased demand for power renewed the simmering feud between public- and private-power interests. This issue would boil over during Rosellini's last years as governor (see chapter 15). Even though eight years had passed since the people had approved liquor-by-the-drink legislation, the regulation of liquor sales continued to be a battlefield. Both sides were quick to condemn anyone involved if they thought the process was being colored by political favoritism, while at the same time the growing hotel and tourism industry was pressuring for a sensible solution (see chapters 3 and 15).

Population growth and the increasing mobility of people and businesses led to more pressure to build and improve bridges, ferries, and highways. The rise of small businesses and the transformation from the prewar big-business versus big-labor struggles had led to numerous national measures, such as the Taft-Hartley Labor Relations Act and attempts in Washington to pass Initiative 198. These "right-to-work" laws were designed to free workers from what was perceived as exploitation by the same unions that had been formed to protect them. An intelligent and sophisticated work force, such as the engineers at Boeing, demanded changes in the old equations. Gone were the days of timber, agriculture, and banking as the major players. For example, the modernization of farming was rapidly changing the political power of the Grange and similar organizations.

The rise of Japan and other Asian countries as trading partners— as well as the growth of world trade generally—was producing pressure in the state for expanded, modern port facilities. Along with this came the need to compete with other western states in attracting new businesses. In early 1952 a small group of civic and government leaders had conceived the idea that Seattle and the state could make its place on the world trade map with a World's Fair, and by 1956 the concept was gaining momentum.

Clearly these problems, challenges, and pressures were not advancing at the same pace, but they were all at work in the political climate of the state in 1956. The sense that the old, traditional methods of Langlie's party could not effect the changes needed—at least with the people at hand—was definitely part of the public mood. The fact that the state had elected a first-generation Italian Catholic was proof of significant changes in the electorate. In contrast to Langlie, the new governor was not the acknowledged philosophical leader of his party, except on certain issues, such as institutions (see chapter 5).[1] This was the setting on November 5, 1956, when Albert D. Rosellini was elected Washington's governor.

Rosellini was not fully prepared to assume the office that he had sought for more than four years. He had few ideas on building a cabinet and staff. He later confided to Warren Bishop (his eventual chief of staff) that he had never considered what would have to happen if he won. The day after the election he met with his closest confidants—Dr. Leo Rosellini, Victor Rosellini, and Judge Hugh Rosellini—and told them that he was overwhelmed by the enormity of what needed to be done and his relative inexperience. While he knew a lot about the senate and the legislature, this did not translate into being an effective chief executive. Years later, Victor recalls Hugh and Leo telling Albert that his name, background, and heritage would make him suspect in most people's minds and that he would have to be very good or he would be ridden out of office at the first opportunity.[2]

That same day Rosellini called on three close friends to join the group and help shape his administration: Charles Hodde, Harold Shefelman, and Joe Dwyer, a Kittitas Valley rancher, lawyer, and businessman. This expanded "brain trust" decided that the highest priority should be the selection of a strong chief of staff, who would be nonpolitical and would have the confidence of legislators, cabinet officers, and the media. Rosellini went to the acting president of the University of Washington, H. P. "Dick" Everest, and sought his help in identifying such a person. Everest, who had been Langlie's administrative assistant from 1941 to 1944, named two possibilities: Lloyd Schram and Warren Bishop. Schram was the director of student services at the university and Bishop was a professor in the school of political science and public administration. Bishop's background appealed to Rosellini because of his work on the King County Metro legislation (a proposal to organize and implement a regional governmental body) as well as his prior service on the Edmonds City Council. At their first meeting a week after the election, Rosellini outlined his plan to reorganize the way state government and the executive office functioned. He explained that the various state departments were loosely coordinated and were not responsible to the governor, even though they were ostensibly under the chief executive's control. The reforms he envisioned would be impossible to effect until the governor's office gained control of the departments and agencies, and this would require fundamental changes in management and budgeting. Bishop had reservations about the governor-elect, but he also was flattered and intrigued. He had studied the state's budget and accounting systems as they affected municipalities, and he considered them to be archaic and ineffective.[3]

The next day Bishop received another call from Rosellini, arranging a meeting that would also include Angelo Pellegrini, Leo, Victor, Hugh, and Harold Shefelman. The group was forthright with Bishop as to the course and direction of the new administration and emphasized that it would be run as nonpolitically as possible. Bishop considered the offer overnight and accepted the position the next day.[4]

The first days were hectic. Rosellini concentrated on identifying key cabinet members, leaving Bishop to oversee the transition. The outgoing administration was uncooperative, as most of Langlie's people had left or were leaving to find other jobs. Many files dealing with state agencies and departments had been destroyed, removed, or did not exist in the first place. Langlie himself was exhausted after his losing effort against Magnuson and had checked himself into a California hospital. There were no funds to cover the transition, and Rosellini paid all expenses. This was onerous because of the large deficit left from the campaign (a debt that was not retired for nearly two years). Since the outgoing staff denied him access to space within the executive office, Bishop was forced to seek offices elsewhere. (Secretary of State Coe, a loser to Rosellini in the primary, generously made offices and some staff available to the governor-elect.) A parting gift of the old administration was a retroactive 5 percent pay raise to all "covered employees," regardless of merit, longevity, or funds available. Because there was no funding, one of Rosellini's first acts was to cancel the raise, setting off accusations of political motivation.[5]

Within his own group of close advisors, Rosellini formed an informal committee to supplement the work of the statutory Standards Committee (certain department heads, with Bishop as the governor-appointed chair), which made personnel decisions for all agencies and departments not covered by the State Personnel Board (see pp. 119–20). The informal committee included Bishop, Hodde, and Joe Davis, executive director of the Washington State Labor Council. They usually followed one guiding principle: no Catholic Italian or close friend of Rosellini was eligible for a key position. Another guideline was that the best person should be hired, even if he or she were outside the Rosellini organization. For example, the selection of Warren Bishop himself was highly criticized by several of Rosellini's Democratic friends, who wanted a more political chief of staff. These same people were equally upset when Hodde, who had backed Earl Coe in the primary, and Earl Coe himself were appointed to major posts within the new administration.[6]

Many department heads were chosen quickly. Among the first were Hodde (chair of the tax commission), Roy Betlach (head of the State Patrol), Don G. Abel (chairman of the Liquor Control Board), John A. Biggs (director of the Department of Game, who also became an invaluable advisor on further appointments and other matters), William A. Bugge (director of the Department of Highways), and Joseph D. Dwyer (director of the Department of Agriculture). Later both Hodde and Betlach would assume other posts within the administration.[7]

Most other appointments were ironed out in the next few weeks. The next group included Jerry Hagan (Department of Labor and Industries), Louise S. Taylor (director of the Department of Licenses), Milo Moore (director of the Department of Fisheries), Peter Giovan (head of the Employment Security Department), John Vanderzicht (director of parks and recreation), Lloyd Nelson (director of the Department of General Administration), and Earl Coe (director of the Department of Conservation).

Except for several minor positions—which were filled by the time of the inaugural—this left two key cabinet posts vacant. The appointment of the director of institutions would have to wait until a thorough nationwide search would be completed. In the interim, Dr. G. Lee Sandritter, head of Eastern State Mental Hospital filled the position. Before the other key cabinet post could be filled, its department had to be created. During the campaign, Rosellini had stressed the need for a Department of Commerce and Economic Development to encourage businesses to locate in the state, thereby creating jobs and increasing the state's economic base. Though his vision as to its function was innovative, it was a misnomer to call it a completely new department.

Functional aspects of its duties had originated in the thirties, with the Washington State Progress Commission, created by the legislature "to promote tourism, industry, investment and immigration to Washington," and the state planning council, whose mission was to analyze the state's resources and recommend ways for developing them. In 1945 both groups were abolished, and their functions were consolidated within the Department of Conservation and Development. For two years the new division of progress and industry did try to encourage investment and development of the state's natural resources. Since 1947, however, the division had focused solely on promoting tourism.[8]

Rosellini planned a department that would take an activist role rather than simply responding to requests by business for assistance—a mission that required more than a mere agency or division within another department. In his view, state government had a duty to "coordinate economic development planning with business, . . . and advise and assist local communities and other governmental agencies in attracting development by both private and public entities." In July 1957, after the required legislation had been passed, Rosellini asked H. Dewayne Kreager to head up the new department. Kreager, a native of Ritzville, Wash., who had worked as an economic advisor to the Truman administration and to Senator Magnuson, and had been secretary of the National Security Resources Board, was first recommended to the new governor by Lacey Murrow. After a three-day visit to the state and a meeting with the newly appointed advisory counsel headed by Stan Donough, Kreager accepted the job and began his duties in October.[9]

The final appointment, director of institutions, was considered by Rosellini and his advisors to be the most critical. The atrocious situation in the state's institutions had been the focal point of his campaign. Rosellini had said that he could turn things around. Failure to do so would be catastrophic not only for the state but for Rosellini politically. During the election campaign, the Seattle *Times* had questioned the legitimacy of his attack on Langlie's institutional program, an attitude which was, in Rosellini's mind, symptomatic of the skepticism his administration faced on that issue. In the past six years, the department had had six directors and one acting director. It would require a leader of national stature to reorganize and rehabilitate the state's institutional facilities.

Rosellini was determined to take the time needed to find the right person. Among the people he consulted was Dr. Will Turnbold, executive director of the National Association of Probation and Parole. After hearing the challenges facing any potential director, Dr. Turnbold mentioned a "fellow in Michigan"—Dr. Garrett Heyns, director of the Michigan Department of Corrections, Probation and Parole. Heyns had molded the Michigan penal institutions into a national model. Before contacting Heyns, Rosellini called Michigan governor G. Mennen "Soapy" Williams and received his reluctant permission to speak to Heyns. The major factors he stressed in their discussions were the need for change and the immense challenges faced by the new director. Rosellini also pledged his full support to help bring about the legislative and administrative changes required, including the necessary funding. On August 3, 1957, Dr. Heyns accepted the position.[10]

By late 1957 Rosellini's major appointments were in place. Charles Hodde had assumed responsibility for the Department of General Administration in place of Lloyd Nelson. A loyal friend and associate, Nelson had proven to be over his head in the position. He got into a needless controversy over purchasing procedures and his performance was highly publicized and criticized by the *Times* (see chapter 14, pp. 181–83). Replacing Hodde at the tax commission was William Schumacher, an accountant who was a former Internal Revenue Service division chief. Hodde turned out to be an outstanding and highly strategic appointment. He was widely viewed as an astute student of government, and he enjoyed excellent rapport with legislators. His position at general administration made him available to troubleshoot for the governor in other areas. According to Bishop and Rosellini, Hodde played a vital role in bringing about budget reform and greater control of the departments and agencies—a high priority for the new administration.[11]

By any standard, the men and women who made up the Rosellini administration were extremely well-qualified. Almost without exception, they were highly educated and experienced in the fields which they managed. And equally important for Rosellini's reputation, of all the group only Francis Pearson—head of the Public Service Commission—had been Rosellini's political ally. Pearson was a man of great personal courage and achievement. Partially blinded at the age of thirteen, he nonetheless earned a high school diploma and went on to a distinguished career as a legislator and civic leader. He and Rosellini became close friends while serving in the state senate, and he had been an early advisor during Rosellini's 1952 campaign. Significantly, Rosellini was willing to appoint former opponents, such as Earl Coe and Charlie Hodde, to important positions. Nor was he reluctant to keep men such as Dr. Bernard Bucove, John Biggs, William Bugge, and Joe Vanderzicht, who had served under Langlie. His one prerequisite, according to Bishop, was that they were the best qualified for the job at hand. Though he was often painted as a governor who abused the patronage system in favor of political friends and contributors, the record of Rosellini's major appointments does not justify that sort of labeling.[12]

In addition to filling key jobs, Rosellini's first weeks after the election were devoted to the coming inauguration and to identifying the themes that would set the tone of his administration's first efforts. Almost immediately, Rosellini listed the kinds of things he wanted to say and the issues he needed to discuss in his inaugural talk. A team of Bob and Lee Schulman at KING TV, Virginia Burnside, and Ed Munro—together with his primary speechwriters, Paul Coughlin and Edward Henry—began to outline his address. Naturally, institutions and children and youth claimed a high priority. As recently as October 10, just prior to the election, a sixteen-year-old boy had died in a fire at Chehalis Green Hill School during a "minor riot." Another priority was Rosellini's plan for a new agency for commerce and economic development. Others that emerged as a result of the team's review of the governor-elect's campaign issues included highways, education, and taxes.[13]

Rosellini had pledged to hold the line on taxes until a full review of government reorganization could be completed. To that end, he decided to appoint a citizens advisory committee to work with the state tax commission to suggest ways for equitably funding the tax

burdens incurred by a growing state and the consequent increased
need for services. This idea was to be highlighted in his inaugural.
Although budget reform was also a high priority, it would be addressed
in a second, later speech.[14]

As themes were discussed and the speech began to develop,
Rosellini felt the need to mention almost every issue he considered
important. As the first Democratic governor in eight years, he wanted
to show how the priorities of his administration would differ from
what had gone before. The result was a lengthy address which took
more than forty minutes to deliver. It did, however, emphasize those
issues which had brought Albert D. Rosellini to the podium to address
the joint session of the thirty-fifth legislature on January 16, 1957, as
Washington's fourteenth governor.

Inauguration

With his father and mother, Giovanni and Annunziata, beaming
proudly—along with Ethel and the children (John, age seventeen;
Janey, fifteen; Sue, thirteen; Lynn, eleven; and Albert, Jr., nearly six)—
on the podium with him, Rosellini formally took office. Chief Justice
Matthew D. Hill handed Rosellini the family Bible, upon which he
swore the oath as governor. Also present on the podium were his friends
and political allies Warren Magnuson, Mon Wallgren, and, from his
own legislative district, John O'Brien. Emmett Anderson, the man he
had just defeated, was present as well. Stopping briefly to kiss his wife
and his mother, Rosellini stepped to the podium and began his first
message as governor.[15]

In many ways, this would be among the most difficult moments
of Rosellini's life. One reason was his discomfort when giving formal
talks of any kind. (David Wood, a media advisor and consultant who
worked with him in later years, explained that the stress caused him
to cut short certain words and to betray a nervous tic which added
to his discomfiture.) Consequently, his speeches were written out to
the last word. Still, the stress required him to be under extremely tight
control when delivering any speech, and particularly his first inaugural.
Even after years in the political arena and two statewide campaigns,
Rosellini lacked the ease of manner and confidence that characterized

Langlie and other skilled orators, who were used to explaining their ideas to others. Another reason for the pressure he felt was the fact that the speech was so long, and he knew that people's attention might fade. He was well aware that he was not a spellbinding speaker.[16]

Even partisan Democratic observers did not think it was a great speech. Rosellini reiterated his belief that there were things the state must do—that it must not wait for events to happen. Beginning with atomic power and ending with the financially troubled metropolitan-area transit systems, he urged action, not concern. "We [the state] have the obligation of *leadership*—and we have the responsibility of *regulation*," he said. He urged "purchasing of park sites while still available," "immediate action to protect against the growing menace of air pollution," "enactment of a sound civil service system," "annual legislative sessions," "immediate construction of a new State Library," "establishment of modern alcoholic treatment programs and facilities," "increased teachers' salaries," "better and more equal allocation of funds among school districts," "better retirement programs for the state colleges of education," and "expansion of the junior colleges of the state." He insisted on "expediting the construction of the second Lake Washington Bridge," the "abolition of lien laws and ratable reductions," "support for a World's Fair," and "passage of laws to strengthen the rights of persons who have been discriminated against because of race, creed or color."[17]

The speech urged action and movement on many fronts. From that standpoint it was no doubt overly ambitious, establishing an agenda that could not succeed except over time. It also gave his opponents a laundry list of issues that they would use against him. But the speech and his constant call for action reflected Rosellini's personality and his approach to government. He was a public servant who acted on ideas when he heard them and they sounded right. His career in the senate was one of action and movement, and he brought the same approach to his administration.

Another facet of the new governor's personality is revealed by an incident that occurred on the night of the inaugural ball. Ethel Rosellini recalled that they were hurrying across the capitol grounds, already late, when they encountered one of the janitors. He stopped them, wanting to talk. Characteristically, Rosellini spent almost twenty minutes visiting with him and listening to what he had to say. "Albert always had time for people—especially people who had little influence or power," said his wife.[18]

When Albert Rosellini took office on January 17, 1957, the fact that he was the first American of Italian parentage to be elected governor in the western states was mentioned prominently in the New York *Times* and the *Christian Science Monitor*. The *Monitor*, in covering his inaugural, quoted one veteran observer of the state political scene as saying that while Rosellini "had a masterly public relations campaign and a good finance procurement set-up . . . he could not have succeeded were it not for himself. He has a golden gift with people. He is charming, attentive and warm. He is genuinely concerned with little people, and has a humility that is very disarming." However, the same article also stated: "Those who know him well also characterize him as extremely ambitious and calculating. They say he makes no moves until he has considered all the angles."[19]

With the advent of Rosellini's first administration, the state's government and the office of governor would be forever changed. Never again would the governor have the luxury of sitting back and letting the legislature decide. A new era of activist government presided over by the governor as chief executive had begun. While it was still a system of checks and balances, the state government that evolved in 1957 had as a central driving force the state's chief executive and his administration—one that pushed, pressured, cajoled, and led the legislature toward his agenda. The emergence into the modern era had begun.

Chapter 9

Budget Reform

O n his first day in office, Rosellini began to work with Bishop on changing the state budgeting procedures, which had been implemented in 1921. Bishop was highly critical of the outdated methods by which state agencies and departments accounted for monies spent. There was no centralized budget office within the executive department; there was only a budget office that was responsible to no one in particular and certainly not to the governor.[1]

Rosellini's years in the state senate had made him aware of the inefficiencies and lack of accountability of the process. He believed someone reporting directly to the governor was needed to reorganize and centralize control of various administrative functions. Consequently, before passage of the Unified Budget and Accounting Act in 1959, Bishop served as the de facto budget director for all agencies accountable to the governor. Rosellini felt that placing his chief of staff in charge of the operation would further emphasize its high priority. The governor also insisted that department directors and staff were to cooperate fully with Bishop and Hodde (who was assisting) so that a unified reform package could be presented to the legislature.[2]

To understand the conditions facing Bishop and the administration requires some background on the then current budgeting process. The state budget and the concomitant appropriation measures were

created by an ad hoc process whereby each unit of government simply requested funds without identifying the programs for which they
would be used. The appropriations bills, likewise, asked for lump-sum
amounts by category—such as overall salaries—without identifying
staff needs or where the salaries would go. In addition, each institution,
facility, agency, and even some sections of departments would prepare
an "object" or "line-item" request for funds for capital expenditures,
such as office furniture. There would be no indication of where the
items purchased would be used, nor would the request reveal whether
an item would achieve program goals of that department.[3] There were
literally hundreds of different funds to which monies were alloted and
from which monies were disbursed. The record-keeping and billing
processes varied greatly from agency to agency and within departments. Some agencies even maintained one accounting system for
their own use and another to meet the demands of the budget office.
It was not uncommon for an office to show a surplus in one report and
a deficit in another. The Seattle *Times* described the budget system as
"crazy-quilt," and compared the process to a giant beer keg with dozens
of different taps operated by people who had no idea what might be
going on at the other taps.[4]

There was no allowance for an ongoing review of agency or departmental needs or programs. Nor were any standard budget procedures
or long-term fiscal guidelines in place. This made it difficult for an
agency or department to overcome the innate skepticism of legislators,
reluctant to increase taxes, as to the need for more money. Similar
skepticism would meet any report by the governor that the state was
in a deficit (or surplus) position. This was one reason that Rosellini
believed that the proper allocation of monies by the administration
was an essential first step, before considering a tax increase. In his
inaugural Rosellini had stated: "We do know that we are going into
the next biennium with a large general fund deficit. We also know that
various departments of the state have overspent by many millions of
dollars. . . . Despite this, it is my firm hope that we will [be able] to
run our state for the next two years without any added taxes." Both
he and Bishop were counting heavily on budget reform to make more
efficient use of funds on hand.[5]

Planning for reform began with a $175,000 appropriation to survey the present system and explore methods for establishing "a modern uniform system of accounting for all State Agencies, together with . . . a related program-type budget." A management consulting firm, Donaho and Associates, was hired to work with a bipartisan advisory committee, which was chaired by Bishop and included Speaker John O'Brien, Hodde, Professor George Shipman, Ed Munro, and Peter Giovan. In addition, Rosellini asked Sen. Marshall Neill and Rep. Joe Chytl, Republican legislators, to participate. That group, along with the consultants, met frequently with the governor to discuss progress and areas of concern.[6]

Bishop's committee and Donaho and Associates appraised existing budgetary practices and found them "mechanical, routine, and overly detailed." There was no substantive review process and "judgement factors as to a particular request are almost wholly lacking." Single-entry bookkeeping was the state's official accounting policy, leading to a "concomitant lack of self-balancing features in financial record-keeping." The activities of the budget sections of agencies consisted mostly of checking for arithmetical mistakes. Further, agencies requested one appropriation for operations and another for salaries and wages and were prevented by law from transfers between the two, "thereby curtailing their freedom in using funds . . . as . . . needs develop during the course of the biennium."

According to Donaho, the "budget process lacks integrity and substantive review . . . the detailed proving, cross-checking, and cross-checking again, which takes place in the budget section and which dominates the time and attention of the staff, is largely misdirected effort and bears only an accidental relationship to a proper budget function."[7]

The 1959 legislature was presented for the first time with a program-oriented budget for all agencies, showing proposed operating budgets by program categories and a six-year capital-improvement program by department. At the same time, the administration introduced a proposed budget and accounting act. If passed, the act would require the governor to submit a balanced budget with revenue sufficient to meet proposed appropriations. (Appropriations for continuing budget reorganization were included in all future appropriation measures—up to and including this current biennium.) It provided for the liquidation of the general-fund deficit left from the 1957 biennium, established a new accounting and reporting system, made the heads of agencies responsible for conducting their business within the budget even if revenues fell, and made the budgets more adaptable to changing needs. In addition, the act established a new central budget agency.

The act was designed to link budgeting and administration so that the governor's programs would not be stymied by the budget process. Although the measure was debated vigorously in both houses, it passed without significant amendment. For the first time in the state's history, the governor could plan agency budgets on a program basis and also know how much money was being spent, and where, for those same programs.[8]

With the passage of the act, the budget office became a part of the executive branch, with its director appointed by the governor. Chief of Staff Warren Bishop was immediately named director and added to Rosellini's cabinet. Bishop set up a new accounting department and hired a permanent staff. In meeting the charge that it "establish the vital link between budgeting and administration," the agency wrote a budget-and-accounting manual, held intensive training sessions with agencies' staff, redesigned state forms, and improved payroll and vendor payment systems.[9]

The act implemented several other changes, including rigorous allocation control by the budget office. This enabled the governor to allot funds to the agencies with his own budgetary or policy goals in mind. Further, the act prohibited agencies from spending monies not allotted to them by the governor. Previously, heads of agencies had personally appeared and defended their budgets before legislative committees. Now the budget director defended the entire budget, leading to more equitable treatment for similar institutions and less lobbying of individual legislators by agency heads. At the same time, regulations concerning travel by state employees, which formerly had varied from agency to agency, were made uniform.[10]

Although for the most part the new act passed in its proposed format, some changes were made. Higher education forces resisted allotment control by the governor, expressing concern about possible favoritism and lack of academic freedom. Hence, the colleges and universities were exempted. An amendment also gave the legislative budget committee a role in preparing the final executive budget. The legislative budget committee, which met between sessions with various institutions and agencies to forecast eventual appropriation levels, was considered powerful and prestigious by legislators, and they were reluctant to eliminate its function. Although Bishop and Rosellini claimed that it represented an unwarranted intrusion by the legislature into the executive planning process, the reform act probably would not have passed without this amendment. In practice, the provision helped to educate the legislature—in advance—as to the administration's proposals and goals under the budget.[11]

The act failed to address two areas of reform initially sought by Rosellini and Bishop. Efforts to include transportation and highway budgets under the governor's allocation process were rejected adamantly by State Rep. Julia Butler Hansen, powerful chair of the House Highways Committee who wanted the Transportation Department to submit a separate budget that would go through her committee. It was still included in the governor's program budget (as part of the 1959 act), but was separately developed by that department. Further, the 1959 act did not create a coordinated planning function for all departments under the governor's direct control.[12] That component was finally added, during Dan Evans's first term.

The state auditor's role in the budget process was also changed, and the auditor's office was revamped. Previously, the state auditor had examined and approved the hundreds of thousands of purchase requisitions generated by state agencies each year—called the preaudit function. The auditor would then permit disbursement of state funds by issuing warrants to pay for these same preaudited requisitions. Then he would approve his own actions—the postaudit function. Donaho and Company stated that this seemed "an unwise mixture of authority" that failed to provide proper review. The consultant recommended that warrant approval and disbursement be moved to the state treasurer's office. This left the auditor with only a postaudit function, since the preaudit function would be performed by the new budget director.[13]

Cliff Yelle, the incumbent auditor, opposed these changes and lobbied hard to maintain his preaudit power. As a result, a number of editorial writers commented unfavorably—accusing Rosellini of trying to usurp powers. C. J. Johns of the Olympia *News* said that the governor was "trying to gain absolute power over the state purse strings." He noted that the consultants hired by Rosellini to overhaul the budget system had "marvelled at the lack of power held by the chief executive over expenditures," adding that they (Donaho and Company) believed that "the Legislature pretty well runs the show, even to the point of exercising some executive prerogative." Even Johns admitted that this move might prove to be efficient, but doubted the legislature would pass it. At one point, due in part to Yelle's efforts, the measure almost failed to clear the senate rules committee. Hearing of the problem in the closing hours of the regular session, Rosellini personally met with the rules committee over dinner, and the bill was finally sent to the floor, where it passed by a large margin.[14]

Ultimately, Yelle filed a lawsuit challenging the constitutionality of the change. The suit was originally argued before the Thurston County superior court, and then was appealed to the state supreme court. Both courts upheld the act's basic constitutionality. At Rosellini's request, his mentor and advisor Harold Shefelman was appointed special assistant attorney general to defend the act. Yelle remained bitter about the law and its changes, blaming Rosellini and Bishop for the erosion of his office's power. In 1960 he organized a Democrats for Andrews group in opposition to Rosellini's reelection.[15]

The importance of the new act to state government and the governor's office cannot be overstated. Years after he left office, Dan Evans commented on the critical importance of the program budget procedure his predessesor had initiated.[16] For the first time, a governor could exert executive leadership over the programs and policies of the various agencies. Working through the budget office, a governor could allocate funds where problems existed—such as at mental institutions and juvenile facilities. In addition to allocation, it provided a critical tool by which both governors and legislatures could monitor performance of state government. For example, it allowed them to ascertain how much money the state was spending per person per day on health care, education, or incarceration. These data could be compared with amounts spent in other states and also with performance goals.

Rosellini's and Bishop's reforms were fully accepted as a method of enabling an administration to be accountable to the taxpayers and legislature. Whereas such reform was long overdue and was, perhaps, inevitable, the fact remains that it was controversial at the time and many predicted it would not win legislative approval. Indeed, without Rosellini's personal involvement, it would not have passed the senate in 1959. Because of his extensive legislative experience, Rosellini knew that efficient and accountable state government could not exist without budget reform, and he made it the first priority of his administration.

Chapter 10

Institutional
Reform

In both 1952 and 1956 Rosellini had charged that the "horse and buggy" Langlie administration's "indifference," "short sighted neglect," and "false economy" had produced "medieval dungeons" rather than institutions. It was clear to everyone that Rosellini had been elected in large part because the voters agreed. Consequently, improvement of prisons, reaccreditation of the state's mental hospitals, building of new juvenile homes, and improved benefits for the 4,000 employees of the department were high priorities for the new administration. Realizing that extraordinary expenditures would be required in order to bring about these reforms, Rosellini began the process by submitting an executive request bill. The legislature responded by passing a supplemental appropriations measure that established a $7 million discretionary fund for the governor to use within the Department of Institutions if budgeted appropriations proved insufficient. Two years later, during the 1959 special session, the legislature approved an additional $1.8 million discretionary fund for the governor to use in achieving reaccreditation of the state's mental institutions.[1]

Prisons

Because of the riots at Monroe and Walla Walla, prisons demanded immediate attention. About one-third of the 1,600 inmates at Walla

Walla were housed in brick cell blocks which had been built in 1886 when Washington was still a territory. These buildings, with no ventilation or plumbing, were known as "bucket cells," because each cell had a bucket for a toilet. The stench, especially during the heat of Walla Walla summers, was unbearable. At both Walla Walla and Monroe, inmate idleness was catastrophic; few prisoners were given any work, training, or education, and recreational programs were limited because of insufficient space. Too little was spent on food, and some of this spoiled due to poor organization and storage facilities. Medical care was often unavailable or unreliable. Power plants at both adult prisons had deteriorated badly due to lack of maintenance funds. Both facilities were overcrowded, and the most dangerous inmates were not always segregated from the others. Problems of supervision and management were compounded by poor accounting and record-keeping procedures.[2]

Rosellini was not willing to ignore the problems at Walla Walla during the lengthy process of hiring a new director of institutions. In February 1957 he appointed B. J. Rhay as the superintendent at Walla Walla. Rhay started a "rehabilitation not custody" program, using an emergency allocation from Rosellini's contingency fund to hire more staff. Before a year had passed, 86 percent of the prisoners had some kind of job.[3]

Heyns's appointment was confirmed in August 1957. He immediately began a complete reorganization of the department to eliminate duplication, streamline the chain of command, and improve communication on policy and personnel matters between divisions. Following still another extensive search, Heyns and Rosellini chose Ernest Timpani to head up the Monroe Reformatory. Emphasizing "rehabilitation through education," Timpani tore down inner fences, planted grass, and asked inmates to suggest improvements. The reformatory's mattress factory, print shop, and farms were reorganized and expanded to create more jobs. A new vocational training building opened at Walla Walla in 1958, enabling the prisoners to learn auto mechanics, metalworking, welding, woodworking, and office machine repair. By mid-1959, idleness on the part of inmates had been "virtually eliminated."[4]

Rosellini's first legislative initiatives involving penal institutions encountered little opposition. In March 1957 the legislature approved a one-time allocation of $2,325,500 for "construction and major repairs at Walla Walla," along with $2,325,928 for operations (a 27.5 percent increase from the previous biennium). The constructions funds, supplemented in later sessions, allowed the penitentiary to build a new hospital wing and a new warehouse by 1963 (in addition to the vocational training center). During that same time Monroe installed a new steam plant, a gymnasium, a remodeled kitchen, and a new "armory tower" to cut down on escapes.[5]

Recognizing that overcrowding at both facilities was due to the need for a new prison, Rosellini obtained a federal grant of $109,552 to design a third prison. In September 1964, the new corrections center opened on a ninety-acre site near Shelton. All convicted felons in the state were sent first to Shelton for diagnosis and classification. After that, the youngest prisoners would generally stay at Shelton, and older convicts would be dispersed to either Monroe or Walla Walla—depending on the security needs of each individual. At the dedication ceremony, the governor called the center "one of the most carefully planned correctional institutions ever built," with the "most enlightened correctional philosophy . . . rehabilitation [of] men, rather [than] mere custody and vengeful punishment." Hopefully, he said, "the unskilled and the unproductive may learn skills and become productive."[6]

Legislative funding for the state's two forestry honor camps, which had been opened by Langlie in 1956, was increased and extended. Two more camps were opened during the 1959–61 biennium. These camps housed low-risk inmates, who, in summer and early fall, were "fully employed at hard labor in snag-felling, reforestation, flood control, building access roads and fire lanes, and as emergency laborers in salvaging harvest crops." Not only did this program relieve idleness and boredom, it also yielded $2 million worth of labor annually. In 1958 the honor camps were commended by the Department of Natural Resources for their firefighting work.[7]

Despite the priority given to prisons, supported in the main by the legislature, improvement of some conditions moved slowly. It was not until February 1963 that the "bucket cells" at Walla Walla were finally abandoned. The "unsanitary, degrading and unhumanitarian conditions" which Rosellini had complained about in 1954 were finally eliminated.[8]

For years Rosellini had advocated a civil-service program and protection of institutional employees from what he called "the harassment of politically-inspired personnel changes." As a first step toward that goal, in February 1957, following one of the recommendations of the 1953 Little Hoover committee report, Rosellini introduced a bill that would give civil-service protection to almost all state employees, including those who worked for the Department of Institutions. The measure encountered the same partisan controversy that had stymied the proposals in 1953. The refusal of the democrats to support passage of the Little Hoover committee civil-service proposal in 1953 led the Seattle *Times* and others to criticize Rosellini's position on civil service and institutions as hypocritical and opportunistic.[9] The *Times*, in particular, castigated Rosellini, saying that many of the management problems blamed on Langlie would have been avoided had the 1953 civil-service proposal passed. This criticism seems misplaced, since both houses were controlled by the Republicans in 1953, Langlie was governor, and it is clear that the Republicans did not want the measure passed. It ignores, as well, the twelve years of lack of funding for institutions under Langlie.

The fact was that civil service and merit-basis hiring for state employees had significant political negatives: (1) the party out of power traditionally looked upon the measure as one which would enable the other party to secure more than 16,000 jobs for its partisans; (2) the party in power, if newly elected, saw the measure as a means whereby the holdovers from a previous administration might be locked in and not replaced; (3) there was a tendency within any legislature to delay passage until after the next election and a possible change in administration; and (4) state employees and their unions opposed any merit system which had an "open back door" and which allowed incompetent or unsatisfactory staff to be fired.

These political liabilities helped defeat Rosellini's civil-service bill in 1957. Despite the fact that the Democrats controlled both houses of the legislature, the bill did not even emerge from the house state government committee. Its proposed effective date was July 1957. Prior to that time, the administration could presumably replace thousands of state employees with Democrats, who would then be protected. Hence, the Republicans refused to support it. The Democrats were concerned that such a short time frame would mean job protection for many Republicans employed by the Langlie administration.[10]

The political climate for civil-service legislation was further clouded by partisan bickering over bills eliminating thirty boards and commissions made up of Langlie appointees, and other measures designed to put Rosellini's appointees into policy-making positions. William Goodloe, Rosellini's political nemesis who was senate minority leader during the session, charged that the "spoils system is the order of the day in Olympia." Rosellini, in response, said such measures were necessary as "a means of giving the party in power the control it needs to be responsible for the government of the state." Even Ross Cunningham concurred generally with Rosellini's position.[11]

From the very first, however, the proposed civil-service legislation had had little chance of success. On the same day that Rosellini introduced that legislation, he revoked, by executive decree, a Langlie-mandated merit system that had covered some 4,000 state employees in five state agencies, including, among others, the state personnel board and the Department of Institutions itself (see p. 100). Rosellini knew that his actions would be seen as incongruous and politically motivated, but he was faced with a dilemma over the role of the state personnel board. At that time, the personnel board was not accountable to the governor, but it had enormous influence over the hiring and retention of employees in policy-making positions within the executive branch. Many of these positions were federally funded. In order to comply with restrictions against using federal funds as part of a patronage or spoils system, these positions had been classified as merit-examination jobs. Implementation of the governor's policies depended on the cooperation of the employees in these positions. Rosellini did not want to have either the personnel board or the people it had placed in policy-making positions locked in under civil service.[12]

Republicans were quick to attack the revocation as proof that Rosellini wanted his own patronage people in place. William Goodloe called on the Democrats to reject the governor's action, saying, "I would hate to see Governor Rosellini become the Huey Long of the State of Washington." In response, Rosellini said that the major reason for his move was that "the State Personnel Board is unable to operate a uniform state merit system because of separate statutes establishing merit systems for different departments of state government. . . . [T]he time has come to have an all-inclusive merit system for all state employees in every agency if all are to have this advantage."[13]

Another reason for Rosellini's revocation of Langlie's merit system was the need to introduce a new order of employee into the Department of Institutions. Gerhart Heyns would arrive on August 3, 1957, and it would take months to hire the staff he needed. Langlie's fiat had frozen a number of appointments that might need to be changed, and continuing the freeze would handicap Heyns's ability to reorganize the department. For example, in late 1957 Heyns requested the resignation of Ray Belknap, superintendent at Monroe, because of philosophical differences; it was not until May 1958 that Ernest Timpani was hired.[14]

The refusal of the 1957 legislature to pass Rosellini's civil-service measures proved even more embarrassing when the situations at various institutions continued to provide politically explosive events. On October 29, 1957, a group of criminally insane inmates at Eastern State Mental Hospital held thirty-six guards hostage for nine hours. It immediately became a political issue when Joseph Lawrence, King County Republican chair, charged that "patronage-hungry democrats have demoralized patients, inmates, and personnel in the state's institutional system." Lawrence also referred to the resignation of Ray Belknap as superintendent at Monroe, commenting that Belknap had "mentioned the constant shadow of partisanship throughout the Department of Institutions" and the "indecision at Olympia." Finally, Lawrence blamed the 51 percent staff-turnover rate in state institutions on Rosellini's abolishment of the civil-service protection provided by Langlie.[15]

It was Rosellini's turn to be on the defensive. He refuted Lawrence's charges, pointing out that Heyns had moved swiftly to control the situation at Eastern State without violence or injury, and that the unfortunate event—as well as the requested resignation of Belknap—

were proof that changes in personnel practices were needed. Rosellini also stated that "as soon as Heyns is able to take a look at the picture," he (Rosellini) would restore some sort of merit-system coverage for all Department of Institutions employees. Heyns and Rosellini were also facing more substantive, nonpolitical pressures for civil-service protection for institutional employees. Most other western states had job-protection systems, which put Washington at a disadvantage in securing competent personnel. The best-qualified applicants were naturally attracted to states where the jobs did not depend on political officeholders and their whims. Heyns was concerned that he would not be able to hire the kind of people he needed.[16]

On December 3, Rosellini put his full support behind a civil-service bill drafted by the legislative council's interim subcommittee on state government. Although the bill would not come before the legislature for fourteen months, Rosellini hoped that the legislative council's proposal, which was designed to overcome objections that had been raised in 1957, would garner enough public support to assure passage at that time. The draft legislation did away with the crazy-quilt situation whereby some employees were already covered by statute and others were dependent on executive proclamations (such as those that Rosellini had revoked earlier in the year). If the measure passed, all state employees currently under such protection would be blanketed in, along with all other state workers who had been employed for two consecutive years prior to January 1, 1959.[17]

The fact that any new legislation would not be adopted until 1959 continued to leave Rosellini vulnerable to partisan accusations. His onetime ally, Neil Hoff, charged that Rosellini had failed to institute reforms the two of them had advocated. He noted that Rosellini had replaced 62 percent of the personnel at institutions since revoking the merit system, and blamed him for the failure of the 1957 bill. Rosellini called the charge "ridiculous" and "politically inspired," and said that, as Hoff knew, Heyns had a "totally free hand to make changes." Rosellini also pointed out that the 1957 turnover rate was 30 percent less than in Langlie's last year. It was clear, however, that until a civil-service system was in place the matter would continue to draw partisan fire.[18]

Republicans were not alone in criticizing the governor and his policies on this issue. In May 1957 a controversy arose between the new administration and the Washington Federation of State Employees, who criticized the governor for removing the merit system for the various state agencies already covered. The union questioned whether the decision was made in order that present state workers within the Department of Institutions could be fired and replaced with Rosellini followers. Because he prided himself on the support of organized labor, Rosellini was upset by the public rift. He and Bishop had already made Joe Davis, executive secretary of the state labor federation, a part of the administration's quasi-official personnel committee, which provided guidelines for the hiring of all state employees not covered by the state personnel board. Rosellini called a press conference to point out that "of the 4,000 employees in the State Department of Institutions . . . only nine have been fired—and every one of them are supervisory people who should be changed. Only two of them have been questioned by the union, and there we have excellent cause." Rosellini went on to add, "we are not going to fire rank-and-file people purely for making political changes . . . we are going to change supervisory personnel—the policy-making heads. But we are going to give job protection to those doing a good job."[19]

By early 1958 Heyns felt that enough qualified new people were in place that proper reforms could begin. Rosellini was feeling pressure from several quarters to reinstate some form of job protection. Numerous professional groups, such as the Washington Citizen's Council of the National Probation and Parole Association, continued to state that a merit system for correctional employees—"by legislation and not by proclamation"—was the number-one need. As a stopgap, in March 1958 Rosellini extended merit-system coverage to the approximately 3,100 employees of both the Department of Institutions and the Board of Prison Terms and Parole. Editorial and professional criticism of a system that could be wiped away as easily as it had been granted continued. Further, Rosellini's action still left several state agencies and their employees without protection.[20]

When the civil-service legislation proposed by the legislative council failed to pass in 1959—despite full support from the administration and the press—for the same basic reasons that it had failed in 1957, Rosellini was convinced that a proper civil-service law could be enacted only by the initiative process. He encouraged the state employees union and the labor movement to sponsor a drive to put the measure before the voters. Initiative 207, sponsored by the Washington Federation of State Employees and endorsed by the Washington State Labor Council, provided civil-service protection for most state employees. (The only exemptions were the state patrol, which kept its own merit system intact, the highway commission, and the five schools of higher education. Each of the latter retained a three-member board to administer its respective programs.) The governor would appoint a three-member state personnel board and a director of personnel to administer the system for all other state departments and employees—some 26,000 in all. The proposed measure did away with the piecemeal approach to civil service. Further, it did away with the independent personnel board that often ran at cross purposes to the administration.[21]

The initiative measure was not perfect. It was patterned after the federal civil service and established overly rigorous procedures to dismiss incompetents or those incapable of performing tasks assigned. The other flaw was that Rosellini and his administration had had nearly four years to place employees. Thus, the initiative's blanketing-in feature was criticized soundly by some groups. Even the *Times*, which had long trumpeted the need for civil service, finally opposed Initiative 207 as providing too much protection for those already on the payroll.*[22]

Some opponents said that the measure should be defeated because it did not require all current employees to take examinations and requalify for jobs they had held for years. Not only was such a task politically unfeasible, it would also have created an administrative

---

*It is difficult to conceptualize how such a measure could be created otherwise. At some point, a civil-service system is supposed to provide long-term protection for qualified state employees who do not hold direct policy-making positions. No matter when it is finally adopted, it protects a group of employees who have been put in place by one or the other political party.

nightmare. Even though there was no organized opposition to the measure, the Seattle *Times* did compile a series of arguments against it. A major objection was that the initiative would create a large political machine of state employees that could influence elections and remove control of state government from the people. According to the *Times*, the measure could never be amended, since the employees' "machine" would be so powerful it could defeat lawmakers in any section of the state.[23]

The measure passed and was signed into law by Rosellini on December 8, 1960. It established a system where few state positions were subject to gubernatorial appointment. The only nonclassified positions within a given department were the director, assistant director, and a confidential secretary. Many department heads felt that this feature was too restrictive and would seriously affect their ability to carry out policies, but Rosellini was convinced that it was either this measure or none at all for the foreseeable future.[24]

Despite the concerns expressed in the Seattle *Times*, the civil-service act has been modified many times by later legislatures. Although state employees are a political force, and they have been effective in advocating for pay raises and career protection, they have not become an entrenched machine of the kind feared by the *Times*.* It is difficult to assess how much the position of the opponents, including the *Times*, was influenced by the facts that the initiative was on the 1960 ballot and Rosellini was already a definite underdog in his race against Lloyd Andrews. Assuming election of a Republican governor, the *Times* may have preferred that the measure be postponed until a new administration could protect its own appointees.

In any event, four years after he became governor, Rosellini's promise of a civil-service and merit system for state employees finally became a reality. Rosellini learned anew, this time from the perspective of the governor's office, that even seemingly noncontroversial subjects had hidden political agendas that could prevent the legislature from

*Dr. William Conte and others, however, attribute the decline in institutions after Rosellini's administration (see pp. 213–14) to the new breed of professional managers spawned, in part, by the Civil Service Act.

acting. Indeed, when asked why he could not successfully push the civil-service bill through a Democratic legislature, he was frank to admit that many powerful members of his own party, such as Sen. Mike Gallagher, were opposed to the idea.[25] Despite friendship and party loyalty, these legislators believed solidly in the spoils system, had been raised on it, and refused to support its demise.

Civil service and merit systems aside, the Rosellini administration continued to place its highest priority on the state's institutions. In many respects, the changes brought about were revolutionary. Under the guidance of Heyns and his staff, remarkable progress was made in modernizing, upgrading, and humanizing the treatment of the state's juveniles, adult felons, mentally ill, mentally retarded, blind, and deaf. The changes brought about in the adult correctional facilities have been chronicled above. Similar improvement occurred in almost ever other area.

Juvenile Facilities

At the time of Heyns's confirmation, all the juvenile institutions were so badly overcrowded that the department asked the superior court judges not to sentence juveniles to its institutions if they could possibly avoid doing so. At Green Hill, for example, more than two hundred boys were housed in facilities designed for half that many. Similar overcrowding existed at Maple Lane School for Girls near Centralia. Conditions at Green Hill, however, were particularly shocking. The so-called cottages were actually overcrowded, messy, unsanitary cell-blocks in which the boys were confined too much of the time. Young, vulnerable boys were not segregated from older, hardened criminals. Morale was low, the academic program was poor, and there were almost no nonschool activities. According to a March 1956 report, the school lacked a "continuity of purpose," "understanding of any overall program," and a "clear chain of authority." After the death of a sixteen-year-old in a fire in October 1956, the acting superintendent stated that he had no backing from Olympia and his school was treated "like a stepchild." In early 1957, an investigating committee called the school's facilities "disgracefully inadequate," its buildings "all wrong for a school," and its budget completely "unrealistic."[26]

Two other schools for delinquents—Martha Washington in Seattle and Luther Burbank on Mercer Island—which the state took over on July 1, 1957, were in "decrepit" condition and unpopular with the surrounding communities because of frequent escapes and behavior problems of the youths housed and treated there. All of the juvenile facilities required immediate improvement and more staff. In addition, the state needed a new diagnostic treatment center for juveniles.[27]

Heyns used monies from the governor's contingency fund to turn Fort Worden into a juvenile diagnostic and treatment center. Located on the Olympic Peninsula near Port Townsend and handed over to the state in mid-1957 by the army, its various buildings later became additional housing for boys. By April 1958 the diagnostic center could handle 144 youths for four to six weeks of evaluation. They were then paroled or sent to another juvenile institution—sometimes to the cottages just across the parade ground. Although it filled a need, Fort Worden's isolated location was a problem for a central diagnostic facility. When the Cushman Indian Hospital in Tacoma (a federal tuberculosis hospital) was deeded to Washington State without charge, it was converted into a "reception-diagnostic-research center" for juveniles, and Fort Worden became solely a residential treatment center.[28]

Rapid improvement was achieved in other areas. Following the passage of funding initiatives during the 1957 legislative session, two new cottages were added at Green Hill, and other cottages and a new recreation building were opened within the next three years. A new machine shop was completed in 1958. New cottages and a treatment center were built for Maple Lane School in the 1959–61 biennium. This relieved overcrowding at the one juvenile institution that had achieved national recognition by virtue of its excellent programs and a rehabilitation rate in excess of 88 percent. Staff and educational improvements were also made at Martha Washington and Luther Burbank. A new gymnasium opened at Burbank in 1959. Both institutions continued to be troubled, however, because of lack of community support, and both were closed in 1967. The approval of a special bond referendum pushed by the Rosellini administration in the 1964 general election allowed the state to build Echo Glen, a new correctional institution near Snoqualmie, which opened in 1967 and absorbed the population of Martha Washington and Luther Burbank.[29]

Both Heyns and Rosellini believed that the main goal for juvenile delinquents had to be rehabilitation. In order to prevent delinquency and to treat juveniles locally, the state had established nineteen child-guidance centers in six different regions. These centers employed "roving psychiatric social workers," psychiatrists, psychologists, juvenile specialists, and a "delinquency prevention consultant" to help local communities develop their own resources. The program received national attention in its efforts to deter delinquency by early intervention. By the end of Rosellini's administration, the number of child guidance centers had risen to twenty-three.[30]

In another area, money from Rosellini's contingency fund was used to hire more parole counselors to supervise young people released from juvenile corrections programs and help prevent recidivism. The added funds also improved the quality of the counseling programs offered to paroled offenders. By August 1958 the department was able to send juvenile court judges follow-up information about the girls and boys they had sentenced—a request that had been pending for years. By 1963 the recidivism rate of paroled youths had decreased from 40 percent to 21.5 percent.[31]

State Mental Hospitals

Few subjects aroused as much passion in Rosellini as did the conditions at the state mental hospitals. Early in his legislative career, he had made official tours of several of these facilities and had come away with a deep sense of sorrow at the condition of the patients confined within their walls. In 1953, he called mental health "the Number One health problem for the state." In November 1957 Rosellini pointed out that the state's mental hospitals had fallen from a rating of seventh in the nation to thirty-second since 1949 and "were no longer recognized as fit training grounds for doctors and nurses." Employees, he said, had recently been sentenced for selling to outsiders "drugs meant to ease the pain of suffering patients . . . and hundreds of pounds of food meant for the plates of bedridden patients were sold into different channels."[32]

The American Psychiatric Association had found conditions at Western State Hospital totally inadequate, with too few professional and semiprofessional staff, few, if any, recreational and occupational programs, no children's unit, and no outpatient clinic. Western State also had far too many children as patients, many of them diagnosed as "psychopathic delinquents." The same type of inspection revealed similar situations at Northern State and Eastern State hospitals. Because the state schools for the mentally retarded were overcrowded, Eastern accepted retarded patients along with psychotic cases, which resulted in several instances of "brutality and maltreatment" of patients by other patients and by employees.[33]

The incident that occurred shortly after Heyns took over the department, in which some of the criminally insane inmates at Eastern State rioted, seized control of the building, and took guards as hostages, was more than just a political embarrassment. It also demonstrated the depths to which the conditions at the state's mental hospitals had fallen. The apparent cause of the uprising was the firing of the chief of the security guards, who had organized a regime of bribes, gambling, homosexuality, and favored treatment for some inmates.[34]

While Rosellini and Heyns believed that new staff and more competent personnel, which were gradually being added, were beginning to solve some of the more immediate concerns, a far more difficult problem was the lack of an effective supervisor for the division of mental health. In fact, this post had never been filled by prior administrations. Finally, after another extensive search, Dr. William Conte was hired in June 1959.[35]

From the outset of his first term, Rosellini was determined to secure the reaccreditation of all three state mental hospitals by the American Psychiatric Association. The 1957 legislature provided a jump start toward this goal when it approved a 37 percent increase in the budget for the division of mental health over the previous biennium. Immediately, with the help of the governor's contingency fund, the hospitals began hiring more staff and raising salaries. At Rosellini's urging, the state personnel board revised the salary schedule, which made Washington's salaries competitive with those elsewhere in the nation. Within two years 248 professionals were in place. By

1963, the ratio of professional staff to patients had been improved from 1:39 to 1:18, and that of registered nurses from 1:220 to 1:39. The legislature appropriated $500,000 for a child study and treatment center to house some of the juveniles inappropriately confined in mental hospitals. The center evaluated, diagnosed, and treated mentally ill children, trained people to work with them, and encouraged parents to participate.[36]

On other fronts, Western and Eastern began a new system of reallocating patients to wards based on age, type of illness, and other criteria, "thereby permitting more concentrated treatment." Doctors at Western State began to try new drugs, such as Deprol, in an effort to cut down on the use of electroshock and restraints. Western also started a new acute treatment center and began to communicate with county mental health associations about paroled and discharged patients in their areas. Northern State improved its nursing training, and medical students once again began to receive training at both Eastern and Western State. Increased professional staff at Western State allowed teaching conferences twice a month and individual psychotherapy sessions with patients three times a week.[37]

By late 1957, Northern State received the American Psychiatric Association's mental health achievement award for showing improvement in patient care "in spite of adverse conditions." All three hospitals began long-needed programs of physical renovation—improving water supplies, roads, plumbing, wiring, metal work, parking lots, covered walkways, and painting. Wards were renovated at all three hospitals, and each received a new occupational therapy and recreation building. The revitalized social services section helped released patients find jobs and placed the non-mentally-ill elderly in nursing homes. At the same time nutritional programs were improved.[38]

By the summer of 1959, Northern State and Western State had been reaccredited by the American Psychiatric Association, and Eastern State followed in 1961. In addition, Northern State was accredited by the Council of Medical Education and Hospitals of the American Medical Association, allowing three-year training programs for psychiatrists. In four years Washington had become one of the few states in the nation to have all of its mental hospitals accredited.[39]

The population of the mental hospitals also began to drop, despite an increasing number of admissions. By 1964 total population had fallen to about 4,300, from 7,500 in 1955. This dramatic decrease was attributed to "improved treatment and rehabilitation programs, which were considered to have cured the patients enough for a return to the community." By 1963, the average length of stay was less than a year.[40]

The Mentally Retarded

When Rosellini took office, the two schools for the retarded were not only run down and inadequate but were so overcrowded that they could accept no more residents—despite a two-year waiting list of more than 750 people approved for admission. The Rainier School at Buckley had more than 1,800 residents—25 percent of whom required full-time nursing care. Forty-three-year-old Lakeland Village near Spokane was deemed "archaic" in a 1957 report. Both schools had been cited by health departments and had inadequate kitchens and laundry facilities. Medical services at Lakeland Village were almost nonexistent and staffing was "grossly inadequate." At Rainier, some residents had been waiting years for needed surgery.[41]

The solution to these problems had to include legislative reform, and Rosellini guided Senate Bill 122 through the 1957 legislature. It defined the duties of the schools' directors, described the educational and vocational services to be maintained, and outlined admission, discharge, transfer, and appeal procedures. At the same time, Heyns moved to turn Firland Sanatorium, a tuberculosis hospital in Seattle, into a third home (Fircrest School) for the mentally retarded. Selah Hospital, also a tuberculosis facility, was obtained in January 1958 for the same purpose and became the Yakima Valley School. Although the 1957 legislature turned down his request for funds to buy the buildings outright, Rosellini provided $1,892,000 from his contingency fund to remodel them pending their ultimate purchase. Fircrest opened in 1959 and began to enlarge its facilities to take in even more residents. Buckley received increased appropriations, and Rosellini added $288,000 from his contingency fund for "program improvement." More staff was hired, including doctors and dentists, new programs were started in research psychology and social services, occupational therapy and recreational programs were significantly improved, and the backlog for required medical treatment was eliminated. The University of Washington began a teaching program for its medical students at Rainier in 1958. At Lakeland Village, sixty-five new staff members were hired, a new hall and classrooms were built, and a 4-H program was started.[42]

In order to ease overcrowding, the Department of Institutions planned to return many mentally retarded persons to their communities, if proper programs and community resources were available. Despite these efforts and the expansion of facilities, waiting lists for treatment and admission continued to grow. By August 1959 the waiting list was 830, in December 1960 it was 900, and by June of 1963 the waiting list had mushroomed to over 1,269 people. The department was trying to cope, to some extent, by using nursing homes and foster homes, and in early 1964 Rosellini recommended that the federal Harrison Memorial Hospital in Bremerton be turned into another state home for mentally retarded children. It later became the Frances Haddon Morgan Center.[43]

Rosellini's record on institutions was one of remarkable achievement. Having hired Garrett Heyns, a near genius in the field, to head the department, Rosellini followed Heyns's advice and lent him total support. Following a 1979 interview with Rosellini, Don Duncan described their teamwork: "Never a week passed . . . but what he and Heyns conferred two or three times—often at great length—about institutional needs. . . . 'He recommended and I followed.' "[44] Rosellini guided and pushed the funding, legislative, and initiative measures needed for reform. He used monies from his contingency fund to assure necessary improvements. He used his years of government experience and political networking to acquire surplus federal or state facilities—for example, even before he took office he had contacted the army about acquiring the surplus property at Fort Worden for use as a juvenile facility. Rosellini was a problem-solver who refused to be diverted by hurdles or roadblocks.

Chapter 11

Higher Education

W hen Rosellini took office in 1957, Washington, like every other state, was faced with a huge expansion of college students, created by the return of veterans from World War II and then Korea as well as the overall increase in the population. There was a tremendous need for more staff, faculty, and buildings at the University of Washington, Washington State College (renamed Washington State University in 1959), and the three teachers' colleges in Bellingham, Ellensburg, and Cheney. Additionally, ever-increasing numbers of adults and high-school graduates were seeking advanced training not necessarily oriented toward a college or professional degree. This placed unprecedented demands on both the state and the traditional institutions of higher education to provide more technical and non-liberal-arts training.[1]

In addition, the successful launching of "Sputnik" by the Soviet Union on October 4, 1957, set off a national debate over the inadequacies of science education in the United States. Within months, literally hundreds of reports were produced concerning the responsibility of schools of higher education in advancing the country's technical and scientific capabilities.[2]

Rosellini's interest in higher education began with his experience at the University of Washington. He was a consistent supporter of the university's needs in the legislature. Upon his election as governor, he looked to the university to provide his chief of staff and eventual budget director, Warren Bishop. Dr. Charles Odegaard, who succeeded Henry Schmitz as president on November 7, 1958, recalls being invited to the governor's mansion prior to his installation. Over lunch Rosellini told Odegaard that his door was always open to university concerns. Rosellini also assured him that the university administration was free to disagree, publicly or privately, with any policies of the state administration, and that he would keep politics out of the university's affairs. Odegaard says Rosellini kept this promise. As he put it, "You could talk about anything with Al, and I had no qualms about disagreeing or dissenting with the administration's financial or budgetary proposals. Al never got angry or annoyed if the university took issue with him or any of his policies." Odegaard then added, "This was a very refreshing quality compared with a number of his successors."[3]

While Rosellini's administration continued to support the University of Washington—for example, by establishing and funding its teaching hospital in 1959—his ties to the UW did not blind him to the needs of the other colleges. His administration initiated measures which brought much needed parity of support to the other schools of higher education. In the years prior to 1957, each of the institutions had lobbied for its own financial needs. This pitted the two major schools against each other, as well as against the teachers' colleges in their requests for funds. Since the schools did not submit program budgets and there were no requirements for recognized standards of measurement—such as faculty-to-student ratios—there was no objective method of gauging the funding each should receive.[4]

Almost immediately, Rosellini asked Bishop, as part of his review of state budget procedures, to explore methods of funding the state's higher education institutions on a more equitable basis. Bishop set up a working group that consisted of representatives from the two universities, the legislative counsel staff, and his own budget people. The group's objective was to develop formulas by which the funding needs of each institution could be compared with those of the other state schools, as well as those of comparable institutions in other states. Through the efforts of this group, the institutions of higher education were asked to itemize their budget requests as to needs for instruction, physical plant, library, and faculty salaries. The group also helped develop and refine other guidelines, such as for full-time employees, faculty-student ratios, and specific program staffing needs. Once these guidelines were in place, the administration and legislature could realistically assess the needs of all the state's schools and also compare Washington's funding practices with those of other states.[5]

The higher education institutions were exempted from the reforms of the state budget procedures adopted in 1959. In particular, Odegaard and the other presidents opposed being subject to the allotment procedure by which the administration would handle the funding requests for each department—including the institutions of higher education. Odegaard argued strenuously that it would constitute state intrusion into the intellectual decisions of the university. Bishop recalled vividly Odegaard's appearance at a legislative hearing on the new act. The hour was late and few committee members were present, but Odegaard was accompanied by the entire board of regents. Using color charts and displays, he argued eloquently against the act's inclusion of the university. Bishop and the administration, concerned about the act's passage, quickly agreed to the exemption.[6]

Even though exempted from the requirements of the new budget and accounting act, the educational institutions were influenced by the budget reform process. They voluntarily accepted many aspects of the new guidelines. In mid-1959, Washington State University began to submit a single biennial budget utilizing the guidelines. The presidents of the five colleges and universities appointed an interinstitutional committee of business officers who worked closely with Bishop and his group. By 1962 the schools were following the requirements of the budget and accounting act.[7]

Another problem was that provisions for faculty and staff retirement were unequal among the colleges and universities. In the 1950s neither of the universities was part of Social Security or the state teachers retirement program. Instead, the faculty—but not the staff—was affiliated with the public employees retirement system. This program was more generous than were those for the faculty of the teachers' colleges. In his 1957 inaugural, Rosellini asked the legislature to cure this imbalance. While it took years and parity was not achieved until 1966 or 1967, Rosellini initiated the measures which eventually provided staff employees with proper benefits and brought the teachers' colleges into line. The passage of the civil-service initiative in 1960 also provided stability and benefits to staff employees not previously covered.[8]

From a purely financial perspective, the administration recognized the increasing revenue needs of higher education. Rosellini's first budget request in 1957 sought appropriations sufficient to increase faculty salaries by more than 4 percent. His request for both operations and capital improvements in the 1957–59 biennium exceeded the 1955–57 expenditures by more than $33 million. Rosellini also proposed that the legislature submit to the people a bond measure (Referendum 10) that would provide $25 million for capital projects. Upon passage in 1958, it provided $15 million to accelerate construction of needed facilities at the universities and teachers' colleges. Even though the measure was a critical part of the administration's drive to improve the state's deteriorated penal and mental institutions, and was designed to take full advantage of the public's support of those efforts, it actually provided more funds for higher education than for other institutions.[9]

In 1959, Rosellini recommended increases of more than $13 million in the operating budgets of the five schools of higher learning. This 18.2 percent increase provided raises each year for faculty and staff, and 195 additional faculty positions. In 1961 the administration's operating budget request for the five schools increased to $103,318,882—a 23.4 percent increase overall for the biennium. The three teachers' colleges received increases of more than 30 percent. In 1963, over the general opposition of the conservative-led coalition in the house of representatives, Rosellini obtained a 16.4 percent increase ($15.7 million) for the state colleges and universities. This enabled all five to maintain the 1962–63 ratio of students to faculty, despite significant increases in enrollment.[10]

Community Colleges

Five weeks after Sputnik, Rosellini invited the presidents of all the state's public and private schools of higher education to attend a meeting that would address concerns over technical and scientific education in the state. At that December 19, 1957 meeting, Rosellini asked the educators to address three questions: "First, what do we want from our schools? Second, are we getting what we want? Third, what concrete action can this state take if we are not getting what we want?"[11]

Although the meeting produced little that was original or profound, the group approved several general resolutions which later became critical guidelines for Rosellini's approach to higher education. Recognizing that proper attention must be given to the humanities, the arts, and the social sciences—while emphasizing science and technical training—the group urged a continuing partnership among the state's public and private colleges and universities. Consistent with national studies, the presidents agreed that higher faculty salaries were crucial to maintaining educational quality. Of greater long-term significance, however, was their final resolution. They unanimously recommended the expansion of community junior colleges. More junior colleges—provided that there was proper business and community support—would enable more of the state's young people and adults to continue their education. The state would also better meet the need for highly trained technicians. Recognizing the limitations of their own institutions, the presidents declared, "[T]his responsibility is apparently falling on the community junior college and other institutions engaged in technical training."[12]

Another recommendation of the presidents' meeting was that a statewide conference on education beyond high school be held the following spring, but Rosellini demurred. There were practical reasons for his hesitation. One was the fact that "everyone on earth" was already giving advice on how the country's and the state's educational problems could be solved. Another was that current estimates of the needed increases in staff and faculty—without any change in emphasis—were staggering. The money would not be available without legislative action and he wanted to make sure the legislature was itself a part of the process.

By late 1958, however, Odegaard was warning Rosellini that a major shift in focus—if not a revolution—was needed among the state's higher education institutions. Odegaard and other of Rosellini's advisors were concerned that simply forcing the universities to admit more students—even if the funding existed—would interfere with the universities' teaching and research functions without solving the underlying problems. Rosellini recommended that the 1959 legislature establish a permanent interim committee, consisting of five senators and five representatives, to study higher education. It would be supported by a fifteen-person advisory committee of educators and community leaders. Although the legislative committee's mission was expanded to include the study of education at all levels, a key subcommittee was the one on education beyond high school. Chaired by Stanley M. Little of the Boeing Company, the subcommittee consisted of Odegaard; C. Clement French, president of Washington State University; Mrs. Henry B. Owen, regent of Washington State University and president of the Seattle School Board; L. H. Bates, director of vocational education in Tacoma; Frederick T. Giles, president of Everett Junior College; and others.[13]

The work of this subcommittee and its report to the legislature turned the administration's focus toward ensuring that the state would provide three levels of higher education: (1) the two universities; (2) the colleges of education; and (3) the community- or junior-college system. For the first time, the state's universities became advocates for the community college movement—arguing for a larger number geographically, as well as greater financial and administrative support by the state. The report and its aftermath also led to the creation of a coordinating council made up of the state's college presidents to advise Rosellini on progress in this and other areas. It was the subcommittee report—shaped to a considerable extent by the academic members— which was responsible for Rosellini's shift in emphasis to the critical role of community colleges in higher education.[14]

Late in his first term, Rosellini pushed measures which, upon adoption in 1961, placed community colleges under the direction of local school boards, subject to state supervision. This made additional state financing possible and facilitated the establishment of additional community colleges. In his 1960 campaign Rosellini criticized Lloyd Andrews, who had been Superintendent of Public Instruction, for "failing to provide a budget request [for the 1961–63 biennium] that fully reflects the construction needs for the junior colleges." In 1961 Rosellini recommended legislation that provided $5.75 million for community college construction. That same session passed an executive request measure removing legal restrictions against use of public funds for community colleges. Rosellini supported the passage of the community college law of 1963, which required the state board of education to present to the 1965 legislature a long-range plan for developing additional community colleges and to define the relationship between community colleges and vocational/technical schools.[15]

In a further effort to broaden access to higher education, Rosellini supported legislation in 1962 and 1963 which renamed the teachers' colleges "state colleges" and permitted them to grant master of arts and master of science degrees. Rosellini's interest in enlarging opportunities for education reflected his own personal experience as well as the changing role of educational institutions that was being described to him as governor. He had benefited greatly from a public education and was convinced that it was the state's obligation to provide educational opportunities to those who might not be motivated or otherwise able to attend the universities. He distrusted any system that promoted an "arbitrarily selected, intellectual elite." In 1960, he said, "It is evident if there is to be equal opportunity to all through education in our democratic society that these opportunities will have to be brought closer to young people in their communities where they have assumed family and job responsibilities." And, in a statement representative of his own life experience, he said, "Our American society has become truly democratic only in that social mobility from one economic class to another has been provided by the opportunities open to all through our [public] educational system."[16]

According to Odegaard, despite the changing role of higher education and the increased emphasis on science and technology, Rosellini understood the necessity of maintaining the integrity of the state's major university. In the midst of the frantic attention paid to the sciences, Odegaard was able to establish the School of Government Affairs, a Far East studies program, the Asian Law Program, and the Middle East Institute for the study of non-European cultures. The expansion of the university into these fields was expensive. Many legislators—and some faculty members—were dubious. To a degree, the universities were still under the cloud of the McCarthy Era, and innovative, nontraditional programs were suspect. As usual, budgets were tight. At a series of private meetings, Odegaard explained to Rosellini the importance of programs such as these to a major research university, and the governor supported the necessary funding.[17]

While the growing student population and changing demands on higher education would have forced any governor to respond, Rosellini met the challenges presented by education in a thoughtful and farsighted manner. Given the shortage of funds and the political pressures faced by a governor forced to raise taxes, it would have been understandable had he merely paid lip service to the long-term goals of higher education. Alternatively, he could have turned the problem back to the legislature, as Langlie did, without pushing for necessary budget increases. Instead, Rosellini acted decisively, seeking the funds and legislation necessary to improve and expand the state's ability to provide post-high-school educational opportunities to its citizens.

Chapter 12

Economic Development

In both his 1952 and 1956 campaigns, Rosellini emphasized Washington's economy and the need for a cabinet-level department to facilitate economic development. He recognized that the state's economic health controlled the revenues available for services, and that cyclical swings created periodic shortages and funding dilemmas for the legislature. Streamlining government to make tax dollars go farther could not bridge these shortfalls, and the most obvious solution—raising taxes—was politically dangerous. Increasing revenues by helping the state's economy prosper was an attractive way to help increase state revenues.

Rosellini's concept for such a department began in early 1953, when he met New York governor Averill Harriman, who was on a swing through the West discussing his state's efforts to rebuild and diversify its economic base. Harriman described efforts by his state to assist and foster new industries and businesses. In Rosellini's approach, a single state department would combine industrial development and tourist promotion with research and community planning. For Washington State, it was an innovative approach to an old idea.

The concept of having state government assist business and industry dates to 1889 and Washington's constitution, which established a bureau of statistics, agriculture, and immigration to "compile

information on Washington's economy, industry, and agriculture."
This information was to be made available to companies and individuals wishing to move to the state. In 1934, alarmed by the Great Depression and a decrease in the state's population during the 1920s, the legislature created the Washington State Planning Council to research and analyze the resources of the state and to make recommendations for their development. In 1937, the Washington State Progress Commission was created to "promote tourism, industry, investment and immigration to Washington," especially with advertising and publicity. In 1945, both the planning council and the progress commission were abolished, and their functions were consolidated within the Department of Conservation and Development as the division of progress and industry. For the next two years, the new division was responsible for advertising, publicity, tourist promotion, the encouragement of investment, and development of natural resources, as well as planning for the inevitable economic changes following World War II. When Langlie was reelected in 1948, he appointed a commission to advise the state on handling its advertising. An industrial utilization committee in the Department of Employment Security handled some industry promotion for the Langlie administration, mainly "from an employment perspective."[1]

Warren Bishop recounts that the creation of the Department of Commerce and Economic Development was one of the first ideas Rosellini discussed with him during his interview for the position of chief of staff. Rosellini believed that the new department could assist and coordinate activities by groups such as the Seattle Chamber of Commerce, the Port of Seattle, the Industrial Development Council of Seattle and King County, and the Puget Sound Industrial Development Council, which had been trying for years to organize efforts to invite new industry and businesses to the Puget Sound region. Seattle's dependence on the Boeing Company raised concerns about the hazards of a "one-industry" town, and the mayor had appointed a committee on industrial development which, in early 1957, had stated that Seattle's future was "in the balance" for this reason. The department could also assist the Port of Seattle with plans to develop new facilities and industrial sites at the mouth of the Duwamish River.[2]

Drafting the legislation that created the department was one of the first assignments given to Max Nicolai and Ed Henry, the governor's staff attorneys. Despite the apparent approval of business groups, many legislators, as well as the 1957 legislative leaders, were hesitant about the idea and failed to see how it could benefit the state. They pointed out that neither Oregon nor California had such a department, but rather utilized other departments or coordinated with local and regional groups to achieve the same objectives. A few legislators were suspicious of potential tax ramifications, such as those in California, where enabling legislation provided substantial funds—primarily from the counties—for development and advertising purposes. Rightly or wrongly, they viewed the new department as another competitor for state funds.[3]

Rosellini refused to be deterred by his legislative advisors' initial coolness to the proposal, and continued to insist on its importance to his administration's goals. Senate Bill 282 was introduced by executive request early in the 1957 session and, despite the concerns described above, passed with relative ease. With an effective date of April 1, 1957, the act provided for a director, a secretary, and an advisory counsel to be appointed by the governor. Concerned that a low salary would make it impossible to attract a director from outside government, Rosellini wanted the director's salary to be higher than all other departments except institutions (at $18,000, it was higher than his own salary). The act also appropriated $1.5 million for operations.[4]

The legislature's accelerated passage of the act creating the department threw Rosellini somewhat off balance. On April 1, he was ill prepared to launch the new department. He was still in the initial stages of locating a director when, almost overnight, requests came in from numerous business groups seeking information about how the department would function. In early responses, the governor was forced to generalize—even to business groups eager for information. Speaking to the Puget Sound Industrial Council in May, he talked about the department as a partner and facilitator and spoke broadly of coordinating, planning, advising, and encouraging economic development.[5]

Rosellini asked A. W. Burchill from the Employment Security Department to act as coordinator and begin organizing the department's activities. Burchill's main job was to study the functions of the advertising commission and industrial utilization committee to ensure that their responsibilities in vital areas—such as tourist promotion—were maintained, and even strengthened if possible. It was necessary to administer a $400,000 appropriation for promotional advertising, publication and printing of travel brochures and maps, administrative costs, and advisory council expenses. The department was also receiving numerous requests for assistance in urban planning. The Langlie administration had not provided state assistance in seeking federal grants-in-aid for any cities under 25,000 in population. Although by 1957 all the other western states had vehicles through which federal grants for community planning could be obtained and administered, Washington did not. The new department immediately began to provide assistance to counties and cities for these grants.[6]

While Burchill was organizing the department, Rosellini continued looking for a director. H. DeWayne Kreager started work on October 30, 1957. He had been away from the state for years, and knew nothing about Rosellini. The image portrayed for him by John Salter, Senator Jackson's administrative assistant, and Irv Hoff of Senator Magnuson's staff was that of an Italian politico tied to liquor interests and local tolerance policies. Nevertheless, Maggie urged Kreager to take the position, calling it a great opportunity. Scoop, however, advised against it and told Kreager he would be cut to pieces by the politics of state government and its operations under Rosellini. Kreager, years later, said that he would not have accepted the job offer had it not been for Rosellini himself—his considerable knowledge of state government and the economics of the state as a whole, his easy informality with people, and his assurances that the department would operate above politics and make a real difference in the economic well-being of the state.[7]

Kreager had also been impressed with the membership of the governor's advisory board, which was chaired by Stanley Donogh of Seattle—a well-known and respected business leader. The other members were equally prominent: Lawrence M. Arnold, Joseph Drumheller, Harold Gibson, Roderick Lindsay, Alfred McVay, Henry B. Owen, William G. Reed, Gerrit Vander Ende, Paul A. Volpe, Sam Volpentest, and Wilfred R. Woods. Gibson was the head of the International Association of Machinists, and Woods was the publisher of the Wenatchee *World*. The rest were successful businessmen and leaders in their various fields. Kreager thought the group could galvanize broad-based support within the business community. Neither he nor Rosellini believed that the new department could accomplish its objectives without that support. Kreager was also impressed by the aspects of the enabling legislation that made it easier to operate within the overall business community. The new department was exempted from revealing confidential and sensitive business information to the legislature, for example, and could accept outside contributions for specific purposes, as long as they were run through the state treasury.[8]

The department's activities were wide-ranging. The industrial development division, directly supervised by Kreager, testified before many state and federal committees in attempts to ease the paths of companies and industries. Examples of activities it supported were dredging rivers and ports, renewing airline licenses, adjusting freight rates, and promoting Puget Sound shipping. The department took credit for the 1958 location of a major electronics and projection equipment plant in Auburn, and in the following years announced the opening or expansion of plants by Intalco Aluminum, Owens-Corning Fiberglass, Joy Manufacturing, Oregon Portland Cement, Bethlehem Steel, American Marietta, Penberthy Instrument company, Sick's Rainier Brewing company, and dozens of others. Another major project was an industrial site survey. Covering more than 300 sites in seventy-four cities and towns, the survey provided information on all sites that were zoned for industry and were suitable for immediate construction. The department concluded that the state had too few industrial parks, and that Seattle, in particular, needed considerable urban renewal in order to expand the industrial sites available. According to the department, all cities and towns in the state needed to prepare and rezone more land.[9]

Expanding trade with Pacific Rim economies such as Japan, Korea, and Singapore placed the state's port districts "in a favorable position to put their communities ahead in the race for new or expanded industry," according to the department. Following up on that analysis, the Rosellini administration recommended and the 1959 legislature passed legislation that strengthened the port districts by expanding their bonding capacity, increasing their right to enter into land leases, permitting higher toll rates, and providing greater ability to create industrial parks. The new laws provided the impetus for the rapid development of the Port of Seattle and its airport, which enhanced the region's ability to handle the flow of goods and passengers necessary to expand trade and economic development.[10]

Another innovative concept was a series of business luncheons in major cities and trade missions to Alaska and Hawaii. The basic purpose was to have businesspeople educate and inform their counterparts and government leaders in other areas about the state's favorable business features and its attractiveness as a location for new businesses. The department developed the necessary information, invited the participants, and coordinated the logistics. The contributions of the participating businesses covered almost all the costs. Following the advice of an economic consultant, the groups visited New York City, Los Angeles, New Orleans, and San Francisco, as well as Alaska, Hawaii, and Japan.[11]

The economic luncheons and trade missions had an added benefit. They provided an opportunity for Kreager to introduce state business leaders to the governor. According to Kreager, Rosellini was at his best in that milieu: "If I could ever get anyone in a room to talk personally to Rosellini, they would come away willing to do anything. I have never known anyone who could make friends so easily in one-on-one situations." Kreager also paid Rosellini a sincere compliment when he said, "Rosellini had the knack of always being prepared and knowing what to say in such situations. He was never off-stride or awkward— although he was just the opposite when asked to take part in formal ceremonies." The result was a greater enthusiasm among these business leaders for the work of the department, as well as increased respect for the governor himself.[12]

The focus on economic and industrial development resulted in less funding for the tourist promotion division in the first two years of Rosellini's administration. This shortfall was remedied in 1959, however, and that division, under the leadership of George Prescott, greatly expanded its activities. The division's work was aided immeasurably by the Seattle World's Fair, which attracted visitors from all over the world to Seattle and the state in 1962.[13]

Century 21: The Seattle World's Fair

Rosellini and his new department were instrumental to the success of the Century 21 Exposition. Even before he became governor, Rosellini had provided legislative assistance to the concept. He and William Goodloe cosponsored the 1955 enabling measure that established a seven-person commission authorized to bring about a world's fair. Langlie appointed the commission in 1955, with Edward E. Carlson as chair; Rosellini reappointed Carlson as chair for three successive two-year terms. Eddie, as he was called by everyone, is recognized as the force who made the Seattle World's Fair a reality. Chairman of Western International Hotels at the time and later head of United Airlines, Carlson was a civic treasure for Seattle and the state. From the fifties through the mid-eighties, it would be hard to name any important civic or public undertaking that required business support that did not have Eddie Carlson leading it or lending his name as a key supporter. As Rosellini put it, "There were a lot of people who were involved and who added input, but when push came to shove it was Eddie who really got things done."[14]

The stories about the original idea for a world's fair in Seattle are legion. It is a matter of public record, however, that Al Rochester pushed a resolution through the Seattle City Council on February 7, 1955, urging the legislature to study the feasibility of holding a world's fair in 1959, and after that the dream began to wind its way toward reality. According to Emmett Watson in a twenty-fifth anniversary article, the notion was a runaway joke at first, with local advertising and public relations executives taking turns making fun of the concept. "[The idea of a world's fair] was a real thigh slapper," Watson wrote. "You see we didn't know much about Eddie Carlson in those days. We had never heard of Ewen Dingwall. We knew that William Street was a big shot at Frederick & Nelson's and some of us had heard about Mike Dederer, State Representative Ray Olson and State Senator William Goodloe. We knew about Joe Gandy, because some of us had bought

Fords from him. Now put all these people together, especially Ray Olson and Bill Goodloe, along with Bob Block and State Senator Al Rosellini, who was bucking for Governor, and Mayor Gordon Clinton, and you had an interesting but not inspiring mix. But among them they got a city bond issue passed for 7.5 million and pried another 7.5 million out of the legislature."[15]

During 1955–57 the state commission concentrated on site se-lection and on building community support in Seattle. The commis-sion coordinated its efforts with two Seattle groups whose missions dovetailed neatly into plans for a world's fair. One was a committee, appointed by Mayor Alan Pomeroy and chaired by Bob Block, to determine the city's needs for sports and cultural facilities. The other, appointed by the city council and chaired by Harold Shefelman, was called the civic center advisory committee. Both groups saw the fair as a way of bringing to the city both a true civic center and buildings that would enhance its cultural and sports capabilities. The site that seemed to meet everyone's needs was a ninety-acre tract north of downtown Seattle. It included the outdated civic auditorium, the ice arena, Memorial Stadium, and the state's fortress-like armory building. In early 1957 the city and the state commission finalized their decision to use this location. An important part of the plan was the acquisition of six acres west of the site. Even before the legislature had passed the necessary appropriation measure, Rosellini approved a request to allow the state to initiate condemnation proceedings on the six-acre parcel. By that time, the city of Seattle had set aside $2.5 million for acquisi-tion, and it was assumed that the state would also devote some funds to that purpose. Rosellini's decision to go forward with condemnation— and to obtain the legal support of Attorney General John O'Connell to do so prior to appropriation of funds by the legislature—demonstrated the governor's commitment to doing what was needed to make the world's fair work.[16]

In the closing days of the 1957 session, the members of the commission were lobbying hard for sufficient funds to assure success. Rosellini's administration was trying to hold the line on taxes and reduce expenditures in every area except institutions and education. But unless the state was willing to commit significant funds toward site acquisition and buildings before the legislature adjourned, there was little chance that the fair could obtain approval from certifying bodies such as the Bureau of International Expositions. Without such approval, other countries would not agree to participate.[17]

One evening in late February 1957, Carlson received a telephone call at home from Rosellini. "Eddie, how much money do you think you will need for the Fair?" he asked. Carlson had no firm figure in mind, but said, "Would it be appropriate to suggest $7.5 million? That is the amount that the City of Seattle has available. That would make the City and State 50–50 partners, which I believe is always a good arrangement." Rosellini agreed without argument, but he needed a means of funding the bonds that would be sold to raise the money. Rep. Ray Olson proposed to the governor that the annual state corporation fee be doubled; the existing annual fee was modest and had not been raised in many years. This change would produce sufficient funds to amortize the $7.5 million in bonds. Within a week after Rosellini's phone call, it was done. Olson and Rosellini, working closely with Senator Goodloe, were able to push the measure through without public hearings or debate—something that would have been impossible in later years. The assurance of state financing gave Carlson much-needed clout with Magnuson and Jackson—whose support was critical in securing financial and diplomatic support from the federal government.[18]

Perhaps as important as the amount of money was the manner in which the legislation was handled by Rosellini and his administration. Had there been any hesitation by the governor or serious debate in the legislature as to the wisdom of supporting a world's fair, the project might have lost momentum. Many months later, the business establishment of Seattle and the state was still skeptical about the idea. In 1959, *Argus* publisher Phil Bailey used his weekly column to blast the notion: "Let's forget the Fair. The search for a proper site has reached the ludicrous stage. . . . We can find little enthusiasm for the Fair except in a small group closely associated with the project. This nearly complete lack of interest on the part of Seattle's business and professional leaders dooms the Fair from achieving an outstanding success. . . . [We] suggest that the time has come to discard the whole World Fair program."[19]

Another key to the fair's success was the announcement of the state's decision to build the Paul Thiery-designed, three-acre coliseum. Kreager had worked closely with the World's Fair Commission and the Century 21 Corporation, the private nonprofit body set up by the enabling legislation to operate the fair, in the process of developing the coliseum plan. The structure would cost nearly $4 million and would house the international science and commercial exhibits. More important, its design would allow conversion into an 18,000-seat sports arena after the fair.[20]

The unveiling of the plans for the Seattle Coliseum in late May 1959 was part of a chain of events which created a "point of no return" for Seattle, the state, and the business community. In June, Senator Magnuson announced that he was proposing an expenditure of $12.5 million by the federal government for a United States science pavilion. Working his usual and accustomed magic, Magnuson succeeded in having both the president and the Bureau of the Budget support the project as well. The appropriation received congressional approval in short order.[21]

Another event, not directly related to the world's fair, played a pivotal role in making Century 21 a reality. Most people scoffed at the notion that Seattle could even contemplate holding such an event. A town of about 400,000 in a state with under three million people located in the far northwest corner of the United States was a most unlikely competitor against New York, Paris, Moscow, and other major cities that were considering world expositions at the same time. Skeptics in Seattle pointed out that the world, as well as the rest of the United States, would never take the idea seriously. Something else was required, something that would galvanize the leaders of Seattle, the state, and the business community.[22]

That event was the Colombo Plan Conference, which was held in Seattle from October 20 through November 14, 1958. The conference was the outgrowth of the 1950 British Commonwealth meetings, which had sought to create a dialogue on trade with the emerging nations of Asia. President Eisenhower and Secretary of State John Foster Dulles headed the list of United States officials who participated in the meetings, along with economic representatives of twenty Pacific Rim nations. Member nations included: Australia, Burma, Cambodia, Ceylon, Laos, The Philippines, United Kingdom, Indonesia, Canada, Malaya, New Zealand, Pakistan, North Borneo, Singapore, India, Thailand, Japan, Nepal, Hong Kong, Vietnam, Sarawak, and the United States. For more than three weeks, Seattle and Washington State were featured. During that time, world attention was focused on discussions of international trade and economic development among the Pacific Rim nations. It was by any measurement the most important international meeting ever held in the Pacific Northwest.[23]

It was not just the fact that the conference was held in Seattle that created a sense that the world's fair could succeed. Rather, it was the manner by which the meeting came to Seattle and the joint state-city-business-community effort required to make it a success. During a trip to Washington, D.C., in early 1958, Carlson and Ewen Dingwall were discussing the fair with Senator Magnuson and with various government agencies that might assist.* While making the rounds, the two men learned that the State Department was looking for a site for an important international meeting. San Francisco, considered the United States gateway to Asia and the Pacific Rim, had already put in a bid, but the final decision had not yet been made.[24]

Carlson called Kreager and Rosellini, as well as Mayor Gordon Clinton of Seattle, and suggested that an effort be made to convince the State Department to hold the meeting in Seattle. Rosellini pledged the financial resources of the state, a critical endorsement of Seattle's bid. The Colombo Conference would be an ideal vehicle for the Department of Commerce and Economic Development. No other single event could match it in placing the area and its resources before

---

*Carlson enjoyed telling about a trip that Joe Gandy made to Paris to lobby for approval from the Bureau of International Expositions. During a meeting, one of the delegates to the bureau recalled his own Washington experience, when "it was raining so hard I couldn't see to the top of the Washington Monument!" It illustrated why the Seattle business community felt the need for greater national (and international) exposure. (Carlson, *Recollections*, 158.)

a worldwide audience. Rosellini directed Kreager and the department to coordinate the effort on behalf of all the interested groups. After several months of negotiations, in March 1959 the State Department advised Kreager that the state's offer to host the conference had been accepted.[25]

Kreager and Carlson were quick to recognize that the conference represented an opportunity to tell the world about Century 21. At a special ceremony upon his arrival at Boeing Field, President Eisenhower pressed a button that set in motion the electronic countdown to the Seattle World's Fair. National and some international news accounts featured stories of how the fair would open just "911 days after the President flashed an Eisenhower smile and the chronometer began flashing lights." (Actually, the timetable was later pushed back eleven months.)[26]

Carlson later summed up the importance of the conference: "First, perhaps, it gave us a sense of cockiness in 'stealing' on short notice this important international gathering . . . from San Francisco; but, more important, it was an opportunity to showcase Seattle and the Pacific Northwest by . . . demonstrating a commitment to expanding Pacific Rim economic opportunities." Coming three years before the fair would open, the Colombo Conference gave the commission and the fair's supporters an enormous confidence boost in approaching the tasks ahead.[27]

Century 21 officially opened on April 21, 1962, a typical overcast and misty day. During the next six months, 9,634,601 people attended the fair, visiting one hundred domestic and fifty-nine international exhibits. More than 125,000 people attended the closing ceremonies, which featured mass bands playing Tchaikovsky's "1812 Overture" while fireworks and rockets lit up Seattle's late twilight sky. The exposition had met or exceeded all expectations, and the state's newest department had played a major role in the cooperative process that had brought it into being. Indeed, the 1957 legislation creating the department stated that it was to "cooperate with the World Fair Commission to the end that the exposition . . . shall become a memorable success." Before Kreager was even appointed, the advisory committee loaned $10,000 to the World's Fair Commission so that it could begin operations. By November 14, 1958, it had advanced $776,000 toward administrative operations and site acquisition. Kreager himself was an important participant in almost every phase of the fair's development.[28]

From the standpoint of the department, the world's fair was a tremendous success. It created an upsurge in tourism, retail sales, and employment for the state and the region. The presence of foreign governments and companies in Seattle introduced many businesses and business people to the area. The same thing was true of United States businesses that participated. Indeed, the world's fair established the position of Seattle and the state on the national and world scene— from a perspective of business, trade, and tourism—in a way that tourist advertising and trade delegations could not. Further, the structures built to house the fair continued to provide economic activity. After the fair, the department sold the Century 21 Coliseum back to Seattle for use as a convention, sports, and entertainment center.[29]

Conflicts

Given the business and economic objectives of the new department and Rosellini's political reliance on Democratic Party and pro-labor support, it seems almost inevitable that conflicts would arise. Rosellini's political and ideological roots were outside the business mainstream. His choice of an independent, business-oriented director from outside the state undoubtedly increased the potential for conflict. In accepting the post, Kreager had requested political independence from Rosellini's ideological position, and Rosellini had agreed to that. The strains between these conflicting forces surfaced rather quickly and continued throughout Kreager's tenure as director.[30]

Following the 1957 session, Rosellini was faced with the potential of a large revenue deficit. By some estimates the budget might be out of balance by as much as $32 million. Some legislators urged a special session in the summer to meet the shortfall with increased taxes or revenue measures, a pattern which had become routine under Langlie. But Rosellini was determined to avoid a special session at all costs. After considerable discussion among his staff and cabinet, in June 1957 Rosellini ordered a 15 percent across-the-board cut for all agencies and departments under his supervision and even a 20 percent cut in some areas. The only department exempted was institutions. In addition, he requested that agencies not directly responsible to the executive also make the cuts.[31]

Kreager and his new department were heavily affected. While the department had received an appropriation of $1.5 million to establish its operations, the tasks of developing economic growth programs literally from scratch and melding in the activities of former divisions were proving to be expensive as well as difficult. It had already been necessary to decrease the budget for tourist advertising. The advisory board and Kreager were upset by Rosellini's mandatory reductions.* The added strain of supporting the world's fair, critically important to many of the advisory board members, was increasing their frustration. The board adopted a resolution, supported by Kreager, which recommended to the governor that the department be ex-empted from part of the 15 percent reduction and that it be exempted from having to absorb extraneous costs on behalf of the fair and the administration. The request was denied by Bishop and the budget committee.[32]

At the same meeting, Kreager proposed another resolution that would direct the department to go on record before the tax advisory committee with facts showing the impact of certain taxes—a rise in unemployment-compensation taxes, for example—that particularly affected businesses. From the outset of his duties, Kreager viewed part of his role as being a spokesman for business. Both Kreager and Rosellini thought it was important to let the business community know that it had a voice within state government and that state government was not always a negative force dedicated to raising taxes or imposing regulations. The resolution and its mandate was a logical outgrowth of Kreager's perceived function, triggered by the 1957 revenue crisis. Rosellini had appointed a tax advisory committee in mid-1957 to

---

*Kreager's and the advisory board's reaction was typical of private, nongovern-mental people frustrated with a process which seems to defy logic. It was not the kind of reaction one would expect from seasoned bureaucrats, who could weather a storm and had done so many times before.

explore new revenue alternatives. Kreager's board was concerned about the kind of alternatives that might be suggested.[33]

Kreager had been promised independence, and these resolutions seemed to be a test of that promise. Eventually this independence, and Kreager's need to express it, would cause him to depart prior to Rosellini's reelection campaign in 1960.

A few examples are illustrative. During the 1959 session, the legislature was considering changes to the state's unemployment compensation laws. Unemployment compensation is basically funded by a tax on businesses—although federal funds may be added to extend the length of benefits. The Association of Washington Industries and many businesses were advocating a change in response to a problem peculiar to Washington State. For years, supported by an alliance between major labor organizations and the lumber and fishing industries, seasonal employees could work just a few weeks and then draw unemployment compensation. As a result, a group of fishermen and loggers would repeatedly work for a few weeks and then draw off large amounts of benefits. Since these benefit funds were pooled, this practice was subsidized by other businesses whose work forces were not seasonal or irregular. Kreager and his board backed the AWB proposal that restricted such practices as representing a fairer tax on the business community.[34]

Unfortunately the issue arose during the 1959 session. At the opening of that session, Rosellini had asked the heavily Democratic legislature to boost taxes by more than $135 million in the coming biennium. His insistence on holding the line on taxes during his first session as governor had prompted the budget cuts in state agencies. Now the demand for services had grown and the trimmed-down agencies were unable to meet it. The prospect of a huge tax increase was very unpopular with the Democrats. Given the Republicans' reluctance to raise taxes at all, Rosellini needed his party to stand together in order to pass the package. In the midst of this battle, Kreager openly came out against any increase in the business-and-occupation (B&O) taxes; he also publicly supported the more restrictive formula for unemployment compensation. Since Kreager's announcement came at a time when the administration was scrambling, along with legislative leaders, to put together a tax package that could pass both houses, it infuriated many legislators. Rosellini was in no position to abandon either of the proposals Kreager had opposed—indeed, he was forced to back the status-quo unemployment compensation system as part of a tax package supported by labor. Kreager actually lobbied against the administration's position and succeeded in getting the status-quo bill stalled in the senate rules committee. In addition, Kreager convinced the senate revenue committee to strike the new B&O taxes.[35]

This open split within the administration caused considerable comment, by the press as well as by legislators. While Rosellini publicly tolerated Kreager's position and understood the reasoning, many Democratic legislative leaders did not. Julia Butler Hansen and Speaker John O'Brien, two of Rosellini's major supporters, were extremely upset. As a result, the Democrats introduced legislation to abolish the department and Kreager's position. Hansen told Kreager at the time, "You embarrassed us. We had to do something." Ironically, the legislation was added to the appropriations measure passed by the house as part of the administration's tax and spending package. Rosellini was forced to announce that he would veto the measure if it passed.* The governor had been forced to defend Kreager and the new department at a time when he was seeking unity for his tax packages. It was difficult for the administration's allies in the legislature to accept open opposition by a cabinet member to the legislative positions of the governor he supposedly served.[36]

Another political firestorm resulted from a speech that Kreager delivered to the Bellingham Chamber of Commerce in 1959, advocating that the ban on Sunday liquor sales in hotels and restaurants be lifted. He pointed out that the Sunday ban was devastating to the tourism industry and to efforts to attract major conventions to the state. While true in every sense, the speech was made without permission and

---

*Rosellini later enlisted Ed Weston and Joe Davis, labor leaders and friends of the administration, to persuade the house not to vote on the measure. It was labor's unhappiness with Kreager's stand on unemployment compensation which had led to the measure's introduction. (*Tribune*, March 20, 1959.)

knowledge of the administration. Indeed, Kreager deliberately did not tell Rosellini in advance because he knew he would be refused permission.[37]

The speech had two immediate effects, both unfortunate for Rosellini. First, it raised the question of whether the administration planned to seek legislation to allow Sunday liquor sales. Having just passed a tax increase of more than $112 million—the largest in the state's history—the Democratic majorities in the house and the senate were already under heavy fire. Adding the liquor issue—with its long history of emotional reactions from the public and the press—to the situation was not pleasing to legislators who had to run for office the following year. Second, it once again tied Rosellini's name to liquor interests at a time when he was preparing for a campaign.

Rosellini's people, particularly some of his close advisors and cabinet members, were enraged. Yet, according to Kreager, Rosellini himself reacted calmly and publicly defended Kreager's right to express his views, although he "pretended to be mad" and told the press that he had called Kreager on the carpet. The press delighted in the apparent clash and continued to imply that the Sunday liquor issue was an administration priority, despite public denials. Kreager, for his part, received a number of nasty letters from emotional opponents of selling liquor at any time, let alone on Sunday. He was even scolded by his mother, who accused him of trying to open bars and taverns on the Sabbath.[38]

At the outset, Kreager had told Rosellini that he would stay for at least two years. Rosellini knew that the $18,000 salary limitation was a hardship for Kreager, who had business opportunities outside government, and in January 1960 Kreager indicated that he would like to leave. The timing was difficult for Rosellini, who was concerned about the impact on his forthcoming campaign. Nonetheless, Rosellini did not try to dissuade Kreager from resigning although he says he wanted Kreager to stay. In an effort to limit the public relations fallout, Kreager agreed to remain with Rosellini as cochair of his reelection campaign. Rosellini's campaign organization still had a considerable debt left from 1956, and Kreager's primary job, along with cochair Ben DiJulio, was fund-raising.[39]

Kreager's new role neither stopped the speculation nor altered the perception among some that the real reason for his leaving was policy differences between the two men. The next director, Robert E. Rose, was much less controversial. Nor did he receive the kind of leeway Kreager had been given. Rose, formerly an executive with General Electric at Hanford, was a businessman in one sense, but his background included working within the restrictions placed on large government contractors. The result was a department whose director, from the date of Kreager's departure, avoided the kind of controversy his predecessor had engendered. Rose did not identify himself, as Kreager had, as more aligned with business than with the administration of the governor under whom he served.[40]

Rosellini also immediately appointed Kreager to membership on the World's Fair Commission. He recognized that the fair's success was crucial and that no one else could step in and take Kreager's place in coordinating activities at the federal, state, and city levels. This was particularly true in 1960, when these efforts were at their most crucial stage. In fact, Kreager's effectiveness was enhanced by his departure.[41]

Despite the department's accomplishments, it had detractors—particularly during the 1960 and 1964 campaigns. This was inevitable, since Rosellini had created the department and considered it a vital part of his administration's program. Several newspapers asserted that it was mainly a political device and had provided no substantive assistance to the state. In 1964 Dan Evans and Joseph Gandy, vying for the Republican nomination, said the department's "record was pretty sad" and that it "was a typical bureaucracy—with no accomplishments on the record." Gandy and William Day, coalition Speaker of the House in the 1963–65 biennium, attacked Rosellini for creating a tax climate that was discouraging business, regardless of the department's efforts. By late 1963 Director Rose lamented that "so much of my time and that of my staff must be spent in explaining or justifying the very existence of the department."[42]

Its detractors missed the mark. Even the most partisan critics of Rosellini at the time—Evans, Lloyd Andrews, Gandy, Newman Clark, and Ross Cunningham—recognized that the state played a critical role in coordinating and assisting industrial and economic growth. Most of their criticism was motivated not only by partisanship but also by dismay (feigned or otherwise) that the department was unable to overcome recessions and other national (or even international) economic forces. Rosellini's typical activist approach had given Washington a running start in the modern economic era. At a time when few states were actively promoting economic growth, Rosellini made it a high priority. His successors not only accepted the department as a necessity but sought to build on its efforts.

Chapter 13

The Second Lake Washington Bridge

The need for comprehensive planning of the state's transportation system was another of Rosellini's 1952 and 1956 campaign themes. Realizing that an expanded transportation system was essential to the state's economic development, he noted in a campaign speech in 1956, "unless we build . . . highways and bridges where they should be, our whole state suffers."[1]

During Rosellini's eight years as governor, four major bridges were completed: the Hood Canal bridge, the Astoria bridge, the Goldendale-Columbia span, and the Evergreen Point bridge. In addition, Highway 18 between Auburn and North Bend, the Olympia-Aberdeen freeway, and the I-5 freeway between Everett and Olympia were either completed or nearing completion by the end of his second term, and major progress had been made on the North Cascades Highway.[2]

A complete chronicle of the Rosellini administration's record on transportation policies, highways, and bridges is beyond the scope of this book. The process by which a second floating bridge came to be built across Lake Washington, however, needs to be recounted for at least two reasons: (1) the bridge was critical to the state's development; and (2) it would not have been built without Rosellini's political leadership.

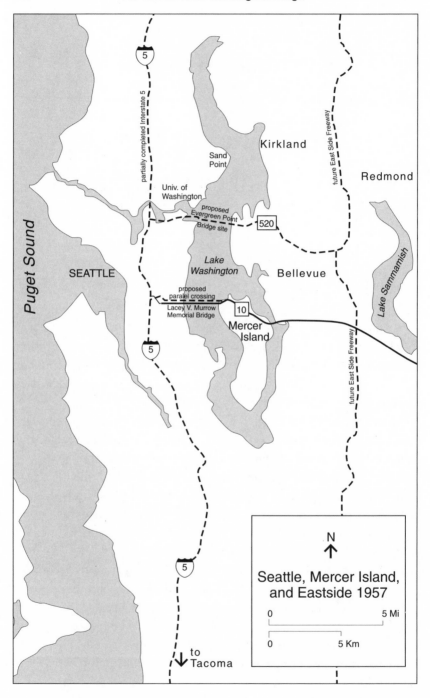

Puget Sound

5

partially completed Interstate 5

Kirkland

Sand
Point

Univ. of
Washington

proposed
Evergreen Point
Bridge site

520

future East Side Freeway

Redmond

SEATTLE

Lake
Washington

Bellevue

Lake Sammamish

proposed
parallel crossing

Lacey V. Murrow
Memorial Bridge

10

Mercer
Island

5

future East Side Freeway

to
Tacoma

N

Seattle, Mercer Island,
and Eastside 1957

0   5 Mi

0   5 Km

Background

The geography of western Washington dictated the course of its economic development and population growth. Seattle, founded in 1851, quickly became the largest city on Puget Sound. Bordered on the west by the Sound and on the east by twenty-two-mile-long Lake Washington, Seattle occupied a narrow isthmus that concentrated the city's business and residential growth through the 1920s. East-west traffic moved by train and road via a southern route through Tacoma and across the Cascade Mountains. As Seattle's limited land area filled to capacity, suburban development expanded east of Lake Washington into the valley that extended to the Cascades. The land routes to the area, known locally as "the Eastside," were congested streets around the north and south ends of Lake Washington, bottlenecks that became more and more limiting as the region developed. The privately owned ferries that crossed the lake could not handle motor vehicles, and the evolution of the automobile age rendered them obsolete.

Another factor creating pressure for direct traffic access to the Eastside was the location of the major highway across the Cascades at Snoqualmie Pass, about fifty miles due east of Seattle. With an elevation of only 3,000 feet at its highest point, it was the most reliable gateway to eastern Washington and the other northern states.

The situation was also affected by the rivalry between Seattle and Tacoma as to which city would constitute the major western terminus for goods and people. Seattle's community leaders were determined to avoid being bypassed because of geographical restrictions. As the automobile continued to change the patterns of life in the region, direct access across Lake Washington emerged as a critical priority for Seattle's leaders, and they used their political and economic influence to gain that objective.[3]

Planning for a bridge across the lake began as early as 1925, but the Great Depression and the inability of available technology to deal with the lake's 100- to 300-foot depths prevented any serious effort until the late 1930s. Even as technologies improved, the nature of the soil beneath Lake Washington added cost complications that made conventional bridging impossible. By 1937 the development of pontoon-bridging technology (concrete floating pontoons capable of sustaining the weight of vehicular traffic) had progressed sufficiently to allow the design of a floating structure that did not require supports driven into the lake bed. This design, developed under the guidance of Lacey V. Murrow as the chief engineer for the state highway department, made possible the bridging of Lake Washington.* The Lacey V. Murrow Bridge was placed at the narrowest midpoint of the lake (the 1.25-mile channel between Seattle and Mercer Island), and construction began on December 29, 1938. When the floating bridge opened for traffic on July 2, 1940, the simultaneous completion of a conventional bridge across the east channel from Mercer Island to the Eastside gave the area a direct east-west link.[4]

The floating bridge was an engineering marvel. It was made up of twenty-five concrete pontoons, each sixty feet wide and averaging 350 feet in length. After being linked together, the pontoons were held in place by sixty-four anchors attached to the lake bed. Weighing more than 100,000 tons, the bridge had four traffic lanes and two sidewalks that floated seven-and-one-half feet above water. Its unique floating structure, which in effect divided Lake Washington into two parts, did draw criticism. During the planning stage, the Seattle *Times*, for one, had lambasted the bridge as a bad idea: "Today a pontoon bridge is as completely outmoded as a stone hatchet." But the finished product, which was named in honor of its designer, was an immediate transportation and financial success.[5]

Despite the twenty-five-cent toll and wartime rationing of gasoline and tires (and contrary to travel trends on other facilities), the average bridge traffic per day doubled from 3,476 vehicles in 1940 to almost 7,000 by 1945. Between 1946 and 1955, average daily traffic increased from 8,820 to more than 30,000. The revenue bonds were retired in 1949 (far ahead of schedule), and tolls were removed that same year.[6]

The completion of the bridge stimulated economic and population growth on Mercer Island and the Eastside. The resulting increase in

---

*Because of the state's depressed financial condition, the $9.5 million cost was a major roadblock. The federal government's WPA grant of $4 million enabled the state to manage the financing through a bond issue.

traffic—spurred by a 50 percent jump immediately after tolls were removed—pushed the bridge above its projected capacity by 1946. Soon the pressures of rapid development made it a bottleneck rather than a facilitator, and forced the state into preliminary planning for a second bridge.[7]

History

Rosellini introduced legislation in 1949 to authorize the Toll Bridge Authority (TBA) to begin consideration of a second bridge, and although his bill did not pass that year, similar legislation was passed in 1951. A series of origin-destination and economic studies led to a 1952 financial feasibility study, prepared by two prominent bonding houses, which confirmed Evergreen Point as the best Eastside connection for a new toll bridge. By the time of public hearings in 1953 and 1954, only two points of connection in Seattle—Sand Point and Montlake—were being considered.[8]

The TBA, chaired by Langlie, had decided on the Evergreen Point–Montlake route in May 1952, and presented that recommendation at a public hearing in October 1953. During that hearing, however, Langlie stated that the TBA was still open-minded on a location, and that a decision was some time away. At another hearing in April 1954, Seattle interests and other groups opposed the Evergreen Point site while the TBA, King County, and numerous Eastside groups supported it. Langlie refused to take sides. Tossing the proposal back into the laps of the various factions, the governor said, "It's up to them now. We've done sound planning for them, but it is not accepted by them. They do nothing but criticize . . . We're not going to force anything on the City of Seattle. It has never been the practice of this administration to ride roughshod over local officials. The next move is up to them."[9]

Rosellini and other critics charged that Langlie's lack of consistent support for expediting the process allowed it to become mired in repetitious studies and battles over location. Studies were done by the Highway Department, the TBA, the Seattle Planning Commission, the combined Eastside chambers of commerce, and the King County Planning Commission, and there were quasi-official studies by the

Lake Washington Good Roads Association and the Bridge Users Association. In addition, the Municipal League issued at least two reports of its own.[10]

In early 1956, Langlie, still vacillating, recommended that a citizens' committee made up of representatives from both sides of the lake retain DeLeuw, Cather and Co., a nationally known engineering firm, to conduct another study and report on the best location for a second bridge. That report, issued in July 1956, recommended construction of a span parallel to the Lacey Murrow bridge, with a northern spur to Bellevue from Mercer Island. Since the DeLeuw report contradicted completely the highway department's studies, the TBA called for a review and evaluation of the report by the highway commission.[11]

The highway commission's analysis criticized many parts of the DeLeuw report and re-confirmed that the Evergreen Point site was "the most feasible of the various alternatives." The primary reasons for the commission's rejection of the DeLeuw report included the following: (1) it was based on seriously flawed traffic-volume and growth data; (2) it greatly increased overall costs with the need for a Mercer Island–Bellevue span; and its financing would rely on federal funds that would supposedly be available in the mid-1960s. The highway commission believed that a bridge needed to be built soon—not sometime in the mid-sixties or beyond—and that waiting for federal funds might delay completion until the early seventies. Further, from every other aspect—such as development of the Eastside, the movement of people and goods, and potential disruption of communities and property—the Evergreen Point site made more sense.[12]

By this time, Rosellini had been elected governor. During the campaign, he had pledged to build a new bridge "wherever the engineers say it should be built," which meant Montlake–Evergreen Point. Recognizing the critical need for leadership, Rosellini was determined to halt the vacillation and get the decision-making process back into the hands of government.[13]

On the day of his election, Rosellini met with members of the highway commission to determine how best to move the process along. He retained William Bugge as director of the Department of Transportation, believing that Bugge had the confidence of the legislature and, in particular, of Julia Butler Hansen, chair of the house committee on roads and bridges.* A powerful legislator and frequent Rosellini ally during his years in the senate, Hansen would be an essential part of the effort to push a decision on siting through the legislature.[14]

In an early meeting, Bugge told Rosellini that the Evergreen Point–Montlake site was the only logical one, and this convinced Rosellini to continue to back that position. Bugge also pledged the support of his department (often the most independent of all departments because of the separate financing it received from federal interstate funds, gasoline taxes, and so forth) in moving the process forward.[15]

However, the mid-1956 publication of the DeLeuw report had solidified opposition to the Evergreen Point–Montlake site. Within a few months, and just as the Rosellini administration was trying to secure construction permits in early 1957, the Seattle Chamber of Commerce, the Seattle City Council, the Seattle Municipal League, the Arboretum Foundation, the Lake Washington Planning Association, the Seattle Garden Club, the Seattle Historical Society, the Corinthian Yacht Club, the Mountaineers Club, and various other groups adopted the DeLeuw report's recommendation and opposed, primarily on environmental grounds, any site other than one parallel to the existing bridge.[16] Many of these groups also believed that federal funding and greater traffic would make the parallel site cheaper and more feasible.

Legislative Action

At the administration's request, House Bill 205, which permitted the TBA to reimpose tolls on the Lacey Murrow bridge and construct a toll bridge at Evergreen Point, was introduced early in the 1957 session.

---

*A widely respected director, Bugge had served as president of the American Association of State Highway Officials, was a member of the Interstate Committee on Highway Policy Problems, and was chair of the committee on design policies of the American Association of Highway Officials. In the latter post he had formulated design policies for the 41,000-mile interstate and defense highway system. (*Cabinet Close-up: Your Guide to Who's Who in the State Capitol* [pamphlet published in Olympia, *ca.* 1960].)

The reimposition of tolls on the existing bridge was considered critical because the presence of a free bridge a mere six or seven miles away might jeopardize financing of revenue bonds for the Evergreen Point span. Reps. Dan Evans and Newman Clark of Seattle introduced bills calling for the construction of a parallel bridge instead. Dan Evans, for the first time an identifiable foe of Rosellini, argued that the parallel site would be financed by federal funds and would cause less environmental damage. Evans and other proponents of a parallel bridge did admit, however, that federal funds would not be available for several years.[17]

With Hansen guiding the process, hearings were held quickly on both the house and the senate versions of the administration's bills. In mid-March, Eastside Republicans joined with the Democrats to pass substitute House Bill 205, which had been amended by Hansen to state a "preference" for the Evergreen Point site, rather than making it a requirement. According to Hansen, it was the sense of the legislature that this "would permit the TBA and Highway Department engineers to make the final determination." Bugge and Rosellini had persuaded the legislature to reimpose tolls on a free bridge—a seemingly impossible political accomplishment.[18]

As it turned out, Rosellini's battle for a bridge was just beginning. The City of Seattle, under the leadership of Mayor Clinton, remained opposed to any bridge other than a parallel one. It was believed that Seattle might have the power to block an Evergreen Point bridge by denying permits for access roads. Something else, however, immediately presented a more difficult obstacle. Before Rosellini could convene the TBA after HB 205 had passed, Bugge was told by the federal bureau of public roads that tolls could not be restored on the existing bridge since the new span would not be part of the federal interstate highway system. Because federal funds had been used to finance the first bridge and it was now part of the interstate system, federal law prohibited tolls that were to be used for nonfederal purposes.[19]

This news was devastating to Rosellini and Bugge. They hoped to finance the second bridge as a separate entity. Reimposition of tolls on the existing span, however, would both provide additional funds and assure greater usage of the new bridge (thereby enhancing its prospects for financing), and would have made construction of the new bridge a certainty. Moreover, a new financial feasibility study would now be needed before revenue bonds could be sold. Regardless, Bugge and Rosellini were determined to press on with the Evergreen Point site, as it was the only option that would not mean multi-year delays.[20]

Although Rosellini told the TBA and the press that the Evergreen Point site could proceed without Seattle approval, he and Bugge knew that delay and the rising costs of construction might make it impossible to obtain financing for that site. Efforts to overcome Seattle's opposition—petition drives, meetings, and negotiations— were uniformly unsuccessful. Consequently, Rosellini stated that if the new feasibility study showed that the second bridge could be financed without reimposing tolls on the old bridge, the TBA would build it in spite of the city's objection. Rosellini believed that the opponents of the Evergreen Point site, aware of the funding delays for a parallel span, were actually against the building of any bridge. In mid-April he said, "We want to get a bridge built, and if we can't build one on the Evergreen Point route we'll have to examine other sites." He pointedly declined to say, however, that the parallel site was a second choice, since he believed that such a decision would mean no bridge at all during his administration.[21]

In a little-noticed but critical session, the King County commissioners, while indicating that they did not want to be drawn into the disagreement between Rosellini and Seattle, readopted resolutions, originally passed in 1953 and 1954, urging that construction begin at once "at a location to be determined by the State Highway Department on a purely technical basis." This position was critical to Rosellini, since he needed their political support for the Evergreen Point site.[22]

Rosellini recommended to the TBA that the state proceed with another study to determine if the Evergreen Point–Montlake site would be financially feasible. Opposition groups immediately raised questions as to why the study was limited and demanded a financial feasibility survey on both the proposed routes. The Seattle *Times* asserted that Rosellini's campaign promise favoring the Evergreen Point route was the motive behind the more limited report, and warned that the narrow focus of the proposed study might force Rosellini to start all over again. Nonetheless, even the *Times* admitted that "Time has become an increasingly acute factor in the bridge problem . . . each year of delay, over the past 5 years, has seen construction costs rise an average of 5 per cent. Each year of delay costs another $1,000,000."[23]

Late in April, Rosellini and Bugge decided to conduct a compromise study. First the consulting firm, Coverdale and Colpitt, would survey the financial feasibility of construction at the Evergreen Point site. If a bridge there could *not* be financed, then the firm would study the feasibility of a parallel bridge. The three- to four-month study would also include traffic surveys. Rosellini felt that this would satisfy, in part at least, the major opponents of the Evergreen Point site by exploring both options. (He was wrong; the decision escalated Rosellini's feud with the city.)[24]

By mid-September 1957, the new traffic and financial-feasibility studies were finished. The results were not good news for the state and Rosellini. Breaking their report into two phases, with phase I the Evergreen Point site (with no tolls on the present bridge), and phase II the parallel site (with tolls on both the new and the existing spans and all bridge approaches financed by bonds), the engineering consultants turned down both sites as financially unfeasible. Even before the findings were made public, Bugge and Rosellini instructed the Coverdale and Colpitts firm to revisit the project and analyze a third proposal—which would involve a multi-phase process. In the third option the Evergreen Point bridge would be built immediately as a toll bridge. Tolls would also be reimposed immediately on the existing bridge. Then, when federal funds became available in the early- to mid-1960s to assist in the construction of the approaches, the combined net revenues of the two bridges would be sufficient to finance the balance of the cost of a parallel bridge and improvements to the existing bridge. This plan would result in two new bridges, not one. Ultimately, this outcome was achieved in 1990, without, however, reimposing tolls on the Lacey Murrow bridge. Although the consultants found the new phase III to be financially feasible, in actuality this was only a face-saving move. Rosellini and Bugge realized that such a long, complicated process was not politically feasible. The negative report on both the proposed bridge sites as stand-alone propositions threw everyone into disarray, at least temporarily. Neither the Evergreen Point supporters nor opponents were pleased.[25]

According to the Coverdale report, the toll revenues on the Evergreen Point site would be $4 million to $5 million less than the amount needed to retire the bonds. Rosellini and the TBA began to explore a number of options: (1) borrowing federal I-5 freeway funds to finance part of the bridge's cost; (2) involving the state's congressional delegation and asking Congress to authorize reimposing tolls on the Lacey Murrow bridge; and (3) using monies that Congress was making available under the Federal Interstate Highway Act in order to combat the national recession. In fairly short order, all these alternatives proved to be politically or legally impossible.[26]

At this juncture Rosellini turned, almost in desperation, to an alternative that would not require a vote by the legislature or Congress. In the late winter of 1957 the governor had appointed Ed Munro to the three-person board of King County commissioners. This gave the Democrats a voting majority, since Howie Odell, board chair, was also a Democrat. Munro, who had served with Rosellini in the legislature and had been an advisor in his campaign, was supportive of Rosellini's position regarding the Evergreen Point span. Additionally, Ray Olson, a longtime Rosellini ally, was Munro's administrative assistant (a position called budget director). In late May 1958, Rosellini asked the King County commissioners to consider raising the additional money by selling limited levy bonds. That amount could be sold within the county's 1.5 percent of assessed valuation limitation without a vote. The funds could be loaned to the state for construction costs, thereby lowering the overall outlay for the project to about $22 million. Under the Coverdale estimates of net revenue, this amount could be financed by tolls from the new bridge, even if tolls were not reimposed on the existing bridge.[27]

This approach was politically sensitive. The City of Seattle, where the bulk of the county's population resided, opposed the Evergreen Point site. Further, since reimbursement of the county's bonds would not begin until after the toll bonds were retired (perhaps twenty-five to forty years), the project would tie up the county's assessed valuation for taxing purposes for an unreasonably long period, and other projects and services would be severely restricted. Opponents immediately shifted their attack to highlight the inadequacy of this approach. The Eastside Commuters Association did its own calculations and arrived at figures showing that even with $4 million in county aid, financing was not feasible.[28]

The incumbent Republican commissioner, Dean McLean, came out against the plan in early summer. In July 1958 he told a gathering of Eastsiders, "No one will benefit from an Evergreen Bridge more than myself. But the County cannot make commitments willy nilly. It would have been foolhardy for the county to go into the situation as it was presented by the state." By then, Rosellini had also concluded that this plan for King County aid was doomed.[29] At the same time, however, political events were occurring that would have a momentous impact on the bridge impasse. A young farmer from the Snoqualmie Valley, Scott Wallace, decided to run for county commissioner against Dean McLean. Aided by his friend and veteran Democratic activist, Henry Seidel, he selected the issues upon which to base his campaign. Both believed that a major issue, which vitally affected Wallace's district, was the need for a bridge at Evergreen Point.[30]

Wallace and Seidel discovered that Eastside residents in his district not only supported the building of a second bridge, but they also wanted it built at Evergreen Point, and not parallel to the existing span. There were two basic reasons: (1) the development potential was primarily north of the old bridge; (2) any Eastside commute would be shorter and less crowded if the bridge was located at Evergreen Point. Soon the bridge became the central focus of Wallace's campaign. His theme was that lack of strong Eastside representation in the county-city building was one reason why opponents of a second bridge had been able to continue delaying tactics against a project that should have been under construction months or years earlier. At a typical meeting at the Happy Valley Grange Hall, twenty-six candidates sought support. A majority, following up on Wallace's remarks, also discussed the need for a bridge or mentioned it in some fashion. While McLean continued his opposition to the Evergreen Point site, Mel Tennant, a Republican candidate for assessor, took issue with him, saying, "King County can well afford to financially back the Evergreen Point Bridge. The increase in property values will more than compensate for any expenses the county incurs."[31]

In view of the outcome, it is ironic that Wallace neither knew Rosellini nor received any support from him or his people. In fact, Wallace's opponent in the primary was Floyd Miller, an associate of Rosellini. Wallace won the primary and went on to defeat McLean. Taking office in early 1959, with Seidel as his administrative assistant-budget director, Wallace gave the Democrats full control of the board of King County commissioners. He also brought to the board a commitment to get a bridge built at Evergreen Point.[32]

By early 1959, Rosellini and Bugge had shifted their attention back to a possible legislative solution to the financing difficulties. More and more pressure was being brought by proponents of a second bridge—regardless of its location—to provide relief from the congestion of the I-10 corridor created by the Lacey Murrow bridge. The opponents of the Evergreen Point site continued to push for a federally funded parallel bridge, ignoring the obvious problems: (1) lack of access roads planning by Seattle and Mercer Island for such a project; (2) lack of available federal funds for any time in the foreseeable future; (3) the added cost of a freeway span from Mercer Island to the Eastside, which would require even more federal funding; (4) the fact that the parallel bridge would still require the state to sell tax revenue bonds to fund its initial cost—something that Julia Butler Hansen opposed and that guaranteed lawsuits (since the uncertainties of future federal funding might jeopardize repayment of the bonds).[33]

Seeking a legislative solution, Rosellini and Bugge turned to the 1959 legislature, which was heavily Democratic. They proposed legislation that permitted the highway department to guarantee up to $850,000 per year from gasoline-excise taxes to meet the interest requirements of toll-bridge bonds. The excise taxes were deposited into the state motor vehicle fund for use by the highway commission. This was a solution that differed dramatically from financing that relied on future federal funds. The legislation—included in an amendment to the supplemental appropriations bill in the special session—passed easily, with an effective date of May 5, 1959. When Cliff Yelle, the state auditor, refused to sign any toll-bridge revenue bonds backed by such a guarantee, Rosellini and the state filed a mandamus action compelling his signature. Opponents of the Evergreen Point site joined in Yelle's opposition, and two months later the state supreme court declared the legislation unconstitutional. The partisan nature of the opposition is illustrated by the fact that Slade Gorton, house minority whip under Dan Evans, appeared for the intervenors who opposed the site. The constitutional defect was technical rather than substantive. The legislature, in its haste, had placed two different revenue measures under the same title. The state's Constitution prohibits this. With yet another financing alternative foreclosed, Rosellini, for the first time, began to doubt whether any bridge would be built.[34]

The court decision triggered another attempt to enlist help from King County. Recognizing the problems inherent in any legislative solution, Rosellini had approached Ed Munro prior to the 1959 session and asked him for other ideas on how King County might assist in financing. Munro promptly referred Rosellini's request to Scott Wallace and his administrative assistant, Seidel, who was chair of the commissioners' budget committee. Seidel began to work closely with Ed Sand, planning director of King County, to craft another approach toward financing assistance from the county. In anticipation of a possible solution from King County, Rosellini asked the legislature to amend RCW 47.56.250 so that the TBA and the highway commission could accept financial assistance from any city or county government that would benefit from a particular toll facility. The amendment received little notice from opponents of the Evergreen Point site and passed the 1959 legislature almost without opposition.[35]

By mid-summer of 1959, Wallace and Seidel developed a plan to use Wallace's own north district road fund to guarantee repayment of the toll-bridge bonds if such a guarantee would assure the building of a bridge. The proposal, which pledged funds from the district that would benefit most from the new bridge, would be politically acceptable in that district. Likewise, the plan removed political pressure from O'Dell and Munro, whose districts contained strong opposition to Evergreen Point. A crucial requirement for the plan was fulfilled on September 30, 1959, when the county planning commission unanimously recommended that a bridge be built at the Evergreen Point site.[36]

As soon as the court decision striking down the state's pledge of gasoline-tax revenues was announced in August, Wallace went public with his own proposal, which drew immediate criticism. The nub of the problem, as pointed out by the opponents, was the question of exactly how much money would be required in order to assure the sale of bonds. Actual construction costs were well known. In March 1959, bids for bridge construction had been opened. Guy F. Atkinson Company of San Francisco was the winner, with a low bid of $10,969,597. Added costs arising from delays were easily estimated. What was uncertain was the interest rate that would be required in order to sell enough revenue bonds to finance construction. The interest debt to bond holders would be by far the largest part of any financial package.[37]

Prior to final approval by the county commissioners, Rosellini and the TBA asked Coverdale to supplement its 1957 report on estimated traffic and toll revenues. According to this supplemental report, the total debt requirement for the project would be approximately $30 million. As calculated by the state and by Wallace, this would require guarantees of up to $750,000 per year if toll revenues fell short. On November 9, 1959, the King County commissioners unanimously adopted a plan to guarantee the bonds necessary to finance the Evergreen Point bridge.[38]

Sensing that this might be the last hope, Rosellini and the TBA moved quickly. Resolutions were passed that permitted the state to utilize this additional guarantee as financing for the bonds to be sold. At the urging of Rosellini, the state had retained Harold Shefelman to pursue the earlier mandamus action against Yelle concerning the gasoline-tax proposal. When Yelle again refused to sign the bonds that would be guaranteed by the county, Shefelman filed a second action. Again the opponents intervened and raised numerous constitutional arguments. Hearings before the state supreme court were scheduled for January 25, 1960.[39]

Meantime, while accusing Rosellini of pushing the bridge only for political reasons, the Seattle *Times* had finally come around to supporting it. An editorial pointed out that opponents of the Evergreen Point route, who were arguing that another bridge could be built with federal funds, were actually engaging in wishful thinking.[40]

The supreme court upheld the validity of the county plan in early April. On April 15, 1960, the TBA announced, through Rosellini, that bids on the bridge bonds would be called immediately. Time was about to run out on the contractor's bid to build the floating pontoon sections at a cost that fit within the financial feasibility parameters. The court's ruling enabled the state to accept the bid and to commence construction procedures—including the immediate sale of bonds.[41]

Rosellini was not the only official who was overjoyed by this turn of events. Almost as one, the respective mayors of the East-side communities of Renton, Issaquah, Bellevue, Clyde Hill, Medina, Hunts Point, Yarrow Point, Houghton, Kirkland, Redmond, and Bothell began planning a ground-breaking celebration. The Evergreen Point toll bridge opened for traffic on August 28, 1963. Its cost of $24,792,000 was under budget, and revenues from tolls exceeded estimates from the outset. Less than two years later, the 1965 legislature passed a measure removing the guarantee obligation of King County. The bonds were retired a year ahead of schedule, and tolls were removed on June 17, 1979. On August 26, 1988, the Washington State Transportation Commission officially named the span "The Albert D. Rosellini Bridge."[42]

Chapter 14

Taxes
and the 1960
Campaign

Rosellini had been elected in 1956 on a platform that emphasized the preceding administration's neglect of institutions and vital services such as education and welfare. Despite pledging to end this neglect and to provide needed services, he also ran on a no-new-taxes platform. Rosellini had said that he wanted to look for more efficient ways to run state government before raising taxes. During the 1953 and 1955 legislative sessions, he had opposed taxes that would disproportionately affect working men and women, such as the sales tax, and had urged the legislature and Langlie to consider placing a state income tax on the ballot. In his 1952 campaign, he had called for the elimination of the sales tax on food and necessities—a position he would continue to espouse as long as he was governor.

Therefore, Rosellini was determined to avoid new taxes during the 1957 legislative session. He also believed that raising taxes during that time would be detrimental to his efforts to build up the state's economy through the Department of Commerce and Economic Development. Recognizing that he was inheriting a large general-fund deficit, he maintained the "firm hope that we will achieve a satisfactory mid-point between income and outgo to run our state for the next two years without any added taxes." This virtually guaranteed that his administration would need to seek substantial tax increases during the

1959 session. Even if immense savings were achieved by streamlining state government, too many areas had been neglected. Institutions and higher education alone required large increases. Their needs would not diminish in the next two or even three biennia.[1]

Rosellini succeeded in increasing the appropriations for institutions and higher education—as well as providing needed funds for budget reform—within a framework that avoided any new taxes. The net result was a budget predicted to be between $25 and $32 million out of balance. Rosellini declined, however, to call a special session to deal with the imbalance. There were several reasons. Among them was the possibility that $5 million that had been appropriated but not used would revert to the general fund. Rosellini wanted to try to postpone the transfer of $11.4 million to the Teachers Retirement Reserve fund—currently operating with a $22 million surplus—and save some of the $16 million of contingency appropriations at his discretionary disposal. He was also hopeful that the budgeting and accounting act, just adopted, would result in substantial savings when Bishop presented the state's first program budget to the 1959 legislature, and that a diversified and growing industrial base, promoted by the new Department of Commerce and Economic Development, would increase the revenue base. Determined to avoid the kind of stopgap measures likely to come from a special session, he wanted to allow his citizens' tax-advisory committee, chaired by Harold Shefelman, time to suggest long-term solutions (see pp. 177–78).[2]

Rosellini recognized that this course was politically dangerous. Conservative critics had already begun to talk about deficits, spending sprees, and fiscal irresponsibility on his part, and there was little doubt that the Republicans would accuse him of reneging on his pledge not to raise taxes. As a fourteen-year senator, he had received the benefit of the doubt on most requests from his recent legislative colleagues, Republicans as well as Democrats. In subsequent sessions this would not be true.[3]

As noted in chapter 10, in June 1957 Rosellini ordered all state agencies under his office, except institutions, to make across-the-board cuts in operating costs of 15 to 20 percent. He also urged state elected officials not under his office to make similar cuts, telling the press that he had received pledges from them to cooperate. By mid-January 1958, however, Rosellini was publicly stating that new or higher taxes would be inevitable. To make matters worse, the state (and the entire country) had entered a full-scale recession, and the declining state economy meant shrinking revenues from sales taxes and higher deficits.* Rosellini warned that services might be affected significantly if tax revenues continued to fall.[4]

The Republicans, at their state convention in July, called for a balanced budget without any new taxes and expressed "shock at the irresponsible fiscal program" of the administration. Although he accused the Republicans of playing politics and said their views were "irresponsible and dishonest," Rosellini was discovering a time-honored political reality: the party out of power will almost always oppose new taxes and raise issues of fiscal responsibility. It was a game that Rosellini had played repeatedly from the other side of the political fence.[5]

In order to minimize the impact of the state's fiscal crisis on the 1958 elections, Rosellini avoided specifics and simply spoke of presenting the upcoming legislature with a tax program aimed at balancing the state budget during the 1959–61 biennium. He wrote a series of articles that outlined the innovative approaches his administration had introduced to improve the state's revenue stream: the program-oriented budget and accounting systems; the Department of Commerce and Economic Development; and the new tax-advisory committee. The committee's report—due in mid-September—would suggest long-term solutions to the state's revenue needs and to the chronic deficits which had been accumulating over the last twelve years and at least six legislative sessions.[6]

The tax-advisory committee's report, when issued, did not ease Rosellini's political dilemma. It warned that Washington's financial situation had "assumed emergency proportions," and asserted that

---

*At a Western Governors' Conference meeting with Eisenhower to discuss federal initiatives to combat the recession, Rosellini joined with eleven other governors in urging more federal building and construction—primarily through the federal interstate highway act—as well as broadened welfare, educational, and health programs. (*Times*, March 20, 1958.)

without drastic revisions in taxation and spending, Washington residents could expect a tax increase at every legislature for the next decade. (That is exactly what occurred.) Additionally, the committee recommended substantial changes in the local property-tax assessment system to equalize assessments among the counties and require assessors to tax property at its increased value. The report also stated that it was imperative to transfer a larger percentage of government from the state to the local level so that spending could be more closely monitored. These findings merely echoed much of what Rosellini had been saying.[7]

It was the committee's revenue proposals that exacerbated the administration's political difficulties. They called for raising the state sales tax from 3⅓ percent to 4 percent and expanding it to services offered by doctors, hospitals, and other previously exempt categories. In total, the group recommended that the legislature raise $120 million in new revenue in the 1959 session. While some commentators applauded the report for its realism, it was clear that Rosellini's administration was facing the unpleasant prospect of asking the next legislature for new taxes in record amounts.[8]

Rosellini's main concern was the impact of the report on the November legislative elections. Without the working majorities in both houses that he had had in the 1957 session, neither his programs nor any tax proposals would have much chance of success. Much to his relief, the 1958 election produced another heavily Democratic legislature. Almost immediately, Rosellini identified the need for additional revenue to run state government in a progressive manner as his number-one priority for the session. At the same time, he wanted to avoid undue increases in taxes, such as the B & O tax, that might hamper economic development.[9]

In mid-January, Rosellini submitted a biennium budget package that totaled $2 billion and revenue proposals that included $135 million in new money—based primarily on an increase in sales taxes. Even this ambitious package, however, would leave a $16 million general-fund deficit. Rosellini's 1959 budget was noteworthy for reasons other than its tax increases. It was the first program budget that detailed the revenues sought by each department as well as the specific programs that would be supported. It was also novel in that it was submitted in its entirety just one week into the session. In another unusual move, Rosellini informed all department heads that they must accept his proposed budget and could not approach the legislature on behalf of any budgetary items not already included.[10]

Response to the record-setting budget and revenue proposals was predictable. The Republicans, who had already cast Rosellini as fiscally irresponsible, said that the budget would create unmanageable tax burdens for the state. It was not long before the term "taxellini" made its appearance. Some Democrats were also appalled by the Rosellini proposals, especially those whose districts bordered Oregon and Idaho, neither of which had state sales taxes.[11]

To no one's surprise, there was considerable momentum against the tax package. Early in the session, Rosellini endorsed bills that would shift some tax responsibilities to county and city governments through higher property taxes. He stated that very low local property taxes "contributed unhealthily to the dependence of schools and other agencies on state money." According to Rosellini, the fact that many county assessors failed to assess property at fair value, thereby providing that county with unreasonably low personal and real property taxes, was one reason that Washington's state taxes were the second or third highest in the nation. Rosellini noted that his executive request bills to correct that situation would follow the recommendations of the state tax advisory commission. His recommendation was strongly opposed by the antitax forces inside and outside the legislature, and it was many years after his administration had ended before legislation was passed to establish equalization commissions that required fair assessments.[12]

Rosellini's efforts to move his revenue measures produced no results. Indeed, all the movement seemed to be in the other direction amid signs that a "taxpayers' revolt" was under way. The barrage of letters against new taxes was growing heavier each day. Despite this pressure from voters, Rosellini continued to urge the passage of his major revenue proposals and maintained that the levying of additional taxes was necessary to keep "essential state services." The degree to which the tax package was in trouble is illustrated by the fact that two Democratic senators from Vancouver (located across the Columbia River from Oregon) forced a vote on postponing the measure indefinitely. It was defeated twenty-nine to twenty-one, but fourteen Democrats voted in favor of postponement. Worse yet, the eight Republicans who voted against the postponement said that they did so simply to guarantee that the important measure would receive a "full and fair test." Despite this discouraging early vote, Rosellini predicted that the "necessary twenty-five votes needed for passage will be there when the chips are down."[13]

On the fifty-first day of the regular session, with no agreement on appropriations in sight, Rosellini called an extraordinary meeting of the 101 house and senate Democrats, who all squeezed into his large office. Rosellini exhorted them to take responsibility for carrying out the Democratic party state platform, which called for sympathetic treatment for schools, public assistance, and the state's institutions. He insisted that they maintain his recommended spending levels, which required substantial new taxes. While encouraging the legislators to submit a graduated net income tax to the voters "as a long-range solution," he reiterated the need to pass an increase in the sales tax. Finally, he pointed out that less than 1 percent of his new taxes was for new services. His unprecedented meeting with the Democrats, excluding the Republicans, made the proposed tax increase his responsibility and provided the Republicans with potent political ammunition.[14]

The regular session failed to pass an appropriations bill. The tax revolt had strengthened, and a large group of "tax rebels" rallied in Olympia during the last few days of the session to speak to legislators who sympathized with their no-tax mood. Not to be outdone, Rosellini welcomed the group with a reminder that only 0.6 percent of his proposed budget for the next two years would be for new services. This was a direct response to those people who had signed petitions stating or pledging that they would not request any new government services if the legislature would not raise taxes.[15]

Rosellini immediately called a special session and reintroduced his overall budget package with few if any changes. He invited the lawmakers to make whatever changes they wished, but insisted that they raise the taxes needed to balance the budget and retire part of the carryover deficit. His stubborn insistence on his tax package and the pressure on the legislators to pass something and go home, gradually

began to bear fruit. The house finally passed an appropriations measure that provided a vehicle for negotiations between the two houses. However, the bill contained a substantial cut in the budget for institutions. Calling the cut unnecessary, Rosellini said he was "very disturbed" and would not allow it to pass. Also, it provided only $77 million in new taxes—leading Rosellini to warn that the proposal was inadequate and that he could call the legislature back in another special session to balance the budget if necessary. He also had to fend off a bill that sought to abolish the Department of Commerce and Economic Development (see p. 155).[16]

The 1959 legislature adjourned on the fifteenth day of the special session. It gave Rosellini the balanced budget he had demanded. It also approved his recommended $2 billion in appropriations for the 1959–61 biennium, as well as $112 million in new taxes to provide the funds. In addition to balancing the general-fund budget, it reduced the deficit carryover from about $80 million to between $36 million and $38 million. While he praised the lawmakers for their hard work and confidently stated that, despite the tax hikes, Washington's citizens would pay less in taxes than those in most other states, Rosellini knew that he had handed the Republicans a major 1960 campaign issue. The press was quick to note that a recent census report—even before the tax increase—had ranked Washington state as having the second highest per capita taxes in the country. Time would tell just how much political damage had been done by Rosellini's efforts to pay for the changes his activist approach to state government demanded.[17]

The Purchasing Department Scandal

Before the 1960 campaign began, however, other events involving Rosellini's administration made news, dampening further his prospects for reelection. In December 1958, Ed Guthman began a series of articles in the Seattle *Times* asserting numerous irregularities and loose practices by the state purchasing department. The problem had been uncovered by studying "thousands of 1957–58 purchases" and questioning scores of state officials and businessmen. According to the articles, *Times* reporters had found instances of state purchasing people favoring certain firms, accepting informal quotes as opposed

to sealed bids, and ignoring Rosellini's mandate that, as of December 1, 1957, the state was to purchase only through use of competitive bidding. They also "uncovered" situations where bids were phoned in or where price quotations were not time-dated or stamped.[18]

The *Times* focused on two irregularities it identified as the most flagrant. One was the purchase of $2,183 in drugs from a store connected with Lloyd Nelson, a pharmacist who was also the director of general administration who supervised the purchasing department. The other was a one-year contract for light bulbs that was awarded to a firm after a lower bid from another company. Despite sensational headlines, the stories revealed that the latter situation was caused by the federal government's refusal to approve use of the lower quality light bulbs of the low bidder, and that the purchases from Nelson's family stores were unknown to him and made by a buyer for price reasons. A later story revealed that the state supervisor of purchasing had placed orders with a firm owned by his brother, although the products mainly involved fair-trade items where no lower price could have been involved. Nothing in the stories implied that any Rosellini appointee or employee—let alone Rosellini himself—had profited from such practices. Guthman, some years later, said he never saw any personal benefit to Rosellini's political organization or people from the state purchasing department practices.[19]

As a result of the stories, Nelson was asked to resign, and Charles Hodde took over as director of general administration. Hodde dismissed the supervisor of purchasing and several buyers whose practices had been suspect or improper. He and Rosellini also retained a consulting firm to modernize the purchasing system. By February 19, 1959, Hodde and Rosellini proposed a new state purchasing act that assured competitive bidding, disqualified any firms where state officials or employees had an interest, and prohibited any form of gifts or favors from firms doing business with the state. The act was signed into law on March 19, 1959.[20]

Rosellini was very upset about the evident bias shown in the articles—though it came as no surprise. In a direct response to the *Times*, he pointed out that they had failed to mention that all the practices uncovered were contrary to his administration's guidelines

and his own orders. He went on to state that many of the situations, and all the loose and irregular procedures of the department, had been inherited by his administration. For example, the contract for the light bulbs had been in existence for seven years. Rosellini, always distrustful of the *Times*, felt the series was slanted to imply that his administration had created the system for personal profit. The Republican minority introduced resolutions in both houses calling for a grand jury investigation (both were defeated by straight party-line votes). Years later, Charles Hodde was interviewed for an oral history project funded by the legislature. Recalling that Guthman had received a Pulitzer Prize for his reporting on the Canwell Committee, he said: "Well, he didn't get a Pulitzer Prize for the investigation of general administration or purchasing."[21]

Political Campaign Funds

In the spring of 1960 when the gubernatorial campaign was starting, Guthman and the *Times* produced another series of articles that clearly targeted Rosellini. In April, Guthman wrote several articles that detailed funds set up to cover Rosellini's political expenses. Under the headline "Rosellini Received Check from A and D Fund," the lead article chronicled Guthman's attempts to track down the source of payment of expenses incurred by Rosellini. One of these expenses was $58.47 charged at the Palmer House in Chicago; another was $455.29 left over from the 1956 campaign, which was paid at Rosellini's secretary's request. A second article pointed out that political funds had been set up by Rosellini's friends and supporters, including various directors of departments. The directors were asked, on a voluntary basis, to contribute, and the articles pointed out that a number of them chose not to do so. (The *Times* later acknowledged that nothing about these funds was illegal.) According to the article, the funds had paid for a dinner for Prince Bertil of Sweden, a reception for President Truman, a press reception, and a reception for the state supreme court, legislators, and elected officials.[22]

In contrast to the "purchasing-department exposé," however, other newspapers were quick to note the inherent unfairness of the *Times* series and the tag-along articles that appeared in the *PI*. The

Eastsider pointed out that the series contained nothing new or unknown: "That's why we view with considerable distaste the Seattle
daily papers' 'exposé' of the Governor's fund to cover his extra expenses
when he is out of town. If the *Times* and *PI* are just now finding out
about these funds that governors have had for several administrations,
they need a fresh staff of correspondents in Olympia. This looks like a
typical, unethical attack during an election year. . . . Langlie's private
fund came from insurance companies doing business with the state. . . .
He now denies this but it was common knowledge at the time." Even
the *Argus* agreed that Rosellini had been treated unfairly.[23]

Rosellini was livid about the series, which he thought was timed
simply to make him look bad before the 1960 election. He issued
a detailed statement in rebuttal, which the *Times* printed in full.
Accusing the *Times* of using a double standard in reporting about
his administration, Rosellini wrote, "They winked at activities of
the previous administration." He noted the Langlie administration's
use of "estate-appraisal fees" and "liquor lines" to reward the party
faithful and its splitting of insurance commissions for work done by
the state.* Responding in great detail about his political expenses,
Rosellini pointed out that Langlie had received free lodging at the
Edmond S. Meany and Olympic hotels (an arrangement acknowledged
even by the *Times* reporters).[24]

In commenting on the purchasing department articles, the governor noted that a study of purchasing practices was already under
way and a consultant hired when the *Times* reporters asked to review
department records. After his administration freely made all records
available—including the preliminary report of the consultants—the
reporters "betrayed a trust," and focused only on what had happened
after 1957. Going on the attack, he described how his administration
had blocked the *Times*'s "attempts to hog liquor advertising," and
concluded that "the other publishers in the state should learn that
recently for the first time in seven and a half years the State Tax

---

*I have confirmed these practices from newspaper accounts and through inter-
views with people in the insurance industry.

Commission audited the *Times*' books and demanded a substantial sum in back taxes." This was a typical Rosellini reaction. He was a fighter and a counterpuncher in the political arena. Using the statement to his political advantage, he attributed the articles not to a dislike for him, but to a realization that the potential Republican candidates would have no issues against him unless some sordid ones of a personal nature were manufactured.[25]

It was a battle he could not win. Though the *Argus* and other papers agreed, to a great extent, with his assessment, the *Times*, and certainly Ross Cunningham, adamantly opposed Rosellini at every opportunity. Guthman acknowledges that the ownership of the *Times* had no use for Rosellini—although he states that he personally maintained a high degree of journalistic integrity in reporting on the Rosellini adminis-tration. Nevertheless, Rosellini was always suspect in the *Times*'s view. As he pointed out during the 1960 campaign, the "distorted, so-called 'Scandal' clippings being used by Lloyd J. Andrews all came from the pages of the Seattle *Times*." But it is also true that, without a crisis, Rosellini was reluctant to give up patronage practices of the type that lent themselves to muckraking headlines even though perfectly lawful. (See also chapter 6.)[26]

The Hood Canal Bridge

Bridges played a major role in the 1960 campaign. In January and February of 1960, while the Hood Canal floating bridge was under con-struction, heavy storms damaged some of the pontoons. Apparently, wind and wave action produced forces that caused metal failure at the bolted joint connections of several pontoons. Repairs and redesign would be costly and would require additional financing. This was not the first problem with the pontoons. Earlier, two of them had sunk at the graving docks in Seattle. Consequently, even though the bridge had been designed and authorized by Langlie and the TBA in 1955, it became a major political issue for Rosellini.[27]

The bridge was also a part of the controversial cross-Sound plan-ning which had begun in 1951 and had involved several other proposed bridges linking Vashon Island and Bremerton. These portions had failed in the legislature by just a few votes after intense fighting between the growth and no-growth factions on both sides of the Sound. Hence, the bridge drew criticism from all directions. Lloyd Andrews and Rep. Richard Ruoff criticized the project because the State Teachers Retirement System had invested funds in the TBA revenue bonds financing it. The bridge was being financed as part of the ferry system, and the ferry users association also expressed concerns over the possible fare increases that might be needed to complete the redesign and construction.[28]

Rosellini had been a vigorous advocate of a cross-Sound bridge system including the Hood Canal Bridge. In response to Andrews and Ruoff, he said that the state would do what was necessary to fund the bridge's completion without jeopardizing ferry commuters. Repairing the storm damage cost $4 million and the bridge was completed without major design changes. However, the fourteen-month delay in completion meant that the legislature later had to act to preserve the viability of the original revenue bonds. As an interim measure, Rosellini allocated an additional $330,000 from his contingency fund to keep the original bond fund reserves at sufficient levels.[29]

The *Times* used the issue as the basis for a cartoon that lampooned Rosellini, who was shown burning money and then having to use magic to build bridges across Lake Washington and Hood Canal. In its editorial comment accompanying the cartoon, the *Times* questioned the entire concept of using toll bonds and toll revenues to finance such projects, saying that due to the second Lake Washington Bridge, Hood Canal, and other toll bridges, the state's bonded indebtedness had risen in five years from $10 million to $44 million. Figuring the total debt at the maximum time period of repayment, the *Times* also pointed out that the state would be paying almost $1.50 in interest for every dollar of cost. It then went on to recommend that the state ought to raise taxes to pay for such facilities rather than relying on user tolls.[30]

Within three weeks of the editorial, both of Rosellini's opponents were using the state's high bonded indebtedness as further evidence of his administration's fiscal irresponsibility. But not everyone was persuaded by the *Times* campaign. The *Eastsider* noted that the *Times*, in 1937, had also editorialized against building the first Lake Washington bridge, saying that it would never float. It accused the *Times* of trying to discredit the Rosellini administration while ignoring the facts that the Hood Canal bridge had been planned, designed, and supported by Langlie's administration, and that it was desperately needed by those who lived on the Kitsap and Olympic peninsulas.[31]

The 1960 Primary

When the 1960 campaign began, Rosellini was unopposed. Two serious candidates for the Republican nomination emerged: Representative Newman Clark from Seattle and Superintendent of Public Instruction Lloyd J. Andrews from Spokane. As early as January 1960, Clark said that the administration was vulnerable because of its ethical practices and spending policies. At the same time, newspapers were reporting that the Republicans, led by state chairman William Goodloe, were planning to attack Rosellini for his role in the financing of the Hood Canal bridge and to link the governor with "various scandals involving the state purchasing agency and the Liquor Control Board." One newspaper said that Goodloe's "story" skated close to the "brink of slander" in trying to convince voters that the state needed a new governor in 1961.[32]

An outspoken critic of the second Lake Washington bridge, Clark was a long shot. His early announcement for the position led Ross Cunningham to speculate that he would be the hatchet man to soften up Rosellini so that Lloyd Andrews could make the final kill. Although the state Superintendent of Public Instruction was a nonpartisan office, Lloyd Andrews, a former state senator, was the only Republican holding a statewide office. However, he was not popular with the western Washington Republican establishment. Early 1960 polls showed Rosellini running strongly throughout the state—even in eastern Washington, where Andrews was expected to do well.[33]

A group of prominent Republicans began a movement to draft Walter L. Williams, a leading Seattle businessman. The Williams group, headed by Joel Pritchard, did not believe that Andrews and Clark had the grass-roots appeal to "oust the well-financed and shrewdly operated political machine of the incumbent governor." Andrews was also hurt by the revelation that his appointee to be supervisor of curriculum for the state's public schools had denounced the

Darwinian theory of evolution, saying that he preferred the Adam and Eve story. When Andrews merely demoted the employee, he seemed to please nobody, failing to appease most of the state's citizens and also outraging the fundamentalists, who were critical of the "advanced thinking" of the Darwinians.[34]

During the summer and early fall, public attention was focused on the Republican gubernatorial race. Williams eventually dropped out, and the race was left to Clark and Andrews. Both continued to attack Rosellini's alleged fiscal irresponsibility, questionable ethical practices, and cronyism. Andrews stressed his own statewide experience and leadership in contrast to Clark. Clark pointed out that Andrews had used his office to staff his campaign and had slanted the state's curriculum guides to match his personal beliefs concerning the United Nations. He also noted that neither Andrews's supervisor of instructional materials nor his administrative assistant had qualifications as educators. As the primary campaign drew to a close, both Andrews and Clark pledged a balanced state budget with no new taxes.[35]

Rosellini opened his reelection bid with an old-style dinner at the Grand Ballroom of the Olympic Hotel in Seattle, with a simultaneous event in Spokane hooked up by radio. Almost two thousand party and administration faithful turned out. His early campaign focused on the accomplishments of his administration and on organizing voter turnout. At the same time he built up campaign organizations in every county and town. He mounted a massive billboard, newspaper, and radio and television effort, spending close to $88,000. (This figure is misleadingly low, since Rosellini did not have to report advertising and printing done by local central committees and labor groups.) After the primary, Andrews charged Rosellini with failing to report all his expenses, claiming that the total figure was at least $133,700, and perhaps as high as $200,000 if all the hidden monies were accounted for. At long last, fund-raising was no problem for Rosellini; his finance committee, headed by Sam Calderhead of Seattle, included powerful business leaders from every part of the state.[36]

With his money and the power of his incumbency, Rosellini was able to mount a sophisticated advertising campaign. His themes were, "Progress you can be proud of," and "Rosellini is doing a great job." As the primary campaign drew to a close, Rosellini was convinced that he would achieve a substantial victory and that the general election would not present a problem.[37]

This confidence was shattered by the election returns on September 13. From the first tally of ballots, Rosellini trailed Andrews in total votes. Ultimately, he received 244,579 votes to Andrews' 263,897. More disturbing was the fact that Clark and Andrews together polled more than 400,000 votes, as contrasted with approximately 296,000 for Rosellini and a scattering of other candidates. The following day, Clark threw his support behind Andrews. Equally worrying was the fact that while Republicans outpolled the Democrats four to three in the governor's race, in other races the Democrats won handily and by large margins. It was clear that many rank-and-file Democrats had crossed over to vote Republican in the governor's race. If that trend continued in the final, there would be a new governor in 1961. The situation in 1960 was completely reversed from that of 1956, when Rosellini had outdistanced Anderson in the primary by almost 50,000 votes, and the Democrats had outpolled Republicans 424,000 to 322,000. Rosellini would have to sell himself to his own party and to those who normally voted Democratic if he was to have any hope of reelection.[38]

Several factors may have contributed to Democratic voters' disaffection. One of Rosellini's advisors believed that in the absence of burning issues it was difficult to sell an incumbent governor on the basis of what he had done as compared with what "needs to be done." For the first time, Rosellini had nothing to attack. High on Rosellini's list, but difficult to quantify, was the influence of the articles implying questionable ethical conduct on his part.[39]

A more troubling factor was the coolness toward his campaign of groups working for various democratic presidential candidates. Except for the Lyndon Johnson supporters, they all avoided coordinating their efforts with Rosellini's campaign. The Stevenson group, with old memories of the Mitchell fight in 1952, was suspicious of Rosellini. While in other states the Kennedy forces were using the old-style party machines to generate delegate support, both the Catholic issue and the ethical cloud kept them aloof from Rosellini's campaign in Washington. The latter two groups represented reformers within the party who wanted to change the old way of doing things. Rosellini was an old-style politician who believed that political spoils went to the victorious party. Although quick to spot areas of government that needed reforming, he was not progressive in sensing that the New Deal partisan approach was becoming outdated.[40]

Senator Magnuson had agreed to support Lyndon Johnson, and he was pressuring Rosellini to stay neutral. Maggie's request presented no problem for Rosellini, because he feared that a too-early endorsement of Kennedy would bring the issue of religion into the governor's race. Scoop Jackson, the de facto head of the state's efforts for Kennedy, already distrusted Rosellini, and the governor's refusal to endorse Kennedy before the convention infuriated Jackson and his people. The situation was complicated by the fact that Jackson was seeking the vice-presidential nomination on a Kennedy ticket. His failure to deliver the Catholic, Democratic governor from his own state for Kennedy rankled Jackson and his staff more than they would ever admit publicly.[41]

After the primary, with Rosellini trailing badly in the polls as well as at the ballot box, the separation increased. Naturally, Rosellini did everything he could to make amends and unite the Democrats. If any coattails existed, he wanted to try to ride them. However, Kennedy was running as a fresh, new idealist who would change the country. The Catholic issue was strong in everyone's mind. Kennedy did not want to tie his campaign in Washington to a Catholic office-holder who was pictured as the ultimate "political pro." Consequently, the local Kennedy organization ignored Rosellini where it really counted—in the doorbelling and get-out-the-vote efforts. Only on the surface was there any pretense of a unified effort.[42]

The General Election Campaign

On primary election night, according to Ethel, Rosellini never stopped smiling. Putting aside his disappointment, he huddled with Maggie and others and began planning what he should do. He told the press that it would be a long campaign and that he had obviously failed to get his story across to the voters. On the night of the primary, he formally challenged Andrews to a series of debates on the issues. Rosellini recalls Maggie's chagrin when he heard about the debate challenge. When Maggie said that an incumbent ought never give his opponent that kind of recognition, Rosellini asked, "What on earth have I got to lose? They already have Andrews in the governor's mansion anyway." Maggie paused a few moments and then slowly nodded his head in agreement.[43]

A basic aspect of Rosellini's character may have been responsible for the calmness with which he reacted that evening. Unlike many other candidates, Rosellini, because of both temperament and background, always saw himself as the underdog. Ambitious as he was, Rosellini was almost always surprised when he did well. Despite his successes in the state senate, he was never sure of his place or position. His treatment by the establishment press and business groups had been grudging acceptance at best, even in areas where his achievements were manifest. Consequently, he took the primary defeat in stride and determined to move forward and fight harder to keep the position he had struggled so long to obtain.

Fortunately for Rosellini, Andrews accepted his challenge and agreed to a series of four debates. In his primary campaign Andrews had mainly tried to discredit Rosellini as fiscally irresponsible because of his tax increases, personally responsible for the financial overruns on the Hood Canal bridge, and ethically suspect for running an office rampant with cronyism and special favors for friends. In the area of taxes, Andrews had been vague and general, saying that he would balance the budget and manage state government on a pay-as-you-go basis. He had criticized Rosellini for not doing enough to improve the state's economy and obtain new jobs. He also tried to take credit for increased budgets for education while he was state superintendent. Claiming that Rosellini had personally jeopardized the teacher's retirement fund by having it invested in revenue bonds to build the Hood Canal bridge, Andrews had mounted a clever primary campaign that featured billboards showing a sinking Hood Canal bridge and the slogan, "Elect Lloyd Andrews—a bridge you can cross." The primary results showed that people believed Andrews and distrusted Rosellini. Without the benefit of debates where the two men could be seen together, it is doubtful that Rosellini could have turned the tide. Years later, Rosellini smiled when he said, "If Andrews had left town for six weeks, he would have been governor."[44]

Between the primary and September 28, the day of the first televised debate, Rosellini's people researched the positions Andrews had taken as a state senator on taxes, education, balanced budgets, and the state's industrial climate. They also prepared position papers on issues where Andrews's management of his state office belied his promises of integrity and morality in government. Rosellini was determined to use the first debate as the springboard for a campaign that would examine the "Andrews record" and make clear what it would mean to the groups of voters that had abandoned Rosellini.[45]

Although Rosellini's advisors had worried about how he would deal with complicated facts and issues before a large audience, most observers believe that the momentum shifted, albeit gradually, immediately after the first debate. Rosellini appeared with charts that demonstrated the accuracy of his own statements, as well as the inconsistencies and inaccuracies of those by Andrews. Although they believed that he had won the debate, both Rosellini and his advisors thought that he had committed a major—perhaps fatal—blunder when he visibly lost his temper in responding to Andrews's assertions that he had misled or lied to voters about taxes and his record. The incident had made Rosellini look undignified and ungovernor-like. It had also increased his nervousness, which in turn made him stutter or pause for words. Rosellini recalls going home tremendously discouraged, unable to sleep. However, during a plant visit early the next morning, his spirits rose when many of the workers, while shaking his hand, told him that he should keep setting the record straight with Andrews.[46]

In the following three debates, which were also televised, Rosellini continued to pound away at Andrews's own record, his obfuscation of the consequences of his proposals, and his lack of professionalism in running his nonpartisan office. As the election neared and as Rosellini continued his theme of showing what Andrews stood for as contrasted with what he was saying, he appeared to gather statewide support. Smaller newspapers, such as the Almira *Herald*, the Renton *Town Talk*, the Columbia Basin *News*, the White Center *News*, the Burlington

Journal, and the Grant County *Journal*, expressed support for Rosellini and commented on Andrews's double-talk.[47]

The larger dailies in Seattle and Spokane were unwavering in their support of Andrews, who put his own spin on many of the issues, denying some and ignoring others. Almost Dewey-like, he continued to portray himself as above the fray and nonpolitical in his speeches and literature. In his major election-day advertisement, a full-length picture of the attractive young candidate was accompanied by a list of simple beliefs—ethical business management; a balanced budget; improving the job climate; accomplishments, not promises; and returning state government to its citizens. The opposite page featured headlines from the Seattle *Times* suggesting scandals or favoritism to friends and cronies on the part of Rosellini. In the center of the page was a box that contained the same listing of Rosellini's state senate voting record, supposedly on gambling and liquor issues, compiled by Willard Wright and used by Republicans in 1956. The advertisement asked, "Which will you choose in Tuesday's election?" The Andrews forces were confident of victory. Two days before the election, William C. Goodloe said, "Andrews will carry the state by 100,000 votes and Nixon will win by 10,000."[48]

Behind in the polls and desperate, Rosellini was not waging a campaign that was "above the fray." In a move that was patently disingenuous, he issued a press release saying that because of Andrews's alleged abuses of his office, education forces had asked Rosellini to introduce legislation at the next session that would prevent the superintendent of public instruction from seeking partisan office until at least two years following his tenure. The same press release asserted that Andrews had turned his office into a three-ring circus and that Andrews, the ringmaster, was carrying his "sucker-born-every-minute philosophy" into his race for governor.[49]

As the long campaign wound down to its final moments, Rosellini returned to the theme that his had been an administration of progress and change and that it should not be brought down by smears, innuendos, misrepresentations, and whispering campaigns. In ending his final debate with Andrews, he said: "Only a man with a name like Rosellini—born of immigrant parents—can appreciate what is meant when you elected me Governor of Washington four years ago. I suppose that name brought some of the whispering campaigns in both 1956 and again now. But people of Washington have dealt with whispering campaigns before—and I know that you will deal with them again. For this, I can only express my appreciation."[50]

As it turned out, Goodloe's predictions were only half right. Although the early returns had him trailing, Rosellini gradually pulled even by late in the evening and went ahead in the vote for the first time a little after midnight. The next morning Andrews's campaign manager conceded, although Andrews himself refused to concede, saying that he would wait for the absentees. The final tally showed Rosellini winning by 27,087 votes out of a total 1,090,053. It was scarcely a mandate, but it was a victory nonetheless. Nixon, who carried the state over Kennedy, outpolled Andrews by some 36,000 votes, while Rosellini topped Kennedy's total by some 13,000. Rosellini had recaptured just enough votes to win. While Ross Cunningham grudgingly credited Rosellini's organizational effort, he mainly blamed the defeat on the GOP's failure to pick a stronger candidate who did not have the "obvious lack of voting booth strengths of Andrews," mentioning the same group of "kingmakers" who had picked Emmett Anderson in 1956. As Cunningham concluded, "The Republican payoff came when Rosellini, who had many political weaknesses—as well as some strengths—led Kennedy and won."[51]

A fairer analysis, however, would have to pay tribute to Rosellini's ability to campaign, organize, and dramatize the weaknesses of his opponent's stand on the issues. The victory was likewise a recognition of the work he had done in important areas, such as institutions, education, and transportation. Yet it was scarcely a positive harbinger. Against a relatively weak opponent, he had trailed badly in the primary. His victory was a negative reaction to Andrews and not an affirmation of his own popularity as governor, despite the significant achievements of his administration. The years of innuendoes and press criticism, together with the natural conservative opposition to an incumbent reform governor had been overcome—but just barely.

Chapter 15

Rosellini, Evans, and the 1964 Campaign

The 1963 legislature convened at the beginning of Rosellini's seventh year as governor. Many of his major objectives had been achieved: budget reform; rehabilitation of institutions; providing for the expanding needs of education; establishing a Department of Commerce and Economic Development; the Seattle World's Fair; civil service for state employees; and constructing a second Lake Washington bridge. His administration had also persuaded the legislature to pass tax increases during both the 1959 and the 1961 sessions sufficient to erase the state's deficit for the first time in twelve years. In almost every respect Rosellini's administration had acted responsibly in meeting the rapidly changing needs of the state.

Despite these accomplishments, Rosellini was not a popular governor. To Republicans and conservatives, he was a "tax-and-spend" Democrat. Although he had delivered on his pledges to achieve major liberal reforms, the liberal groups rarely supported him publicly. The 1960 election had provided graphic proof of their lack of enthusiasm, and they did not warm to him as his second term went on. Past primary wounds, political attacks, and press allegations of cronyism and misdeeds had taken their toll. A major political battle in 1963 was the catalyst that spotlighted Rosellini's political vulnerability and brought to power the man who could take full advantage of that vulnerability in the 1964 campaign.

House Bill 197

It all began during the 1961 session with yet another dispute between private and public power and a procedural battle that centered on House Speaker John L. O'Brien. In 1955, 1957, and 1959, O'Brien had been speaker of the heavily Democratic house of representatives (which meant that he was also chair of the legislative council). During those years O'Brien was easily elected speaker, even though he was relatively liberal and his policies were not popular with a number of conservative Democrats.[1]

In the 1961 session, however, the Democratic margin in the house dropped to nine votes (a net loss of seven seats), and a coalition of forces that would control the house and the legislative council in 1963 began to emerge. During the routine preliminaries of the 1961 session, a bloc of private-power Democrats threatened to withhold its votes for O'Brien as speaker. This maneuver, led by Len Sawyer from Tacoma—who was doing legal work for Puget Sound Power and Light and covertly helping with fund-raising for legislators in PUD districts—caught O'Brien and the Democratic caucus by surprise. Four-term legislator Dan Evans, the minority leader with forty solid Republican votes, would be elected speaker if the bloc carried out its threat. Only last-minute maneuvering among the Democrats, which gave chairmanships to Sawyer and Robert Perry, a union-backed legislator with strong ties to private power, prevented this result.* Dick Kink (who, it was later discovered, was on the Puget Sound Power and Light payroll) was appointed chair of the public utilities committee. Other compromises assured private-power supporters that their bills would reach the house floor for debate. While this maneuvering gave

*Years later, Washington Water Power, its CEO, and its chief lobbyist during the 1950s and 1960s, Jerry Buckley, were indicted for allegedly paying Perry illegally via his employer, Tyee Construction Company. These indictments resulted from Perry's guilty pleas to federal charges based on violations of the state's public disclosure laws. The 1984 trial led to convictions of Buckley and Washington Water Power that were ultimately overturned on appeal.

O'Brien the speaker's chair, it also set into motion a struggle between public- and private-power forces in the house that led to O'Brien's defeat in 1963.[2]

House Bill 197 was the focus. Introduced by private-power forces on January 23, 1961, it would require all PUDs seeking to condemn and take over private-power facilities to submit the issue to the voters of the district and to reveal, as well, the acquisition price contemplated by the action. If passed, its practical effect would be to prohibit PUDs from expanding into any area already served by a private-power company. Private-power forces were confident that they had adequate votes to pass the bill in the house—as many as fifty-nine votes by some estimates.[3]

When the bill first emerged from Kink's committee, public-power forces assumed that the rules committee would hold the bill and not let it reach the house floor. However, as part of the compromise giving him the speaker's post, O'Brien had pledged to Rep. Maggie Hurley that he would allow a secret ballot in the rules committee on any public-power bill. With support from several Democrats (protected by the secret ballot), the bill passed out of the committee. It was scheduled for the second-reading calendar the next day, February 21. With no time for the supporters of public power to prepare any kind of filibuster, the private-power forces, under Evans's leadership, were confident of an easy victory by the end of the day.[4]

The February 21 session opened at 1:30 p.m. with a barrage of emotional speeches for and against the bill. Due to convoluted and diversified loyalties to the respective positions of parties and caucuses, however, the proponents could not produce fifty votes. On the other hand, the opponents could not muster fifty votes to re-refer the bill to the rules committee, where it would probably die. In what astute observers call the bitterest and most divisive legislative session ever, tempers grew more and more heated as the evening wore on. Legislators shouted down speakers and broke into small groups where bickering and even name-calling predominated. Several near shoving matches occurred. Speaker O'Brien, who said he feared that decorum would never be restored, waited until the disorder had continued for almost thirty minutes. At 10:30 p.m. he instructed majority leader

Mark Litchman to make a motion to adjourn. O'Brien called for an immediate voice vote and declared the session adjourned—breaking his gavel in the process—and quickly left the rostrum.[5]

The private-power supporters were livid, feeling that they had been cheated of eventual victory that evening. The adjournment allowed the public-power forces to reorganize and plan delaying tactics. For the next four days the house devoted its attention exclusively to HB-197. Opponents mounted a filibuster with an endless series of amendments—each of which was debated and subject to a roll call of the full membership. During the four days there were more than 45 roll-call votes—unprecedented for a single measure. Meantime, both public-power and private-power forces were pressuring fellow legislators. Senators Magnuson and Jackson both sent telegrams opposing the measure. On the fourth day, Republican Morrill Folsom from Lewis County—a PUD stronghold—switched his vote, telling the house that he had stayed with his caucus as long as possible on the assurance that a compromise could be achieved, but that it could not be done. This gave the opponents their fiftieth vote. Private-power Democrat Avery Garrett, one of the sponsors of the measure, immediately moved to re-refer HB-197 to the rules committee. His motion passed by a vote of 51 to 47, and no further attempts were made to resurrect the measure.[6]

It had been O'Brien's finest hour as speaker. Beset by pressures from all sides, he rarely left the podium for fear that the delaying tactics of the public-power forces might fail. His knowledge of parliamentary procedures and timing was prodigious. For one of the few times during his four terms as speaker, he showed zeal and all-out advocacy for a cause—a luxury a speaker cannot indulge in and survive. It is hard to know why O'Brien became so uncharacteristically involved in this issue. He may have sensed that this was to be his last term as speaker and was determined to achieve one last victory over the private-power Democrats who had nearly toppled him at the beginning of the session. O'Brien, in a later interview, said that one of the dissidents, Robert Perry, had told him that they would pass HB-197 regardless of what he might do as speaker. Perhaps it was this challenge to his authority and tenure that led to his commitment. It proved to be his undoing, since Evans later confirmed that O'Brien's actions—particularly his dictatorial use of his "power of the gavel"—strengthened Republican resolve to oust him as speaker.[7]

In retrospect, the fight over HB-197 seems senseless. Rosellini had told legislators in both houses that he would veto the bill. Democrats had a thirty-six to thirteen majority in the senate, and even though there were divided loyalties within both parties on the issue, it is clear that neither chamber could have overridden a veto. It is possible that the private-power forces and Evans chose the measure as a way to test their political muscle, and the public-power forces welcomed it as an ideological battle for much the same reason. Regardless, the fight over HB-197 and the emotional energy expended on both sides left an indelible mark on the 1961 session and its two leaders. O'Brien, despite his short-term triumph, lost his leadership base, and Evans became an acknowledged leader of the Republican party inside and outside the legislature.[8]

The 1963 Legislative Council Fight

When the 1963 legislature convened, the Republicans had gained eight more seats, for a total of forty-eight. Faced with a numerical Democratic majority and the probability that O'Brien would again be speaker, Evans and the Republicans joined forces with seven Democrats (all of whom had supported HB-197) to elect conservative Democrat William Day from Spokane as speaker. Day appointed coalition Democrats and Republicans to all key committee chairmanships. Although the Democratic caucus once again elected John O'Brien as its leader, Evans was the acknowledged leader of the coalition, and as such was the de facto "majority" leader of the house.[9]

Day and the other coalition Democrats considered Rosellini their political enemy because of his identification with O'Brien and public power, as well as his administration's progressive positions on civil rights, conservation, and institutions. Most, and particularly those from eastern Washington, had also opposed the tax increases sought to fund expanded services. Day, in particular, had purportedly promised to give Evans and the Republicans "all the investigations of Rosellini they wanted" through the legislative council in the eighteen months leading up to the 1964 campaign. By packing the council with conservative

Democrats and ignoring the "regular" Democrats, who would have neutralized the Republicans and prevented use of the council for political purposes, Day lived up to his promise.[10]

Calling the coalition an "unholy alliance," Rosellini accused the dissident Democrats of working against him and handing control of the legislative agenda to Evans in an effort to blunt his chances for a third term. Fully aware of the power of interim investigations by the council, having used them himself, Rosellini also knew how such investigations could be fashioned for partisan advantage. Rosellini's suspicions were confirmed during the 1963 session, when the council decided to investigate the financial affairs of the world's fair, contributions to Rosellini's 1960 campaign, and, possibly, the state liquor control board. Rosellini knew that all these investigations, if carried out by a council controlled by Day and Evans, would most likely end up as attempts to embarrass his administration.[11]

Although it was the 1961 fight over HB-197 that paved the way for the 1963 coalition, it soon became clear that the power grab was to be utilized for much broader purposes. For example, despite their control of the house, Day and Evans made no attempt to reintroduce the measure, which had been so narrowly defeated in 1961. It seems obvious that Evans and the Republicans decided not to waste any more political capital on the issue of public versus private power. Instead, they focused on partisan issues and investigations of Rosellini.[12]

The method the governor used to counter these activities was perhaps more questionable than the tactics of the coalition. On April 18, 1963, after the special session had adjourned, Rosellini vetoed the appropriation for all interim committees, including the legislative council. But his veto also took away the funds of the legislative budget committee, an important nonpartisan group that played a key role in the planning process for the coming biennium. While his message explaining the veto complained of deficit spending, attempts to hide the legislative council funds in a lump-sum appropriation, a plethora of legislative studies, and violation of the council's bipartisan purpose, it fooled no one. The governor's veto made it clear that he considered himself to be the target of the Day-Evans coalition. Ultimately, his action played into the hands of the Republicans. It created the kind of controversy, investigations, and political debate that severely weakened his bid for a third term—the exact result he had hoped to avoid.[13]

As in the past, Rosellini demonstrated his mastery of the political process and timed his veto so that it could not be overridden. Under the constitution at that time, only the governor could call the legislature back into session, so there was no way for legislators to force an override vote. There is little doubt that the governor considered the veto the proper way to deal with the situation.* In his view he was using legitimate governmental tools to counter a politically motivated ploy masterminded by a likely opponent in the 1964 election. What he failed to realize was that the procedural astuteness of the veto, together with its broad punitive effect, made it easier to criticize and gave credence to the coalition's counterattacks. It appeared to substantiate allegations that he was a sharp politician who had much to hide.[14]

Media reaction was overwhelmingly negative. The veto was called "shocking," a "childish act," an "overstepping of his authority . . . for political reasons," a "usurpation of the powers of the Legislature," and "a threat to the very democratic processes under which this state and nation operate." Editorials stated that Rosellini did not want aspects of his administration investigated. Evans called the veto "the most shameful political act in the last thirty years in this state," and asked, "What has the governor got to hide?" Stating that they would ask the council members to serve without pay, Day and Evans declared that the campaign expenditure probe would go ahead, even without staff for the council.[15]

A few voices, however, said the veto was proper. The Montesano *Gazette* agreed with Rosellini that the council had been unduly political and partisan, and "a sounding board for the politically ambitious." The conservative-leaning *Argus* said it was "a mere tool for the exercise of political gymnast[s] and their attempted satisfaction of a variety of partisan and political ambitions." Even the Seattle *Times* admitted that the council was accused by some of trying to conduct a witch hunt.[16]

---

*In 1995 he reiterated that he felt he had little choice and did not regret his veto (ADR, Sept. 13, 1995).

The protestations of Rosellini and his supporters concerning the actions of the council in 1963, however, applied with equal force to the situation in 1951–53, when it was Rosellini calling for investigations. Rosellini also ignored the political axiom that any administration is easily put on the defensive by calls for an investigation—a tactic that Rosellini himself had used to great advantage during the Langlie years. In fact, in 1949 Langlie had vetoed funds for the house interim committee on institutions for much the same reasons, and Rosellini and Knoblauch had made similar accusations (see p. 39). For more than a year, legal challenges to the veto by the council, efforts to force the treasurer to honor council warrants, and attempts by the council to fund its operations by other means made headlines and focused public attention on the feud and the council's desire to investigate the administration.[17]

While this maneuvering was going on, the council, over the objections of the regular Democrats, voted to investigate the operations of the state liquor control board. At the time, the council was using general-purpose funds, on a limited basis, to finance its activities. Robert Perry's subcommittee on state government set hearings for early October 1963. On the first day, liquor control board members answered general questions about the applicable statutes and whether they were being obeyed, whether the board had adopted a code of ethics, and whether it had too much power. Before the hearings could deal with any specific allegations about the administration, however, the supreme court unanimously upheld Rosellini's veto, and all funding was withdrawn, which brought the hearings to a halt.*[18]

---

*Apparently Rosellini expected the investigation to go forward—regardless of the outcome before the supreme court—since his files contain "Information Reports" from 1963 on the personal background and police records of William Day and Robert Perry (information reports, Feb. 7, 1964; March 30, 1964 [Rosellini Papers, Box 2R-3-4]). Rosellini said later that he knew nothing about the reports or why they were made. On its face there is no indication of who conducted this investigation into the lives of two men who were such thorns in Rosellini's side, but it is hard to believe that Rosellini was unaware of it at the time. The reports also contain loose, unverified information on bribe attempts, liquor theft, and other malfeasances on the part of liquor stores, clubs, and liquor board employees.

This created a new round of public charges and counter-charges. Day and Evans immediately accused Rosellini and Attorney General John O'Connell (who had instructed Treasurer Tom Martin and Budget Director Warren Bishop to reject all further council vouchers following the ruling) of conspiring to block any "further" investigation of the liquor control board and the administration. Sensing a public relations victory, Day and Evans pressed forward with other legal challenges and stated the council's intention to proceed without funding.[19]

Shortly thereafter, Sen. Mike Gallagher, seeking a declaration that the council was improperly constituted and could not proceed, filed suit. Gallagher's membership on the council and his close political ties to Rosellini simply reinforced claims that Rosellini must have something to hide. Although rather quickly dismissed by the courts, the suit strengthened the resolve of the coalition to go forward with its investigations.[20]

Six months later, in April 1964, the council was preparing to reopen the liquor board investigation. Even without funding, their staff investigator had found at least one former liquor control board employee who admitted to taking payoffs. Interestingly, while this information appears in minutes of the council and in newspaper accounts, even Perry denied that this had anything to do with Rosellini. In fact, the employee had been fired immediately as a result of the board's own internal investigation. Attacking the motivation for the hearings, all three members of the liquor control board and the board's license supervisor swore in front of a notary public that subcommittee member Sen. Al Thompson had told them that the purpose of the investigation was "not to condemn the Liquor Board" but rather to "embarrass the Democratic Party and Governor Rosellini, or words to that effect."[21]

The revived hearings, which began in June 1964, received a great deal of press coverage. Much of the testimony was vague and general, and highly inflammatory. The liquor control board was portrayed as being overpowerful and accustomed to encouraging bribes. Several witnesses accused the governor of having too much control over the board. Other allegations by Thompson, Perry, and Evans charged that the administration had handed out lucrative liquor representative contracts (on behalf of large distillers who sell to the state) and that there was a going rate of $5,000 in political payouts required to get a license to run a cocktail lounge. The *PI* called the latter charges preposterous, and even the *Times*'s Ross Cunningham admitted that the liquor representative issue was scarcely new, since every previous administration had also viewed these positions as a form of political patronage. Perry's subcommittee also subpoenaed records from the governor's office and then accused him of withholding them. Rosellini's representative at the hearing denied withholding records and cited examples of requests for records that did not exist and could not be found. Rosellini called the hearings "mumbo jumbo histrionics."[22]

Even before the June hearings began, several newspapers concurred with Rosellini's view. The *PI* accused the probers of hiding or overlooking documents which either exonerated Rosellini or implicated Republicans in years before Rosellini was governor. The same article pointed out that the probers had subpoenaed only files with Italian names and had refused to disclose a list of fifteen prominent Seattlites, presumably Republican, who were investigated for bootlegging liquor from California to avoid tax. The *Argus*'s Phil Bailey challenged the hearing's premise and pointed out that the president of one of the largest national liquor companies had said Washington State was "one of the cleanest states in the Union as far as his company was concerned." A *PI* editorial on June 2, 1964, castigated Perry and Thompson for reckless rumor-mongering. Pointing out that throughout the previous seven and one-half years the liquor board had been controlled by non-Rosellini appointees, it asked how Rosellini could have directed them to engage in any kind of chicanery. It then made a telling comment: "Liquor, here and elsewhere, has always been fair game for critics and an easy mark for those bent on taking potshots at the administration in power. Liquor, by its nature, is controversial and will always be so. There are still plenty of people who would like to see Washington State go dry."[23]

As predicted by Bailey and the *PI*, the hearings did not substantiate any of the allegations of administration impropriety, nor did they lead to any criminal charges or indictments. They did result in the board's adopting a code of ethics (something Rosellini had proposed four years earlier), strengthening compliance with laws on leasing, and providing "clearer directives to employees" on political activities and "pushing brands of liquor." By late summer of 1964, Perry and Thompson quietly ended the investigation by not scheduling further hearings.[24]

The liquor board hearings' major accomplishment, thanks to the controversy over legislative council funding, was the implication that Rosellini still practiced government by patronage and did not run a professional operation. The Republicans exploited this in the 1964 primary, and Evans used it to great effect in the final. On several occasions he alleged that Rosellini had improperly used liquor inspectors to pressure people into donating money to his 1960 campaign. This accusation made good copy as 1964 campaign fund-raising began.[25]

The 1964 Campaign

No previous Washington governor had served three consecutive terms, although Langlie had been governor for a total of twelve years. While there was no legal bar to three terms, the national prohibition against a president serving more than two terms was often seen as precedent. Several western states did not permit a governor even a second consecutive term. Consequently, some party and media observers felt that the third-term issue would deter Rosellini from running.

During 1963, Attorney General John O'Connell, Lt. Gov. John Cherberg, and Speaker William Day were discussed as possible Democratic candidates. O'Connell publicly stated that Rosellini should not seek a third term because it would damage the party. Day, perhaps in anticipation of his own candidacy, attacked Rosellini in a government forum hosted by the state Junior Chamber of Commerce in mid-January 1964: "First and foremost, we must get rid of the Rosellini administration and get rid of fiscal irresponsibility." By the end of his talk he had blamed Rosellini for almost everything wrong with the state's economy and government.[26]

Throughout 1963 and early 1964, Rosellini was undecided about running. The third-term issue was bothersome and his early polling, which concentrated mainly on the strength of possible opponents, revealed his own lack of popularity. Although the governor was encouraged by an *Argus* article in which 56 percent of its readers predicted that Rosellini would win reelection, more reliable polls showed that less than 44 percent of Democrats favored his candidacy. Indeed, by May, polls indicated that any one of the three potential Republican nominees would have defeated him.[27]

Despite these difficulties, by March 1964 Rosellini was determined to run. He believed his record of progress could overcome the daunting negatives, and his experience in 1960 reinforced that belief. He had unparalleled knowledge of the state, a well-organized political base, and support of many friends. The governor's strengths were obvious to others as well. The *Argus*'s Melvin Voorhees wrote: "No single individual knows or has known this state and its people—county by county, town by town—as does Rosellini. This results from systematic study for 20 years, constant travel, close attention to correspondence, up-to-date homework, a continuous willingness to zero in on trouble spots. . . . He is genuinely compassionate; [and] practices patience to a degree close to phenomenal." Voorhees also pointed out the Rosellini administration's remarkable record on universities, education, highways, bridges, a modern financial and budgetary system, civil service, and, most of all, institutions.[28]

On May 11, 1964, Rosellini announced his candidacy before more than twelve hundred people in the Spokane Armory, while another five thousand participated by video hookup in Seattle. Ironically, given the third-term issue, he was introduced by Franklin D. Roosevelt, Jr. As in 1960, it was an old-fashioned political banquet, and Roosevelt's remarks often harked back to the war his father had waged on poverty and the Great Depression. Rosellini stressed his administration's accomplishments and attacked what he referred to as the "gloom and doom boys" critical of him. He promised "to use facts to counter fiction and information to confound innuendo."[29]

By then, three Republican candidates had emerged: Richard G. Christianson, a Lutheran minister who had made a strong showing against Warren Magnuson in 1962; Joseph E. Gandy, Seattle businessman and president of the Seattle World's Fair; and Daniel J. Evans,

Republican leader in the state house of representatives. Because of Christianson's recent statewide campaign and his oratorical skills, he was the early favorite. The Christianson senate race against Magnuson in 1962 and his candidacy for governor in 1964 illuminated Rosellini's potentially fatal flaws. C. E. Johns accurately pointed out that Christianson's favorable showing was based on an "image of honesty and integrity" and that this image also was responsible for Langlie's reelection to a third term. Turning to Rosellini, Johns noted that critics had raised enough doubts about his personal integrity—admittedly without substantiation—that it could cause political trouble. Contrasting the two, he stated: "Whether it is right, or makes sense, that he [Christianson] is this symbol of all that is pure as opposed to [Rosellini] who at one time was the legal representative of at least some of the tavern interests, the wine merchants, and a segment of the people which favored wide open policies . . . the image is there. It is image that elects candidates to office."[30]

Yet it was not Christianson, but Evans, thanks to his leadership of the coalition in the 1963 legislature and the legislative council, who was quickly emerging as a solid candidate with an excellent grasp of the issues on which Rosellini might be vulnerable. Not only had he and Day used the council to attack Rosellini, but he and a cadre of young Republican leaders, such as Joel Pritchard and Slade Gorton, were quietly rebuilding the Republican party organization with new, progressive conservatives. Gandy, the candidate of what remained of the "Langlie machine," had entered the campaign in late January 1964, but was seen as a spoiler at best.[31]

By early summer of 1964, Evans was closing the gap with Christianson. Gandy, unable to garner financial support, was trailing badly in the polls, and on July 7 he withdrew and threw his support to Evans. Gandy's endorsement benefited Evans, particularly in eastern Washington, and gave his campaign significant momentum during the last four weeks of the primary.[32]

From the beginning, the three Republican candidates primarily attacked Rosellini. Little of the governor's record was untouched: education, economic development, ethics of fundraising, cronyism, bridges and freeways, taxes, and the prisons and parole board. Gandy, in particular, attacked Rosellini's attempt to block the liquor-control-board investigation. Evans stressed that Rosellini should be defeated on the "issues" because he (Evans) would be governor with "integrity." Astutely avoiding his own advisors' recommendation to attack Christianson, Evans emphasized what he alleged were "ethical improprieties" and government by "cronyism" on Rosellini's part. For example, he produced documents purporting to show that some state liquor board employees had sold tickets to a Rosellini campaign dinner almost four years earlier.[33]

Aside from Rosellini's own people, there were few groups who stood up for his administration. Some of the attacks, particularly by Gandy on Rosellini's Department of Economic Development, drew responses from neutral businessmen, who said Gandy, Evans, and others were "distorting the record" and "speaking from ignorance." With no opposition, Rosellini ran a primary that stressed his record and responded to the charges of the Republicans. He tirelessly visited plants and shook hands. At a Bothell cafe he said, "just call me Al . . . state employee." He attacked Evans and Christianson as mouthing "loose and damaging propaganda" about the state's economic health, and said Evans's voting record in the house belied his claim of leadership on progressive issues such as education, food for the needy, funds for community colleges, and the state's need for bridges and highways.[34]

On September 15, Evans routed Christianson by more than 100,000 votes. Wearing an Evans campaign button, Christianson conceded early in the evening. Despite a huge Democratic turnout for Scoop Jackson (who ran ahead of Lloyd Andrews by more than two to one) Evans drew 70,000 more votes than Rosellini. Evans's showing was particularly impressive as other statewide Democratic officeholders drew huge majorities. For example, John O'Connell and Bert Cole both received 65 percent of the votes cast. Many observers, as well as Evans himself, were surprised by the size of both his victory over Christianson and his margin over Rosellini. The primary showed not only that Rosellini was unpopular among Democrats, but that Evans had unified his party and built a broad base of support. Tremendously disappointed, Rosellini admitted that a heavy crossover of Democrats was responsible for Evans's strong showing. The governor noted that he had rebounded after the primary in 1960 and predicted that he would do so again. Mirroring his 1960 campaign, he challenged Evans to debate the issues, particularly Evans's legislative record.[35]

The outcome of the November election was never really in doubt. However, there were elements at work nationally that encouraged Rosellini and concerned Evans and his supporters. Lyndon Johnson's campaign against Barry Goldwater gave indications of a landslide victory for Democrats. The country's emotional response to the death of John Kennedy and the right-wing attacks while he was in office was at its zenith. If Rosellini could attract that Democratic support, he might still prevail. Rosellini quickly joined forces with the state's Johnson organization, headed by his old friend Warren Magnuson, and tried to tie Evans to Goldwater.[36]

Nothing worked. Dan Evans ran a masterful campaign and refused to let the governor take the offensive. At thirty-eight, Evans was young, knowledgeable, articulate, and attractive, with a charming wife and family. In many respects he resembled the handsome, youthful president the country had lost less than a year earlier and whose memory was reaching heroic proportions. Like Kennedy, Evans's "Blueprint for Progress" campaign theme emphasized the need for reform and challenged the state's voters to create a government based on "professionalism," not the spoils system and cronyism of the past. He appealed directly to Democrats and labor groups in advertisements and with endorsements, and said that he would work with them against what he termed "Rosellini's third party." To avoid Lloyd Andrews' major mistake, Evans refused to debate unless Rosellini agreed not to use charts (which had effectively illustrated the critical difference between what Andrews was saying and his past voting record) or notes.[37]

Evans never let up on the issues of ethics and cronyism, leveling almost daily charges. Some examples of his allegations: Rosellini pressured businessmen for contributions through the Purchasing Department; Rosellini did nothing about a negligent liquor-license holder; the Rosellini administration had placed a price-tag on political service; Rosellini obtained thousands of dollars improperly through liquor inspectors in 1960; Rosellini used the state road program for political influence; Rosellini used highway funds to favor rural areas. These charges were usually accompanied by an appeal to Democrats to help Evans end these practices. The Republican candidate would then add that "political integrity" was the cornerstone of his "Blueprint for Progress."[38]

Rosellini tried to take the offensive by alleging that Evans's voting record demonstrated that (1) he had consistently voted against money for schools and kindergartens; (2) he opposed expansion of junior colleges; (3) he voted against a youth conservation corps; (4) he had been against the state Department of Economic Development; (5) he had opposed consumer protection legislation; (6) he had refused to support a resolution condemning the John Birch Society; and (7) on numerous occasions he had voted against the interests of senior citizens and organized labor.[39]

The final few weeks deteriorated into name-calling by both candidates. While saying he would not "let the governor's brand of brawling draw us into a gutter campaign," Evans charged "deceit by the administration on freeway completion priorities" and that "Rosellini's control of liquor sales in this state is so complete he can dictate the placement of liquor advertisements." Evans also denounced Rosellini as being the "sole cause" of the coalition by which he became leader of the house. Rosellini alleged that Evans would "close the state's Veteran Homes," had actively led a fight to make liquor available "to the kids in the University District," and that his voting record as a legislator was a "briar patch of anti-education voting."[40]

The Seattle *Times* produced its own exposés of the administration —the most damaging, a piece published the week of the primary featuring blown-up facsimiles of personal checks from state liquor board employees for tickets to a Democratic picnic and Rosellini campaign dinner in 1960. Ross Cunningham criticized Rosellini's spending and said that much of his attack on Evans's voting record was "untruthful." The *Times* not only favored Evans editorially but also chose to publish an editorial that criticized Rosellini's record on economic development, saying that Rosellini had, in effect, promised "jobs for all" and "a utopia where no tax increases would ever occur" but had not delivered. The *Times*'s obvious preference for Evans was clear to several observers, including the editors of the University of

1000 county employees are a dagger at the heart of every Republican candidate." Despite such talk, throughout much of 1965, Scott Wallace, the commissioner who had saved the Evergreen Point bridge for Rosellini—much to the chagrin of Evans, Slade Gorton, and King County's Republican leadership—was seen as a strong candidate for reelection. The situation changed, however, when John Spellman, a moderate Republican who had lost a close race for mayor of Seattle in 1965, announced that he would run against Wallace.[4]

At the same time, King County Prosecutor Charles O. Carroll announced his intention to utilize a current grand jury, which had been called to investigate scandals in the assessor's office, to probe alleged irregularities in the remodeling and expansion of the King County courthouse. Throughout January, February, and March, Carroll called a string of county employees and the commissioners themselves as witnesses before his grand jury, with concomitant headlines about possible irregularities. Yet, despite the headlines, the grand jury returned only one indictment, which was immediately dismissed by the courts.[5]

Nevertheless, Carroll managed to have a report prepared by the grand jury made public. Blatantly partisan toward Carroll's viewpoint and without any legal precedent for its issuance (since the only indictment substantiating it was dismissed), the report criticized the county commissioners for negligence. Leaving nothing to chance, the foreman of the grand jury later held a press conference and stated that he was voting for Spellman because of the purported findings of irregularities.

By the time the grand jury's work was finished, Wallace was damaged goods. Carroll's maneuvering of the grand jury and his intentions toward Wallace were hardly a secret. Robert Cour of the *PI* reported that "many GOP leaders figure that Prosecutor Carroll will generate enough heat from his grand jury investigation of court house remodeling to make Wallace vulnerable." Carroll even went so far as to say publicly that "last spring's grand jury investigation of the court house remodeling project was responsible for Wallace's defeat."[6]

More important from the standpoint of county government, the probe forced the two Democratic commissioners, Wallace and Ed Munro, to admit that the commission form of government, in which they acted both as the executive and the legislative branch, was inadequate. The League of Women Voters and the Municipal League urged Wallace and Munro to set a freeholder election in the fall of 1966 (Johnny O'Brien, the Republican commissioner, was in favor). While both Wallace and Munro publicly endorsed reform, they resisted putting it on the ballot in the fall of 1966, primarily because it would be used against Wallace, who would be running at the same time. Wallace's opponent, John Spellman, on the other hand, heartily endorsed the home-rule charter proposal and made frequent headlines by criticizing Wallace for his refusal to expedite the process, while blaming him for the mess that made it necessary. When Wallace and Munro continued to say it was too soon to put a freeholder election on the ballot, the charter's supporters formed a citizens' committee to gather signatures to force a freeholder election. Even though it failed, the effort proved to be extremely damaging for Wallace. The drive remained an issue throughout his entire campaign.[7]

Wallace's refusal to put the reform matter on the 1966 ballot, as well as the allegations and aftermath of the grand jury investigation, combined to sweep Spellman into office. He defeated Wallace by 30,000 votes. Equally important, he continued to push for the modernization of the county's government and identified himself as the champion of reform. Since Spellman had been elected on the issue, he and Commissioner O'Brien immediately announced that they would put the freeholder election on the ballot in 1967 so that a new form of government could be submitted the following year. Almost overnight Spellman became not only the most powerful Republican officeholder in King County but the logical candidate to seek the executive post that the charter would create upon its adoption in 1968. In retrospect, Rosellini's close friendship with Wallace and Munro, as well as his reputation for intense partisanship, irreparably damaged his candidacy for the "reform" position of King County executive.

Lacking the luxury of hindsight, Rosellini saw only that the position was a powerful one involving more than one-third of the state's residents. In addition, the most immediate tasks confronting the new form of government would be to establish a new performance budget and accounting system, a new purchasing system, and a merit personnel system—areas in which Rosellini had proven expertise. Likewise, as chief executive of the state for eight years, he felt he had the experience necessary to guide the county effectively and efficiently. Further, he would be in a logical position to challenge Evans or any other incumbent governor, should he decide to do so.[8] It was also obvious that Spellman would easily defeat the nonpartisan candidates who were filing. Rosellini and other political professionals felt that only a well-known figure with experience could mount a credible challenge.

Rosellini was upset with Spellman over the abusive campaign the Republicans—mainly Carroll and Spellman—had waged against Scott Wallace in 1966. Rosellini was quoted as saying that Spellman had gone "to excessive lengths to destroy the reputation of former commissioner Scott Wallace, one of the finest young men ever to serve this country."[9] He was determined to deny Spellman a free ride into office. He also believed that, if elected, he could do the job much better than Spellman or any of the other candidates.

Recognizing that he needed to present a united front and to gain the support of the liberal wing of his party, Rosellini selected David G. Wood, a liberal with strong ties to the McCarthy-Kennedy peace faction, as his campaign manager. Running as a "proven executive," Rosellini stressed his experience as governor and his successes in solving the kinds of problems facing the county. For his part, Spellman campaigned as a new, progressive leader without ties to the parties of the past. He stated that the new position required nonpartisan intergovernmental cooperation. While Rosellini tried to tie Spellman to various irregularities with overruns in the courthouse remodeling project and sweetheart leases at Boeing Field, Spellman was adeptly referring to Rosellini's past and the unfavorable innuendoes that had surrounded his administration. One of his finance letters said, "King County can't be turned over to Al and his friends."[10]

The election result was determined, however, by factors other than the specific nature of the two campaigns and the qualities of the candidates. The first was the fact that the modernization movement in King County was a popular one. Most Democrats supported the reforms adopted by the freeholders. The 1966 King County Democratic convention had endorsed charter reform almost unanimously. Many Democrats, the author among them, viewed Rosellini as a

step back into the past, while they equated Spellman with reform.*
Consequently, Rosellini was never able to develop partisan enthusiasm
for his candidacy. Once again, despite the efforts of Wood, Rosellini
failed to secure the support of the liberals within his own party. Rightly
or wrongly, he was seen as a politician who operated under the old rules
and the patronage approach of an earlier era. The fact that it was not
true—given Rosellini's record of support for civil service at the state
level, as well as the positions he espoused during his campaign—was
beside the point.

Second, because it was the only election on the ballot in an off
year and one involving a new office for which no one had previously
voted, the voter turnout in the primary indicated that any Democrat—
especially a partisan one such as Rosellini—was in trouble. The heavily
Republican precincts had a 60 to 70 percent turnout, whereas only
10 to 15 percent voted in the traditionally Democratic precincts.
Further exacerbating Rosellini's problems was the fact that it was
these Republican precincts which had most heavily supported the
new charter movement. Even worse was the apparent voter apathy
about the race. A poll taken two weeks after the primary showed that
more than 55 percent of the voters were unsure as to whether they
had even voted in the primary.[11] Even an energetic voter turnout
drive could not stem the tide, and Spellman rolled to an easy and
overwhelming victory in the final. Once again Rosellini had been
rejected by the voters.

The Governor's Race, 1972

In June of 1972, only three weeks before filings opened, Rosellini
decided to oppose Dan Evans's bid for a third term as governor. This
caught almost everyone, including most of his closest friends and
longtime supporters, totally by surprise. Since Rosellini's defeat by
Spellman in 1969, leadership of the state Democratic party had passed,
in the main, to State Sen. Martin Durkan. Durkan, from Renton, had
been chair of the powerful Ways and Means Committee for seven years,

*The author was co-chair of the committee to modernize county government.

and was believed by most pundits and insiders to be the clear choice to oppose Evans. Utilizing his position in the senate effectively, Durkan had succeeded in developing broad backing by conservative business groups—particularly in the private-power and real-estate sectors—as well as from most of the party that was not dedicated to the peace movement and Vietnam war protests. Durkan was widely seen as the quintessential legislator and power-broker.[12]

As for Rosellini, his defeat by Spellman in 1969 had been seen by most political professionals and reporters as the end of his career in public office. In the months leading up to the 1972 election, no Democrats even gave Rosellini consideration, and he made no effort to generate support. The other Democratic candidate who was seriously considering the race was State Sen. James McDermott. While he was the liberal alternative to Durkan, he was not considered to be a realistic threat to either Durkan or Evans.[13]

Rosellini, when questioned in early 1996, was not able to explain fully why he entered the contest. The late declaration, totally out of character, illustrates that it was not something he had been planning for any time. He says he was frustrated at what he perceived to be the alarming growth of state government managers at the expense of programs and the continued deterioration of his beloved institutions. For example, he points to the fact that when he left office in January 1965 he had a staff of nine people in his office, with a monthly payroll of $7,765. Eight years later Evans had twenty-one people on staff, with a monthly payroll in excess of $21,000. (Rosellini comments that this trend never seems to stop. By 1981 Governor Spellman began his term with a staff of thirty-two—including a chief of staff, a deputy chief of staff, and a special counselor—whose payroll exceeded $56,000 per month. This at the same time that Spellman was requesting a 10.1 percent cut in state spending.) Rosellini was also troubled by the burgeoning staffs of the legislature at every level, as well as the explosive growth of middle managers in most areas of government. The creation of the Department of Social and Human Services on January 1, 1971, and the abolition of the Department of Institutions as a separate entity was a step he bitterly resented as well. Rosellini believed that Durkan was as responsible as Evans for these changes—

since the legislation and tax increases to accomplish them had been partnered to a large degree by the Durkan-controlled state senate. In his terms as governor, Rosellini had always tied tax increases to specific increases in services, and not to the growth of government itself.[14]

But there was more than just Rosellini's feelings about institutions and growth of government that led to his decision to file. By late 1971, several major newspapers had pointed out that Rosellini's approach to government and taxes was not being followed by his successor. The *Times*, in an article published long before Rosellini was considered a possible candidate, ran a comparison of state treasury expenditures under Rosellini and Evans. The *Times* concluded that general government expenditures had risen 464 percent in 1965–73, as compared with an increase of about 14 percent under Rosellini. In fact, it pointed out that general government expenditures had actually declined in Rosellini's second term. During the next eight years under Evans, by the calculation of the *Times* and others, such as the Association of Washington Business, property taxes had increased by more than 266 percent, sales and use taxes by more than 50 percent, license fees by 33 percent, tobacco and alcohol taxes by more than 50 percent, while the number of state-government employees had increased more than 50 percent. Despite the growth in various taxes, for more than twenty-two consecutive months the state had operated in a deficit position. Ross Cunningham, an ardent Evans supporter, had concluded in 1967 that Evans's taxing and spending policies made all former governors (including Rosellini) look like "pikers." This was prior to Evans second term bid and matters had not improved, in the *Times* view, by 1972.[15]

Evans as a two-term governor had generated his own set of alleged irregularities and scandals, and the headlines surrounding them undoubtedly contributed to Rosellini's feelings that the governor was vulnerable. Even Rosellini's enemies must have chuckled over the fact that—despite the endless allegations of illegal liquor ties involving Rosellini—it was Evans's three appointees to the liquor board who were indicted in 1971 by a Republican County Prosecutor (the indictments were ultimately dismissed in June 1971 for lack of jurisdiction and because of the board's partial immunity from prosecution). Other headlines trumpeted, over the years, Evans's tax vetoes to help Boeing, his recommending removal of a property-tax lid, his raising sales taxes while cutting teachers' salaries, his forecast and endorsement of the need for a state income tax, his failures to complete highway projects, and on and on.[16]

According to Rosellini, however, other factors ultimately led him to enter the race at the last minute. While he may have been eager in some sense to show Evans that an incumbent governor can be easily put on the defensive, it was conversations with several reporters and political allies that convinced Rosellini that Durkan simply could not win against Evans. In May 1972, after a long conversation with the editorial staff of the *Daily Olympian*, in which tax issues and the decline of institutions were discussed, he became determined to run and began discussions with close friends and former supporters. Some of them, such as Bill Gissberg and Luke Graham, frankly told him he was too late and had no chance of beating Durkan in the primary. Scott Wallace and others, however, encouraged him, and he quickly began to put together an organization and plan his campaign.[17]

From the outset Rosellini focused on two key issues: the growth in taxes and government, and the almost complete reversal in the conditions of institutions. In his statements and literature, Rosellini tied Durkan and Evans together as the architects of an unprecedented spending binge and the creation of bigger and bigger state government—to the detriment of the services he had advocated for years. In the June 19, 1972, press release announcing his candidacy, he said that the other candidates are all part of the "Olympia Scene" that had created the problems. He vowed to abolish the State Department of Social and Health Services, eliminate more than $100 million from the state's budget, and restore the state's mental hospitals and prisons to the high standards that had prevailed when he left office. Realizing that he could not match campaign funds, he asked for volunteers and small donations of one to five dollars. Finally, he pointed out that although the number of state-government employees had doubled, the state's property taxes had risen by almost 100 percent, and the state budget was 137.8 percent higher than when he left office, the state itself was in the grips of its worst economic recession in more than twenty years.

Clearly he was using against Evans exactly the same kinds of material that had been used against him just eight years earlier.[18]

Rosellini's primary literature ignored McDermott and always tied Evans and Durkan together as the two men responsible for the current state of affairs. His campaign against Durkan was hard-hitting and one which Durkan later described as vicious and unfair. The most damaging element, according to most observers, was a series of advertisements that highlighted "The Two Faces of Martin Durkan," comparing Durkan's actions in the legislature with his posture as a candidate on issues such as property taxes, tax benefits for businesses, ties to real estate and liquor, and accusations that special interests controlled his votes. One advertisement highlighted Durkan's call to close Northern State Hospital at a time when facilities were already overcrowded. Rosellini admitted later that the ads were very tough and said that at one point he almost decided against running them. But his people insisted that they were factually accurate, and he decided to use them.[19]

Rosellini's message of bloated government spending and runaway bureaucracy, and his own ideas about saving money for the state, quickly took hold. He criss-crossed the state preaching a balanced state budget, limitation of state employment, and better management of state agencies. He also said that increased efficiency at the state level could return more money to schools and thus reduce property taxes at the local level. He attacked the notion of a state income tax as unnecessary, given the other tax increases already levied over the past eight years. By late August he had begun to lead Durkan in the polls, and after a strong editorial supporting his candidacy appeared in the *Daily Olympian* on August 29, he assumed a commanding lead. The newspaper's endorsement commented on the major candidates and their positions. It was strongly critical of both Evans and Durkan, charging that they were calling for more and more taxes because they were unwilling to rein in government. While the editorial writers concluded that inflation, increased demands for services, and the need to meet federal matching programs had played a part, they noted a tendency in the executive and legislative branches to expand without good reason. The *Olympian* concluded its endorsement by saying:

"Rosellini is the one major candidate who has recognized where the most urgent state problem lies and has brought forth a plan to solve it. He has the know-how and will to carry out that plan."[20]

Despite being outspent by more than $50,000, Rosellini easily defeated Durkan in the primary. He outpolled Durkan by 60,000 votes and Evans by more than 50,000 votes. The *Times* and Ross Cunningham, now more muted in their treatment of Rosellini and more critical of Evans's policies, reported on the concern and anxiety felt by the Evans forces. Dick Larsen analyzed key precincts and discovered that minorities, the elderly, blue-collar workers, and education forces were solidly behind Rosellini. Highlighting Evans's concern, Larsen also reported that the governor had called on Durkan to ask his support. Prior to the primary, the word was out that Evans's people felt that Rosellini would be the easiest candidate to defeat. Now that no longer seemed to be true. The *Argus* commented that Evans was in for a very tough race and was behind in the polls, primarily because of two issues—taxes and institutions—and that Rosellini had strong positions on both.[21] Through late September and most of October, Rosellini's campaign against Evans's third-term bid gained momentum and support. Evans replayed his 1964 allegations of cronyism, mismanagement in government, and questionable ties to liquor interests, but it was clear that these efforts were falling short. Evans also charged that Rosellini failed to report his income properly and reveal who his real campaign contributors were—again implying, as in 1964, that unseemly forces were behind Rosellini. To counter these charges, Rosellini used hard-hitting advertisements targeting weak spots in the Evans administration. This time around it was Evans who had scandals to explain, as news stories accused him of cronyism, back-door spending for friends, and a mini-purchasing scandal—all this in addition to indictments of his three liquor board members by a grand jury controlled by a Republican. Equally effective was the fact that at every opportunity Rosellini pointed out that just eight years earlier Evans had said that no governor should serve three consecutive terms, that he would oppose sales tax increases, and that he would never support an income tax. Rosellini usually ended these talks with the comment that, "Today the story is different. Evans can no longer rely on promises or his "Blueprint for Progress." . . . Now he is a known quality and cannot hide."[22]

Finally, Rosellini was assisted by the bitter conservative-liberal split within Evans's own party. State Sen. Perry Woodall, the ranking Republican senator, opposed Evans in the primary. He campaigned vigorously against Evans's taxing and spending policies. Many of his statements about Evans were highly quotable. One that Rosellini found particularly useful was the following: "After serving in the State House and Senate under five Governors, I know Dan Evans to be the most inefficient, spendthrift, tax hungry Governor to ever hold the office."[23]

By mid-October 1972, Rosellini was leading in the polls by thirteen percentage points, and his momentum seemed to be upward. However, two events disrupted this momentum and effectively ended Rosellini's bid to return to the governor's mansion.

The first event was a slip of the tongue during an impromptu debate with Evans on October 17. Rosellini was upset that the debate was even occurring. Leading in the polls, he had decided to refuse to debate Evans. Evans was correspondingly anxious to debate because he was trailing. When Rosellini refused, Evans showed up—with a full camera crew in tow—during a speech by Rosellini at Seattle Community College and challenged him to debate. Although totally unprepared, Rosellini believed that it would look worse if he appeared afraid to debate, and so he agreed. Responding to Evans's pointed assertions of cronyism, an irritated Rosellini lashed out. In the heat of the moment, he referred to Evans as "Danny Boy." In fact, he did so at least twice. The demeaning term, he realized, was a mistake, and his advisors pointed out that it could be interpreted as a lack of respect for the governor's office. Naturally, the newspaper stories played up his use of the derogatory nickname. The Seattle *Times* and Ross Cunningham opined that the "Danny Boy taunt may backfire."[24] Once again his discomfort with public speaking in a formal setting and his quick temper had betrayed him. Still, since it was not a scheduled debate, it is doubtful that many people saw the actual film footage. Even though he regretted the incident, Rosellini did not feel it had irreparably damaged his campaign or his chances of defeating Evans.

However, that mistake of judgment paled into insignificance when compared with the second event, which occurred four days later, just two weeks before the election. The *PI*, with a front-page banner headline, published a sensational article by Lou Guzzo that tried to link Rosellini to a notorious local gambling and racketeering figure, Frank Colacurcio.[25] Guzzo's article, printed without giving Rosellini any opportunity to respond, detailed a telephone call Rosellini had made on behalf of a relative of Colacurcio in 1968, when Rosellini was no longer governor, regarding a club license transfer in Hawaii. The article also recounted Rosellini's legal representation, in the distant past, of a Seattle bingo and club operator "purportedly" tied to Colacurcio. Hawaiian authorities had found nothing improper about Rosellini's contact in Hawaii, and Rosellini had readily acknowledged that in the 1940s, as a young lawyer and former prosecutor, he had represented the then-teenaged Frank Colacurcio on a charge of statutory rape. The Colacurcio family were longtime friends of the Rosellinis.

Rosellini felt that Guzzo's article was another example of "Wop-baiting" and baseless innuendo. Other press accounts confirm that Rosellini did nothing wrong and label the Guzzo story as a "cheap shot" designed to play on the worst of public prejudices and fears. Nothing in the story supports any inference of improper or illegal conduct. Guzzo, years later, could not add any substance to his allegations, but he unreservedly stated his personal animosity toward Rosellini and his pride in the fact that his story "finally got Rosellini out of politics once and for all." Called a "baseless smear" by KING TV, the story was deliberately planted by Keith Dysart,* a deputy to Attorney General Slade Gorton, with the full knowledge of high operatives in the Evans campaign. At the same time, supporters of Gorton and Evans distributed "We Don't Need a Godfather" bumper stickers. This occurred at the height of the popularity of the "Godfather" movies, which depicted in graphic detail the corruption and violence of the Mafia in America. The inferences sought to be drawn from Rosellini's

*Always a marginal political hanger-on with Gorton and the Republicans, Dysart eventually resigned after being placed on leave with pay because of the incident and his actions.

Italian background were obvious. (In typical fashion, Evans's managers apologized for the bumper stickers two days before the election.) Even Sen. Henry M. Jackson, who had traditionally distanced himself from Rosellini, was outraged by the tactics of Evans and Gorton and spoke out against them.[26]

Just three days later the polls showed that Rosellini had dropped more than 13 percentage points and that Evans and he were in a dead heat. Even though Rosellini launched a last-minute media blitz seeking to refute the inferences of the Guzzo article, borrowing money to do so, he continued to slide in the polls. In the general election, held two weeks after the appearance of the sensational article, Evans defeated Rosellini by approximately 50,000 votes. It is of course difficult to say that the article was the sole cause of Rosellini's defeat. As in 1952, Rosellini's hard-hitting tactics against Durkan left behind a Democratic opponent who may have worked with his opponent in the general election. As in 1964, most of the major newspapers endorsed Evans, with some significant exceptions, such as the *Daily Olympian*. On balance, however, one can only conclude that the Guzzo smear destroyed any chance Rosellini had to win the race. Almost every political observer, when asked, concurs that Rosellini was winning until the article appeared, and that without it Evans most likely would have been defeated.[27]

Chapter 17

Epilogue and Conclusion

Public Life, 1972–96

Although Rosellini remained politically active, the 1972 campaign was to be his last. Rosellini said that the loss—given the circumstances—was painful and difficult to accept. It convinced him he should not seek public office again. However, his service to his state was not ended. In 1979, at the urging of Julia Butler Hansen and a number of others knowledgeable about transportation needs, Gov. Dixy Lee Ray appointed Rosellini to a six-year term on the State Highway Commission—later to become known as the Washington State Transportation Commission. Gov. Booth Gardner reappointed him for a second term in 1985, and he served as the commission's chair from 1990 to 1992. According to Duane Berentson, a Spellman appointee who served as secretary of the commission for many years, Rosellini always advocated a balanced and forward-looking transportation policy that followed the advice of the experts and would insure the future development of the state.[1]

In 1992 Rosellini was appointed to a six-year term as a director of the Washington Trade and Convention Center by Governor Gardner. In a private capacity, Rosellini has also continued to serve his state with his usual vigor. In 1969 he agreed to serve as chair of the state's United States Olympic Committee, a position he still holds. During his stewardship the committee has raised more than $2 million to maintain Olympic training centers and provide financial support for Olympic athletes from Washington state.

As this is written, Rosellini is eighty-six years old and is in his office at least five days a week, maintaining a schedule that would tax a person twenty-five years his junior. He rarely takes a vacation. When asked why he doesn't take it easy, he says, "I can't stand to be still." As nearly as one can tell, he has never been still for long. Even after his disappointing loss in 1972, his advice and support were sought by candidates and political hopefuls. In particular, he was a confidant to Booth Gardner as he began to consider running for governor. He remained a close advisor and member of Gardner's kitchen cabinet during his two terms. Rosellini was an early mentor to Sen. Patty Murray and encouraged her bid to become Washington's first woman United States senator. He is still among her closest advisors on sensitive political issues. He was also a strong supporter of Christine Gregoire in her successful race for Attorney General.

Conclusion

Albert Rosellini brought significant strengths to the governor's office. He had an empathy which enabled him to listen to people and care about their concerns. If he could not move crowds by his oratory, he could reach out and touch tremendous numbers by his personality and passionate devotion to improving their lives.

He was healthy, energetic, smart, personable, and hard-working. His humility enabled him to choose excellent advisors, listen to them, and support them in the actions of government. He was quick to note ideas of others, such as Averill Harriman, and meld them into his own vision for his state. He had a remarkable insight into the legislative process and its use to achieve his objectives. His work habits and tenacity enabled him to focus on specific goals, such as juvenile justice reform, the establishment of the University of Washington medical and dental schools, and improvement of institutions. His dedication to public education, which was driven by his personal experiences, never waned. Finally, and perhaps most important, he loved what he did in state government and enjoyed going to work every day. He never pretended to be "bigger than the job" or "above politics," nor did he see his role as governor as a stepping stone to federal office or a judicial appointment. State government was his specialty and his passion.

Most of all, however, Albert Rosellini is a man of action—a quality that is reflected in only a partial listing of his administration's accomplishments:

1. Rosellini's budget reform and executive leadership transformed the governor's office into the central policy-making apparatus of state government. By giving the governor the responsibility for budgeting and planning, Rosellini, reinforced by his successor, created a state government in which the governor—not the legislature, independent commissions, or other offices—generated all major policy initiatives.

2. The Rosellini administration's program of institutional rehabilitation and reform was and is without equal in the state's history. Whether it was a deep-seated empathy that sprang from memories of his own father's incarceration or simply a concern for the less fortunate, he demonstrated a steadfast devotion to this cause.

3. In the area of higher education, Rosellini brought funding equity to the state's colleges, nourished its two universities, and established a sound, expanded community-college system. Dr. Charles Odegaard, who served as president of the University of Washington under four governors, called Rosellini, without qualification, "the best governor the state has ever had."[2]

4. Rosellini's record in transportation was one of decision and leadership. He was committed to building highways and bridges where the experts said they should be located, understanding that this was necessary for the development of the state's economy. Given the impetus provided by the federal interstate highway funding programs, any governor would have been forced to provide some leadership in this area. But Rosellini's record, time and again, demonstrated his commitment to making things happen—not simply being controlled by events. The Hood Canal Bridge saga and his unsuccessful initiative to build a cross-sound bridge are examples of his determination to lead, not follow, regardless of political consequences. It is hard to imagine the impact on the Puget Sound region if the second Lake Washington bridge had been completed in the late 1970s or mid-1980s, rather

than in 1963. Rosellini's decision to act in the face of vituperative opposition was tremendously important for the state and the region.

5. Rosellini believed that state government had an obligation to work with the private sector to encourage economic development. In order to fulfill this obligation, he created a new department and recruited a highly qualified professional to define its mission and purpose. The complex of activities that led up to the Seattle World's Fair coincided fortuitously with the early development of the new department, and both the fair and the department were beneficiaries. Today the state of Washington has formal trade offices in Japan and China, and exports more goods per capita than any other state.

Any governor in 1957 would no doubt have been forced to address many of the issues listed above, simply because of the pressure of growth. Washington State, however, was fortunate that its governor was Albert Rosellini—a man whose ambition had driven him to become a master of government, whose origins had created a dedication to using government to improve social conditions, and whose relentless drive refused to admit that problems could not be solved. Ironically, it was a Seattle *Times* editorial columnist, Don Hannula, who paid Rosellini the ultimate accolade. Pointing out that he had covered politics for four decades (spanning the administrations of Rosellini, Evans, Ray, Spellman, and Gardner) Hannula states: "I'm . . . often asked to name the best governor. My answer is: Al Rosellini. He was not a man of empty rhetoric. He got things done. His legacy is everywhere."[3]

A fair assessment of a governor's administration must also address areas where he failed to accomplish stated objectives or provide political leadership. The checks and balances of the two-party system, as well as the leavening effect of special-interest groups, automatically modify a governor's legislative and political agenda. Rosellini's broad approach to the problems of state government left many of his stated objectives unfulfilled. Executive leadership in state government is a continuum where initiatives begun at one point in time often take years to evolve successfully. Rosellini, an action-oriented governor, was never content with the status quo, and he was destined to leave a laundry list of such matters.

Rosellini's critical weakness as a governor was his inability to inspire by example and to articulate his philosophy of government. Many of the strengths which made him successful as a politician also worked to undermine his political leadership: (1) his immigrant, blue-collar ambition; (2) his innate sense of the value of publicity and willingness to exploit it; (3) his combative and partisan political style; (4) his moral neutrality toward controversial political issues, such as liquor and gambling; (5) his willingness to confront middle-class mores and the conservative establishment; (6) his unwillingness to keep his law practice separate from his political life; (7) his grass-roots fund-raising and organization; and (8) his reliance on family and close friends for political advice.

Rosellini enjoyed a political fight. The insecurities of his immigrant upbringing, his combative instincts, and his uncertain grasp of the niceties of spoken English made him prone to sensationalism and inflammatory excesses in political debates. Nor was he particularly sensitive to the nuances and protocol of fund-raising. He was equally blunt about seeking office. There was no pretense, coyness, or guile; once the decision was made, you did not want to get in his way. He lacked the cultural background necessary to develop a broad intellectual and political vision of his own, although he quickly assimilated the ideas of others and often improved on them.

These traits, together with the social prejudices toward an Italian-Catholic politician, resulted in an administration constantly embroiled in controversy, rumor, and suspicion. The establishment press and media—particularly the Seattle *Times* and Ross Cunningham—never trusted Rosellini. This bias was confirmed repeatedly. Melvin Voorhees of the *Argus*, in late 1959, wrote: "Most of the press of the state has displayed a studied, persistent hostility to the Rosellini Administration since it took office almost three years ago." In the same article Voorhees went on to observe, "it is equally evident that most newspaper owners and publishers and many editors are unfriendly to him. When it comes to defining the 'why' of this, they seem to find meaningful articulation difficult."[4] This combination of factors meant that Rosellini was not popular with the public at large or with the voters who did not consider themselves members of any particular party. It also led, at critical times, to a lack of enthusiasm among segments of his own party. Thus, as a political leader, he was unable to cross party and philosophical lines, which made a number of his goals and objectives even more difficult to achieve.

Rosellini's position on tax increases was often ambivalent and confusing. Always concerned about the voters' negative reactions, he was rarely forthright with the public about the need to increase taxes, preferring to deal with the issue candidly in the legislative process. His consistent opposition to new taxes during election campaigns was countered by the tax increases that he knew were necessary for progress and which he demanded in 1959, 1961, and 1963. His political opponents naturally accused him of being two-faced and reneging on no-new-tax pledges.

In retrospect, Rosellini's shortcomings were not so much political as they were personal. Despite hard work and ceaseless devotion to the office, he never achieved the popularity and respect as governor that he believed would be the ultimate tribute to his father and his family. His personal and cultural background made it difficult to adapt to the evolution in political style which rendered government by party patronage outmoded even though he consistently advocated and helped bring about a civil service system for all state employees. He was only forty-seven when he became governor. Yet by that time Rosellini had already served almost twenty years as a liberal, New Deal politician. In order to be elected governor, he had devoted himself to gaining acceptance within his party—as it was, and not as the progressives wanted it to be. Rosellini was elected because the voters wanted changes in state government and its delivery of services. Having overcome seemingly impossible odds, he was not going to alter the political style that had made him successful.

As this book is written, Rosellini is still unfailingly generous to those who seek him out—regardless of the reason. His desk is covered with literature for candidates for city council, superior court judge, county council, and school boards. He is besieged with calls from friends, old political foes, and former associates seeking advice on a myriad of problems concerning government. No question is ever too small or unimportant. He has never lost his friendly warmth or his "golden touch with people" from all walks of life. Equally important, he has never lost his concern for the ways that state government affects the lives of those around him and his desire to help make it work the way it should.

Chronology: Albert D. Rosellini

January 21, 1910: Born, Tacoma, Washington

June 1927: Graduated from Stadium High School, Tacoma

June 1933: Graduated from the University of Washington (joint BA/Law degree)

Fall 1933: Passed Washington State Bar Exam

September 1934: Candidate, Washington State Senate primary, 33rd Legislative District

January 1935: Appointed deputy prosecuting attorney by Warren G. Magnuson

June 1, 1937: Married Ethel McNeil at Our Lady of Mt. Virgin Church, Seattle

November 1938: Elected to State Senate from 33rd Legislative District

January 1941: Elected Senate Majority Leader for the first time

January–March 1945: Introduced and helped pass bill establishing University of Washington Medical/Dental schools

1941: Appointed to Board of Trustees, Harborview and Georgetown hospitals. Served until 1946 (chair 1942–46)

February–June 1949: Chair of Senate-House joint committee to study juvenile confinement facilities

June 1949–December 1950: Chair of subcommittee of legislative council's state and local government committee to study juvenile justice system

1951 session: Introduced and helped pass bill to create University of Washington Hospital

June 1951–June 1952: Chair of legislative council state and local government subcommittee to study organized crime

June 1951–December 1952: Chair of legislative council state and local government subcommittee to study government reorganization— the "Little Hoover" Committee

September 1952: Candidate for Democratic nomination for Governor

November 1956: Elected Governor. Took office on January 16, 1957

November 1960: Re-elected Governor

November 1964: Lost 3rd term bid to Daniel J. Evans

February 11, 1969: Won Democratic nomination for King County Executive

March 11, 1969: Lost general election for King County Executive to John Spellman

September 1972: Won Democratic nomination for Governor

November 1972: Lost general election for Governor to Dan Evans

June 1979– : Chair, Washington State Olympic Committee

July 1979–July 1991: Member, Washington State Transportation Commission (chair 1990–91)

1993– : Director, Washington Convention Center

1994– : Member, King County Kingdome Advisory Committee

A Note on Sources

A brief explanation of sources and citations in the notes is necessary. As indicated in the Acknowledgments, a number of books and articles were extremely helpful to my research and writing. I have tried to give proper citations in the notes to these works so that the interested reader can pursue the areas discussed. In chapters 5 and 7, in particular, I have used the same references and abbreviations to the Langlie Papers as were used by George Scott in his detailed study of Governor Langlie and upon which I relied. The Langlie papers at the University of Washington (at lease at the time of Scott's thesis) were designated by a capital "L" followed by numbers indicating the box and folder number. These papers are still maintained at the University's Library. Langlie's official papers in the State Governors' Collection at the Washington State Archives were kept as part of the Archives Record Group and designated as "WSAARG" and then numbered. These have now been reorganized and renumbered to give a more accurate inventory. The Langlie papers are now designated within the Archives as "Record Group—Langlie" and then given a box number. While I made no reference to them, Governor's Langlie's son, Arthur S. Langlie, has a private collection utilized by Mr. Scott.

The Archives also carried the files of all departmental directors, such H. D. VanEaton, under the same type of prefix—"Institutions Directors files." At times, however, the sources reference such files by the name of the director. I have tried to accurately cite these sources but realize there may be some confusion inherent in the process.

Unless otherwise noted, all references to Rosellini papers are in the Washington State Archives under the box number cited as, for example, Rosellini Papers, Box 2R-1–13. Additionally, I had access to Warren Bishop's collection of papers which had just been turned over to the Archives. I have referred to these as Bishop Papers without a box number since they had not yet been organized into that format.

Notes

Introduction

1. David L. Nicandri, *Italians in Washington State: Emigration, 1853–1924* (Tacoma: Washington State American Revolutionary Bicentennial Commission, 1978), pp. 17–23; Eric Scigliano, "Italian Seattle: Good-by, Garlic Gulch," *The Weekly* (Seattle), Apr. 29-May 5, 1987, p. 30.

2. Nicandri, *Italians in Washington State*, pp. 17–23.

3. *Ibid.*, p. 54.

4. *Ibid.*, p. 47.

5. *Ibid.*, p. 21.

6. Nellie Virginia Roe, "The Italian Immigrant in Seattle" (MA thesis, University of Washington, 1915), pp. 5, 43, 47.

7. Nicandri, *Italians in Washington State*, pp. 37–39.

8. Scigliano, "Italian Seattle," p. 24; interview, Gerald A. Hoeck, May 12, 1994.

9. Interview, Hoeck; interview, Dan Evans, Sept. 23, 1991.

10. Angelo Pellegrini, *Immigrant's Return* (New York: Knopf, 1951).

11. Nicandri, *Italians in Washington State, passim.*

12. Interviews, Ed Guthman, July 18, 1994; Louis Guzzo, Nov. 25, 1995; Shelby Scates, Dec. 13, 1995; Guzzo, quoted in Scigliano, "Italian Seattle," p. 35.

13. Interview, Hoeck.

Chapter 1. The Early Years

1. The information on the Rosellini family is largely based on extensive interviews with Albert Rosellini from 1990 through 1995. Where other informants or sources have been used, references are included in the notes.

2. Interview, Ida Bachechi, Nov. 28, 1992.

3. Interview, Victor Rosellini, June 21, 1991.

4. *Ibid.*

5. Interview, Ida Bachechi; interview, Victor Rosellini.

6. Seattle *Post-Intelligencer* (*PI*), Nov. 7, 1932.

7. Laws 1935, Chapter 18, sections 1–14 (see RRS, section 9871–1, Revised Code of Washington 88.16.010–040).

8. Seattle *Times* (*Times*), Aug. 13, 1933; Tacoma *News Tribune* (*Tribune*), Aug. 14, 1933.

9. *PI*, Apr. 14, 1934; Seattle *Star*, Apr. 17, 1934; interview, Ethel Rosellini, June 19, 1991.

10. *Times*, Sept. 1, 1934.

11. *Ibid.*

12. For an excellent treatise on Pro-

hibition in Washington State and its aftermath, see Norman H. Clark, *The Dry Years: Prohibition and Social Change in Washington* (Seattle: University of Washington Press, 1965). This brief background is based on information from Clark's book.

13. *Ibid.*, pp. 164, 159–60.

14. *Ibid.*, p. 58.

15. *Ibid.*, pp. 239, 240.

16. *Times*, Sept. 1, 1934.

17. Undated and unidentified newspaper clipping, but *ca.* Sept. 2, 1934.

18. Clark, *The Dry Years*, pp. 240–41.

Chapter 2. The State Senate

1. Interview, Albert D. Rosellini (ADR), Oct. 12, 1990.

2. *Ibid.*

3. *Ibid.*

4. *Ibid.*; ADR, Dec. 27, 1990; *PI*, July 11, 1934.

5. ADR, Sept. 21, Dec. 27, 1990.

6. *PI*, Jan. 9, 1937; Seattle *Star* (*Star*), Dec. 28, 1935.

7. ADR, Sept. 21, Dec. 27, 1990.

8. ADR, Sept. 21, Dec. 27, 1990.

9. ADR, Sept. 21, Dec. 27, 1990.

10. ADR, Sept. 21, Dec. 27, 1990; 1939 Senate Journal.

11. ADR, Sept. 21, Dec. 27, 1990.

12. ADR, Sept. 21, Dec. 27, 1990; Ken Billington, *People, Politics and Public Power* (Seattle: Washington Public Utility Districts' Association, 1988), pp. 4–11.

13. Billington, *People, Politics and Public Power*, pp. 9–15; *PI*, Feb. 19, 1941.

14. ADR, Sept. 21, Dec. 27, 1990.

15. ADR, Sept. 21, Dec. 27, 1990.

16. ADR, Sept. 21, Dec. 27, 1990; *PI*, July 28, 1940; Revised Code of Washing-

ton 19.89.010, 19.90.010, Laws 1935, ch. 177, sec. 3; Laws 1937, ch. 176, section 2, RRC 5854–3-22; repealed by Laws 1975, ch. 59, section 1 et seq.

17. ADR, Sept. 21, Dec. 27, 1990; *PI*, July 16, 1942.

18. ADR, Oct. 12, 1990.

19. *Ibid.*; *PI*, Jan. 14, 1941.

20. *PI*, Jan. 14, 21, 1941; *Times*, Jan. 14, 1941; ADR, Oct. 12, 1990.

21. ADR, Oct. 12, Dec. 27, 1990.

22. *PI*, Jan. 24, Feb. 6, March 7, 1941; *Times*, Feb. 7, March 5, 1941.

23. *PI*, Feb. 26, 1941; ADR, Oct. 12, 1990.

24. *PI*, June 13, 1942; ADR, Oct. 12, 1990.

25. ADR, Sept. 21, Oct. 12, 1990; Laws 1943, ch. 254, section 1, codified as RRS, section 7636–1; Revised Code of Washington, sec. 49.12.210, recodified as RCW, sec. 49.12.175.

26. *PI*, Jan. 10, 1943; Billington, *People, Politics and Public Power*, p. 25.

27. *PI*, March 4, 1943.

28. ADR, Sept. 27, Oct. 12, Dec. 27, 1990.

29. ADR, Sept. 27, Oct. 12, Dec. 27, 1990; *Times*, Feb. 29, 1943.

Chapter 3. Legislative Priorities

1. ADR, Oct. 12, 1990.

2. *Star*, Jan. 17, 18, 1945.

3. *Star*, Jan. 17, 18, 1945; ADR, Oct. 12, 1990; *Star*, Jan. 10, 26, Feb. 3, Mar. 2, 1945; *Times*, Feb. 17, Mar. 12, 1945; *PI*, Jan. 18, 31, Mar. 2, 1945; ADR, Jan. 15, 25, 1994.

4. *PI*, Feb. 17, Jan. 31, Jan. 18, 1945; ADR, Oct. 12, 1990, Feb. 28, 1992.

5. ADR, Oct. 12, 1990, Feb. 28, 1992; *PI*, Jan. 21, 1945.

6. *PI*, Jan. 19, 1945; *Times*, Jan. 31, 1945; *PI*, Jan. 31, 1945.

7. *PI*, Jan. 24, 1945.

8. *PI*, Jan. 24, 31, 1945; ADR, Feb. 28, 1992.

9. ADR, Oct. 12, 1990; *PI*, Apr. 14, 1945.

10. ADR, Oct. 12, 1990, Feb. 28, 1992; *PI*, April 14, 13, 1945, Feb. 26, 1946; *Times*, March 12, 1946.

11. *PI*, Jan. 29, 13, 1947; ADR, Oct. 12, 1990.

12. ADR, Oct. 12, 1990, Feb. 28, 1992.

13. ADR, Oct. 12, 1990, Feb. 28, 1992; Vancouver *Sun*, Apr. 14, 1947; *Times*, May 2, 1947.

14. *PI*, Nov. 14, 1948, Jan. 10, 12, 1949; *Times*, Jan. 11, 1949; Rainier *Reporter*, Mar. 3, 1949; *PI*, Feb. 8, 1949.

15. Legislative Council, Third Biennial Report, Jan. 1953; *Tribune*, Feb. 3, 1963; ADR, Feb. 28, 1992; *Times*, May 8, 1949.

16. *Times*, May 8, 1949; ADR, Feb. 28, 1992; *PI*, Sept. 17, 18, 1950; *Times*, June 6, Sept. 16, 1950.

17. *Times*, June 6, 1950; ADR, Oct. 12, 1990.

18. *PI*, Aug. 6, 16, 1950; *Times*, Sept. 17, 1950.

19. *Times*, Sept. 17, 1950; Lewiston *Tribune*, Mar. 16, 1956; Walla Walla *Union Bulletin*, Oct. 14, 1956; Session Laws 1961, vol. 1, no. 1, ch. 1; *Perspective* (Department of Institutions Newsletter), April 1958 (Rosellini Papers, Box 2R-1–56).

20. Yakima *Herald*, undated, *circa* April 1950; *PI*, Mar. 23, 1951.

21. *PI*, Nov. 15, 1950; ADR, Oct. 12, 1990; Rainier *Reporter*, Aug. 15, 1951; *Times*, Jan. 9, 11, 1951.

22. *Times*, Dec. 5, 1950; *PI*, Dec. 4, 1950; *Times*, Jan. 10, 1951; *PI*, Nov. 19, 1950; *Times*, Dec. 19, 1950; ADR, Oct. 12, 1990, Feb. 28, 1992, Feb. 12, 1994; *PI*, Mar. 2, 1951; *Times*, Mar. 21, 1951; Yakima *Herald*, ca. April 1950.

23. *PI*, Jan. 9, 1951; *Times*, Jan. 9, 1951.

24. *Times*, Dec. 29, 1950, Jan. 11, 12, 1951; *PI*, Dec. 28, 1950, Feb. 7, 1951.

Chapter 4. Statewide Investigations

1. ADR, Oct. 12, 1990; Sept. 21, 1991; *PI*, Sept. 18, 1950; *Times*, June 6, Sept. 16, 1950.

2. ADR, Oct. 12, 1990; "ADR Report from Olympia," Rainier *News*, February 1951; *PI*, July 17, 1950; *Times*, Aug. 28, 1951; *PI*, Mar. 16, 1951; *Times*, Mar. 13, 1951.

3. *Times*, Mar. 2, 12, 13, 1951; *PI*, Mar. 2, 1951.

4. *Times*, Mar. 2, 12, 13, 1951; *PI*, Mar. 2, 1951; *Times*, March 3, 1951.

5. *Times*, Jan. 13, 1949, Mar. 2, 3, 12, 13, 1951; *PI*, Aug. 29, Mar. 2, 1951; "ADR Report from Olympia," Rainier *News*, February, March 1949; ADR, Sept. 12, 1990.

6. *Times*, Jan. 13, 1949, Mar. 2, 3, 12, 13, 1951; *PI*, Aug. 29, Mar. 2, 1951; "ADR Report from Olympia," Rainier *News*, February, March 1949; ADR, Sept. 12, 1990.

7. "ADR Report from Olympia," Rainier *News*, March 1949; February 1951; ADR, Sept. 21, 1990.

8. *Times*, Aug. 30, 1950; undated article, *circa* August 1950.

9. *PI*, Oct. 12, 1951; *Times*, Feb. 26, 1952. See also chapters 9 and 14.

10. *Times*, Aug. 29, 1951; Associated Press article, *Times*, June 1951; *Times*, Apr. 29, 1949; ADR, Sept. 21, 1990.

11. *Times*, Oct. 9, 20, 1951; *PI*, Oct. 1, 10, 11, 1951.

12. *Times*, Oct. 6, 9, 10, 1951; ADR, Oct. 12, 1990.

13. *Times*, Oct. 20, 1951.

14. *Ibid.*; First Report of Committee on State Government Organization, Jan. 5, 1953; Shefelman committee papers, Washington State Archives, Box D-8 ADR, Oct. 12, 1990.

15. ADR, Oct. 12. 1990.

16. *Ibid.*; Vancouver *Sun*, Oct. 5, 1951; *PI*, Oct. 11, Nov. 25, 1951; *Tribune*, Nov. 2, 1951.

17. Vancouver *Sun*, Oct. 5, 1951; *PI*, Oct. 14, 19, 1951; *Tribune*, Nov. 25, 1951.

18. Portland *Oregonian*, Oct. 12, 1951; *PI*, Nov. 29, 1951.

19. *PI*, June 6, 1952; *Times*, Jan. 19, 1952; Port Angeles *News*, June 27, 1952.

20. Omak *Chronicle*, June 19, 1952; ADR, Oct. 12, 1990, Mar. 21, 1994.

21. Vancouver *Columbian*, Oct. 15, 1951; *Tribune*, Oct. 15, 1951.

22. Vancouver *Columbian*, Oct. 15, 1951; *Tribune*, Oct. 15, 1951; Columbia Basin *News*, May 24, 1952.

23. Vancouver *Columbian*, Oct. 15, 1951; *Tribune*, Oct. 15, 1951; *PI*, Oct. 14, 1951.

24. Portland *Journal*, Oct. 14, 1951; ADR, Mar. 21, 1994.

25. *Tribune*, Oct. 15, Nov. 2, 1951; Bellingham *Herald*, Oct. 24, Nov. 25, 1951; ADR, Oct. 12, 1990.

26. ADR, Oct. 12, 1990; *PI*, Nov. 25, 30, 1951; *Times*, Nov. 29, 1951.

27. ADR, Oct. 12, 1990; *PI*, Nov. 25, 30, 1951; *Times*, Nov. 29, 30, 1951; *Tribune*, Nov. 28, 1951.

28. *Times*, Dec. 1, 1951; *PI*, Nov. 27, 1951.

29. ADR, Oct. 12, 1990; *Times*, Nov. 27, 1951.

30. *PI*, Nov. 27, 29, 1951; ADR, Oct. 12, 1990.

31. Everett *Herald*, Mar. 11, 1952; Yakima *Herald*, Mar. 19, 1952.

32. Everett *Herald*, Mar. 11, 1952; Yakima *Herald*, Mar. 19, 1952; *PI*, Feb. 27, 1952; *Times*, May 1, 1952; *Olympian*, May 11, 1952.

33. Everett *Herald*, Mar. 11, 1952; Yakima *Herald*, Mar. 19, 1952; *PI*, Feb. 27, 1952; *Times*, May 1, 1952; *Olympian*, May 11, 1952.

34. *Times*, May 2, 9, 1952.

35. ADR, Oct. 12, 1990.

36. Anacortes *Daily World*, May 22, 1952; Everett *Herald*, Jan. 22, 1952; Yakima *Republic*, Jan. 17, 1952; Kelso *Tribune*, April 10, 1952; Aberdeen *World*, Mar. 5, 1952; Spokane *Chronicle*, May 15, 1952; *PI*, Apr. 2, 1952; Longview *Daily News*, Apr. 5, 1952.

37. Omak *Chronicle*, June 19, 1952; Ellensburg *Record*, June 11, 1952; Columbia Basin *News*, June 12, 1952.

38. Spokane *Chronicle*, June 20, 1952; Walla Walla *Herald*, June 20, 1952; Wenatchee *World*, June 21, 1952.

39. ADR, Oct. 12, 1990.

40. Vancouver *Columbian*, Apr. 22, 1952; Spokane *Chronicle*, May 15, 1952.

Chapter 5. First Campaign for Governor

1. ADR, Oct. 12, 1990; *PI*, Aug. 10, 1952; *Times*, Apr. 23, 1952.

2. ADR, Oct. 12, 1990; *PI*, Dec. 31, 1951.

3. ADR, March 30, July 11, 1991; *PI*, Nov. 2, 1951; Mary L. Harris to Hugh B. Mitchell, June 4, 1952 (Mitchell Papers, Box 1); George Scott, "Arthur B. Langlie: Republican Governor in a Democratic Age" (Ph.D. diss., Univ. of Washington, 1971), pp. 233–34.

4. ADR, Oct. 12, 1990, Apr. 13, 1994; *Times*, Aug. 22, 1952; *Tribune*, Aug. 17, 1952.

5. ADR, Oct. 12, 1990; Rainier *Reporter*, July 3, 1952.

6. ADR, Oct. 12, 1990; *PI*, Aug. 18, 1952.

7. Yakima *Herald*, July 3, 1952; Bellingham *Herald*, June 29, 1952; Yakima *Republic*, Aug. 12, 1952; Chelan Valley *Mirror*, July 3, 1952; Ballard *Herald*, Aug. 14, 1952; ADR, Oct. 12, 1990; *Times*, Aug. 8, 19, 22, Sept. 1, 2, 1952; Spokane *Chronicle*, Aug. 19, 1952.

8. Spokane *Chronicle*, Aug. 18, 1952; *Times*, Aug. 7, 21, 22, 1952; Bellingham *Herald*, Sept. 1, 1952.

9. *Times*, Sept. 4, 1952; ADR, Oct. 12, 1990.

10. *Times*, Sept. 4, 1952; ADR, Oct. 12, 1990.

11. *PI*, Aug. 6, 18, 19, 1952; *Tribune*, Aug. 17, 1952; *Times*, Aug. 19, 1952.

12. *PI*, Aug. 19, 1952; *Times*, Aug. 19, 1952; interview, David G. Sprague, Aug. 4, 1995.

13. *PI*, Aug. 28, 1952.

14. Interview, David G. Sprague, Aug. 4, 1995; interview, Robert J. Block, Feb. 8, 1991; interview, Herb Legg, April 3, 1991; *Times*, Sept. 5, 17, 1952; Scott, "Langlie," pp. 242–43, 254–56; "Langlie Rally Norway Hall," 1952 speeches, Lan-glie Papers, Box L-28; Bremerton *Sun*, Oct. 10, 1952; interview, Ancil Payne, Nov. 2, 1995.

15. David McCullough, *Truman* (New York: Simon & Schuster, 1992), pp. 903–6; Scott, "Langlie," p. 245; *Times*, Sept. 17, 1952; ADR, Oct. 12, 1990, May 9, 1994.

16. *Times*, Aug. 7, 1952; *PI*, Aug. 10, 1952.

17. ADR, Oct. 12, 1990.

18. *Ibid.*

19. *Times*, Sept. 7, 1952; ADR, Oct. 12, 1990.

Chapter 6. Public Perceptions

1. ADR, July 11, 1991; interview, H. DeWayne Kreager, Dec. 20, 1990.

2. *Ibid.*; interview, Ethel Rosellini, June 19, 1991.

3. ADR, March 30, 1991.

4. *PI*, Aug. 22, 1945; Lucille Cohen, "Hospital Hit by Politics," *PI*, August 1945; Seattle *Star*, Aug. 27, 1945.

5. Seattle *Star*, September 1945; *PI*, September 1945 (Lucille Cohen article, exact date unknown); ADR, July 11, 1991.

6. *PI*, Jan. 25, 1946.

7. *PI*, Jan. 25, 17, 1946.

8. *PI*, Feb. 17, 19, 1946; ADR, Sept. 21, 1990; *Times*, June 6, 1946.

9. *Times*, undated, October 1946; ADR, Oct. 12, 1990, July 14, 1992.

10. ADR, Sept. 21, 1990; *PI*, Feb. 17, 1946, Oct. 4, 24, 1947; *Times*, Oct. 3, 4, 25, 1947; *Star*, Oct. 24, 1947.

11. *Times*, Oct. 26, 1947; *PI*, Feb. 24, 1949.

12. *PI*, Feb. 4, 1948.

13. *PI*, Mar. 4, 1949; *Times*, Mar. 6, 1949; ADR, Sept. 21, 1990.

14. ADR, July 14, 1992.

Chapter 7. Langlie and Rosellini

1. *Times*, Nov. 7, 1952; ADR, Oct. 12, 1990, Apr. 13, 1994; *PI*, Sept. 12, 1952.

2. ADR, Oct. 12, 1990, Apr. 13, 1994.

3. Scott, "Langlie," pp. 230–31, 262–63; *Times*, Apr. 28, 1950; ADR, Oct. 12, 1990, Apr. 13, 1994.

4. ADR, Apr. 13, 1994.

5. Scott, "Langlie," pp. 313–14.

6. *Ibid.*; *PI*, Feb. 19, 1949; ADR, Oct. 12, 1990.

7. *PI*, Aug. 13, 1950; Scott, "Langlie," pp. 313–14; memorandum, H. D. Van Eaton to Arthur B. Langlie, Jan. 3, 1949, in "Report of the Interim Committee on State Institutions" (Langlie Papers, Box 25).

8. Scott, "Langlie," p. 315.

9. Yakima *Herald*, April 1950.

10. ADR, Oct. 12, 1990; Scott, "Langlie," pp. 314–17.

11. *PI*, Aug. 22, 1953; Scott, "Langlie," pp. 317–18.

12. *PI*, Sept. 2, 3, 1953; Scott, "Langlie," pp. 317–18.

13. *PI*, Sept. 4, 5, 7, 1953.

14. ADR, Oct. 12, 1990, Mar. 23, 1994; *PI*, Sept. 5, 6, 1953.

15. ADR, Oct. 12, 1990, Mar. 23, 1994; *PI*, Sept. 5, 6, 1953.

16. *PI*, Sept. 5, 1953.

17. *PI*, Aug. 12, 1950, Sept. 5, 7, 1953; P. J. Squire to Van Eaton, Aug. 13, 1953, in Institutions Directors' Files, L111–2; Norman Hayner to Arthur B. Langlie, Dec. 3, 1952, in Institutions Directors' Files, L111–2.

18. *PI*, Dec. 2, 1953.

19. *PI*, Sept. 10, 1953; Spokane *Chronicle*, Sept. 7, 1953; *Tribune*, Sept. 10, 1953; Scott, "Langlie," p. 318.

20. *PI*, Sept. 10, 14, 1953; *Tribune*, Sept. 10, 1953.

21. ADR, Apr. 13, 1994; *PI*, Sept. 17, 1953.

22. *PI*, Sept. 17, 18, 1953.

23. *PI*, Sept. 22, 1953; Hayner to Langlie, Sept. 26, 1953, in Institutions Directors' Files, L111–2.

24. *PI*, Nov. 14, 1953.

25. *PI*, Nov. 15, 17, 1953.

26. *Ibid.*

27. *PI*, Nov. 15, 17, 19, 1953; Scott, "Langlie," pp. 319–32.

28. Scott, "Langlie," pp. 319–32; F. R. Dickson to Langlie, July 27, 1954, Institutions Directors' Files; *PI*, Dec. 21, 1954.

29. Scott, "Langlie," pp. 319–21; Van Eaton to Langlie, Dec. 17, 1953, H. D. Van Eaton Papers; ADR, Oct. 12, 1990.

30. Washington State Parole Board to Langlie, May 21, 1953 (Washington State Archives, ARG, Box 34); H. Hess to Hoff, Oct. 29, 1953 (Washington State Archives, ARG, Box 26).

31. Hayner to Langlie, Feb. 23, 1953 (Washington State Archives, ARG, Box L-111–2); Scott, "Langlie," pp. 321–22.

32. ADR, Apr. 13, 1994; Spokane *Chronicle*, July 9, 1955; Shrag to R. F. Dickson, Jan. 27, 1955 (Washington State Archives, ARG, L-111–2).

33. Press release, Aug. 18, 1955 (Langlie Papers, L-17–2); Scott, "Langlie," p. 322; Longview *Daily News*, July 9, 1955; Bremerton *Sun*, Sept. 2, 1955; ADR, Apr. 8, 1994.

34. Shrag to Langlie, Oct. 21, 1955 (Langlie Papers, L-17–2).

Papers, Box 2R-3–32); Department of Institutions, Budget (Rosellini Papers, Box 2R-1–17); Department of Institutions, monthly reports, May 27, Sept. 29, 1958 (Rosellini Papers, Box 2R-1–56); Department of Institutions, Advisory Committee minutes, Oct. 3, 1958 (Rosellini Papers, Box 2R-1–57); Division of Mental Health, 1957 Annual Report (Rosellini Papers, Box 2R-1–19); "Washington State Mental Hospital Population Trends, Length of Stay, Personnel Indices, 1955–1963" (Rosellini Papers, Box 2R-3–4); Heyns to Stanley J. Stamm, Oct. 7, 1958 (Rosellini Papers, Box 2R-1–56); undated press release, probably 1961 (Rosellini Papers, Box 2R-1–216, file called "Dept. of Institutions— Children and Youth Services").

37. Department of Institutions, monthly reports, Apr. 29, May 27, Sept. 28, Dec. 29, 1958, May 29, Sept. 28, 1959 (Rosellini Papers, Box 2R-1–56); Department of Institutions, Biennial Report, 1959–61; *Perspective*, November 1958.

38. Department of Institutions, Biennial Reports, 1957–59; 1959–61; "Remarks of ADR," dedication of Northern State recreation building, Apr. 4, 1964 (Rosellini Papers, Box 2R-3–45); "Accomplishments of the Department of Institutions"; "Washington State Mental Hospital Population Trends."

39. *Perspective*, September 1959; October 1959 (Rosellini Papers, Box 2R-1–111); Francis Hoague to ADR, Aug. 29, 1959 (Rosellini Papers, Box 2R-1–112); press release, Aug. 3, 1959 (Rosellini Papers, Box 2R-3–33).

40. Department of Institutions, Budget, 1957–59 (Rosellini Papers, Box 2R-

1–17); *Perspective*, Summer 1963 (Rosellini Papers, Box 2R-3–9); Heyns to Bishop, May 5, 1964 (Rosellini Papers, Box 2R-3–3); Charles Jones to Friends of Northern State Hospital, Christmas 1958 (Rosellini Papers, Box 2R-1–58); Calvin Johnson to Carl Downing, Aug. 31, 1964 (Rosellini Papers, Box 2R-3–4).

41. Edna D. Ferguson to A. A. Murry, Aug. 22, 1957 (Rosellini Papers, Box 2R-1–19); Department of Institutions, Budget, 1957–59 (Rosellini Papers, Box 2R-1–17); Department of Institutions, monthly report, May 27, 1958 (Rosellini Papers, Box 2R-1–56); G. Lee Sandritter, "Consolidated Budget Request," Feb. 25, 1957 (Rosellini Papers, Box 2R-1–18).

42. Washington State Legislature, Session Laws, 1957, ch. 102; press release, March 13, 1957 (Rosellini Papers, Box 2R-3–31); Kitsap County Democratic Central Committee, Resolution, June 19, 1957 (Rosellini Papers, Box 2R-1–8); "Accomplishments of the Department," July 17, 1959; Department of Institutions, Biennial Report, 1957–59; press release, March 3, 1958 (Rosellini Papers, Box 2R-3–32); "Progress in State Institutions" (Rosellini Papers, Box 2R-1–110).

43. "Schools for the Mentally Deficient Waiting List Summary Report," June 1963 (Rosellini Papers, Box 2R-1–298); Bainbridge Island *Review*, Jan. 8, 1964; *PI*, Dec. 27, 1963.

44. *Times*, July 8, 1979.

Chapter 11. Higher Education

1. John Fuller to ADR, Jan. 25, 1956 (Rosellini Papers, Box 2R-1–3); press release, Oct. 6, 1960 (Rosellini Papers, Box 2R-1–147); Charles E. Odegaard to ADR, Dec. 4, 1963 (Rosellini Papers,

Box 2R-1–313); interview, Charles E. Odegaard, Jan. 5, 1991.

2. ADR, "Remarks to Conference of School Presidents," Dec. 19, 1957 (Rosellini Papers, Box 2R-1–043).

3. ADR, Dec. 27, 1990; interview, Odegaard; interview, Warren Bishop, Jan. 15, 1994.

4. Interview, Bishop, Jan. 15, 1994.

5. Interview, Bishop, June 25, 1995.

6. Interviews, Bishop, June 25, 1995, and Odegaard, Jan. 5, 1991.

7. Carl Pettibone to Bishop, Nov. 21, 1963 (Rosellini Papers, Box 2R-1–314).

8. "Inaugural Message of Albert D. Rosellini, Governor of Washington, to the Thirty-fifth Legislature" (Olympia, Wash., Jan. 16, 1957); interview, Bishop, June 25, 1995.

9. "Inaugural Message"; Robert E. McConnell to ADR, Oct. 11, 1958 (Rosellini Papers, Box 2R-1–38); "Higher Education Budget Comparison," undated, *ca.* 1961 (Rosellini Papers, Box 2R-1–220).

10. "Higher Education Budget Comparison"; ADR Address to Wenatchee Valley Community College, May 1, 1964 (Rosellini Papers, Box 2R-3–079); Governor's Budget Request and Message to the Legislature, 1963, p. 15 (Rosellini Papers, Box 2R-3–067).

11. ADR, "Remarks to School Presidents," Dec. 17, 1957.

12. Press release, Dec. 19, 1957 (Rosellini Papers, Box 2R-1–043).

13. ADR, Dec. 27, 1990; interview, Bishop, Jan. 5, 1991; Charles E. Odegaard, "Annual Report to the University Community," October 1973 (Odegaard, private collection); ADR, state-

ment, Jan. 27, 1959 (Rosellini Papers, Box 2R-1–097).

14. Charles E. Odegaard, "Annual Report to the University Community," October 1979 (Odegaard, private collection); ADR, Dec. 27, 1990; interviews, Bishop, Jan. 21, 1991, Odegaard, Jan. 5, 1991.

15. Charles M. Gates, "Higher Education in the State of Washington," Apr. 23, 1962 (Rosellini Papers, Box 2R-1–244); press release, Oct. 4, 1960 (Rosellini Papers, Box 2R-1–147); summary of higher education initiatives by the Rosellini administration, 1963 (Rosellini Papers, Box 2R-1–002).

16. "Legislation Permitting the Three State Colleges to Grant Master of Arts and Master of Science Degrees" (Rosellini Papers, Box 2R-1–259); "Master's Degree Programs" (Rosellini Papers, *ibid.*); interviews, Odegaard, Jan. 5, 1991; Bishop, Jan. 15, 1991; ADR, "Suggested Thoughts for a Major Educational Address," *ca.* 1959–60 (Rosellini Papers, Box 2R-1–096); ADR to Margarite Cross, Apr. 1, 1958 (Rosellini Papers, Box 2R-1–58).

17. Interview, Odegaard, Jan. 5, 1991.

Chapter 12. Economic Development

1. "Records of Promotion and Development in Washington State, 1889–1972," July 1988 (Rosellini Papers, Box 2R-1–5); Alfred McVay to ADR and Department of Commerce and Economic Development (DCED) Advisory Board, Aug. 29, 1957 (Rosellini Papers, Box 2R-1–5).

2. Interview, Warren Bishop, Jan. 15, 1991; *Times*, Apr. 11, 1957.

3. Interview, Bishop, Jan. 15, 1991; ADR, Dec. 27, 1990; McVay to ADR et al., Aug. 29, 1957.

4. Interview, Bishop, Jan. 15, 1991; ADR, Dec. 27, 1990; Washington State Legislature, Session Laws, 1957, ch. 215.

5. Interviews, Bishop, Nov. 30, 1990, Jan. 15, 1991; ADR, address to Puget Sound Industrial Council, May 10, 1957 (Rosellini Papers, Box 2R-1-15).

6. A. W. Burchill to John A. Cherberg, Aug. 27, 1957 (Rosellini Papers, Box 2R-1-15).

7. Interview, H. DeWayne Kreager, Dec. 20, 1990.

8. Ibid.; interview, Bishop, Jan. 15, 1991; memorandum, July 30, 1957 (Rosellini Papers, Box 2R-1-15).

9. Memorandum, "Announced New Industry Plant Expansion and Major Construction in the State of Washington," July 1964 (Rosellini Papers, Box 2R-3-1); Progress (bulletin of the DCED), Feb. 1, July 1, Aug. 1, 1959; DCED, First Biennial Report, 1957–59; Second Biennial Report, 1958–60 (Rosellini Papers, Box 2R-1-02); "Summary of Accomplishments to Date," ca. 1959 (Rosellini Papers, Box 2R-1-39).

10. Memorandum, "Announced New Industry Plant Expansion," July 1964; Progress, Feb. 1, July 1, Aug. 1, 1959; DCED, First Biennial Report, 1957–59; Second Biennial Report, 1958–60; "Summary of Accomplishments to Date."

11. Progress, Aug. 1, Sept. 1, 1959; DCED, Fifth Biennial Report, 1964–66 (Rosellini Papers, Box 2R-1-02); Odessa Record, Apr. 16, 1959; William Goodloe to Kreager, Sept. 29, 1959 (Rosellini Papers, Box 2R-1–92); Times, Sept. 16, 1959; Tribune, Apr. 3, 1963.

12. Interview, Kreager, Dec. 20, 1990.

13. DCED, First Biennial Report; Burchill to Cherberg, Aug. 27, 1957.

14. Edward E. Carlson, Recollections of a Lucky Fellow (Seattle: privately published, 1989), pp. 144–74; Murray Morgan, Century 21: The Story of the Seattle World's Fair Successful Eight-Year Effort (Seattle: Acme Press, distributed by the University of Washington Press, 1963); ADR, Dec. 29, 1994.

15. PI, Apr. 21, 1987.

16. Carlson, Recollections, pp. 144–74; interview, Kreager, Feb. 28, 1995.

17. ADR, Dec. 29, 1994; Carlson, Recollections, pp. 144–74.

18. Carlson, Recollections, pp. 147–48.

19. Ibid., p. 148.

20. Progress, July 1, 1959.

21. Carlson, Recollections, p. 154.

22. Ibid., pp. 144–46.

23. DCED, First Biennial Report.

24. Interview, Kreager, Feb. 28, 1995; Carlson, Recollections, p. 153.

25. DCED, First Biennial Report.

26. Carlson, Recollections, pp. 144–74; DCED, First Biennial Report; Kreager to Jay Larson, May 27, 1958 (Rosellini Papers, Box 2R-1-41).

27. Carlson, Recollections, p. 153; interview, Kreager, Feb. 28, 1995.

28. Carlson, Recollections, pp. 163; DCED, First Biennial Report.

29. DCED, Third Biennial Report; DCED, Fourth Biennial Report.

30. Interview, Kreager, Dec. 20, 1990.

31. PI, March 26, 1957; ADR, Dec. 27, 1990; Columbia Basin News (Ephrata), June 12, 1957.

32. DCED Advisory Board, minutes, Jan. 20, 1958 (Rosellini Papers, Box 2R-1–40); interview, Kreager, Dec. 20, 1990; interview, Bishop, Nov. 13, 1990.

33. DCED Advisory Board, minutes, Jan. 20, 1958; interview, Kreager, Dec. 20, 1990; interview, Bishop, Nov. 13, 1990.

34. Interview, Kreager, Dec. 20, 1990; Tri-City Herald, Nov. 7, 1958.

35. Spokane Chronicle, Jan. 17, 1959; PI, Jan. 26, 1959; Tribune, March 20, 1959; ADR, Dec. 27, 1990; interview, Kreager, Dec. 20, 1990.

36. Tribune, March 20, 1959; interview, Kreager, Feb. 28, 1995.

37. Interview, Kreager, Dec. 20, 1990.

38. Ibid. and Feb. 28, 1995; ADR, Feb. 28, 1995.

39. ADR, March 30, 1991, Feb. 28, 1995.

40. Tribune, Apr. 3, 1963; ADR, Mar. 30, 1991, Oct. 3, 1995; interview, Kreager, October 3, 1995.

41. Carlson, Recollections, pp. 144–74; ADR, Feb. 28, 1995.

42. Odessa Record, Apr. 16, 1959; Spokane Spokesman-Review, May 22, 23, 1963; Tribune, Mar. 13, 1964; Argus, Apr. 27, 1962; William Day, address to state Junior Chamber of Commerce, Jan. 18, 1964 (Rosellini Papers, 2R-3–010).

Chapter 13. Second Lake Washington Bridge

1. ADR, address to Evergreen Bridge Association, May 15, 1956 (Rosellini Papers, Box 2R-1–032); press release, October 1956 (Rosellini Papers, ibid.).

2. Times, Aug. 31, 1988; ADR, address to North Cascades Highway Association,

June 7, 1963 (Rosellini Papers, Box 2R-3–074); Toll Bridge Authority (TBA), minutes, October 1960 (Rosellini Papers, Box 2R-1–233).

3. Tudor Engineering, "Lake Washington Bridge Crossings," Dec. 13, 1968 (Seattle Public Library); DeLeuw, Cather and Co., "Report," esp. the foreword (Seattle Public Library).

4. Tudor Engineering, "Lake Washington Bridge Crossings"; DeLeuw et al., "Report."

5. Tudor Engineering, "Lake Washington Bridge Crossings"; DeLeuw et al., "Report"; Times, Dec. 12, 1938.

6. Tudor Engineering, "Lake Washington Bridge Crossings"; DeLeuw et al., "Report."

7. Tudor Engineering, "Lake Washington Bridge Crossings"; DeLeuw et al., "Report."

8. ADR, Feb. 28, 1992; "History: Second Lake Washington Floating Bridge," program for ground-breaking ceremonies, Aug. 29, 1960 (Rosellini Papers, Box 2R,1–358); ADR, address to Evergreen Bridge Association, May 15, 1957.

9. Times, Oct. 19, 1953, Apr. 20, 1954, Jan. 18, 22, 24, 1957.

10. ADR, Feb. 28, 1992; "History: Second Lake Washington Floating Bridge."

11. Bridge Builder (newsletter of the Eastside Commuters Association), Oct. 16, 1958 (Rosellini Papers, Box 2R-1–082); Times, Apr. 18, 1957; ADR, address to Evergreen Bridge Association.

12. Washington State Highway Commission, "Review and Analysis," Dec. 10, 1956 (Seattle Public Library); ADR, Sept. 8, 1994; Municipal League of Seat-

tle and King County, "Proposed Report of the Second Lake Washington Bridge Committee," March 17, 1958 (Rosellini Papers, 2R-1-082).

13. ADR, Feb. 28, 1992.

14. *Ibid.*; *Times*, Jan. 24, 1957.

15. ADR, Feb. 28, 1992.

16. *Bridge Builder*, Aug. 14, 1959; *Argus*, Aug. 7, 1959.

17. *Times*, Jan. 18, 1957; *Bridge Builder*, Oct. 16, 1958.

18. Interview, John L. O'Brien, Sept. 13, 1994; *Times*, Jan. 22, 24, Feb. 6, 19, 27, 28, Mar. 3, 1957.

19. *Times*, Mar. 24, 27, 1957.

20. ADR, Sept. 8, 1994.

21. *Times*, Apr. 18, 1957; ADR, Feb. 28, 1992, Sept. 8, 1994.

22. *Times*, Apr. 15, 1957; ADR, Feb. 28, 1992.

23. *Times*, Apr. 18, 1957.

24. *Bridge Builder*, May 12, 1958; ADR, Feb. 28, 1992, Oct. 14, 1994.

25. Coverdale and Colpitts, "Report," Oct. 11, 1957 (Rosellini Papers, Box 2R-1-033); ADR, Feb. 28, 1992, Oct. 24, 1994.

26. ADR, Feb. 28, 1992; *Times*, Jan. 5, 16, Mar. 20, 1958; *Bridge Builder*, May 12, Oct. 16, 1958; Bishop to Bugge, Mar. 26, 1958 (Rosellini Papers, 2R-1-054).

27. *Bridge Builder*, May 12, 1958; interview, Henry Seidel, Oct. 17, 1994.

28. *Bridge Builder*, May 12, 1958; interview, Seidel, Oct. 17, 1994.

29. Sammamish Valley *News*, July 31, 1958.

30. *Ibid.*; interview, Seidel, Oct. 17, 1994; interview, Scott Wallace, Mar. 15, 1996.

31. Sammamish Valley *News*, July 31,

1958; interview, Seidel, Oct. 17, 1994; interview, Wallace, Mar. 15, 1996.

32. Interview, Seidel, Oct. 17, 1994.

33. *Times*, Mar. 3, Apr. 27, May 15, 1957; *Bridge Builder*, Aug. 14, 1959; Municipal League of Seattle and King County, "Resolution," March 17, 1958 (Rosellini Papers, Box 2R-1-082); *Argus*, Aug. 7, 1959; interview, Seidel, Oct. 17, 1994.

34. ADR, Oct. 14, 1994; Washington State Legislature, Session Laws, Extraordinary Session, 1959, ch. 11; *Bridge Builder*, Aug. 14, 1959; State ex. rel. *Toll Bridge Authority (TBA)* v. *Yelle*, 54 W (2) 545 (1959); press release, Aug. 8, 1959 (Rosellini Papers, Box 2R-1-132).

35. Interview, Seidel, Oct. 17, 1994; State ex. rel. *Washington TBA* v. *Yelle*, 56 W (2) 86, 89 (1960).

36. Interview, Seidel, Oct. 17, 1994.

37. *Bridge Builder*, Aug. 14, 1959; press release, Aug. 15, 1960 (Rosellini Papers, Box 2R-1-188).

38. ADR, Feb. 28, 1992; "History: Second Lake Washington Bridge."

39. ADR, Feb. 28, 1992; interview, Seidel, Oct. 17, 1994; State ex. rel. *Washington TBA* v. *Yelle*, 56 W (2) 86, 89 (1960).

40. *Times*, Jan. 3, 1960.

41. State ex. rel. *Washington TBA* v. *Yelle*, 56 W (2) 86, 89 (1960); press release, Apr. 15, 1960 (Rosellini Papers, 2R-1-188).

42. "History: Second Lake Washington Bridge"; *Times*, Aug. 29, 1988.

Chapter 14. Taxes and the 1960 Campaign

1. ADR, Dec. 27, 1990; "Inaugural Message of Albert D. Rosellini, Governor

of Washington, to the Thirty-fifth Legislature" (Olympia, Wash., Jan. 16, 1957); interview, Warren Bishop, Jan. 15, 1991.

2. *PI*, March 26, 1957; *Times*, April 1957 (undated); *Tribune*, Oct. 18, 1957.

3. *Columbia Basin News* (Ephrata), June 12, 1957; ADR, Dec. 27, 1990; *PI*, Aug. 17, 1957; interview, Bishop, Jan. 15, 1991.

4. *Times*, June 1957 (undated); *Columbia Basin News*, June 12, 1957; Olympia *News*, Jan. 16, 1958; *Times*, Mar. 20, 1958.

5. *Times*, July 21, 1958.

6. *PI*, Sept. 15, 1958; Clarkston *Herald*, Aug. 14, 1958.

7. *PI*, Sept. 25, 1958.

8. *Ibid.*

9. ADR, Dec. 27, 1990, Feb. 28, 1992, May 3, 1995; Tri-City *Herald*, Nov. 7, 1958.

10. *Tribune*, Jan. 19, 1959; Tacoma *Labor Advocate*, Jan. 30, 1959; interview, Bishop, Jan. 15, 1991; Governor's Message to the Legislature, Jan. 14, 1959; *Washington Public Employee*, Jan. 15, 1959.

11. Olympia *Chronicle*, Jan. 17, 1959.

12. Bellingham *Herald*, Jan. 19, 1959; *American Bulletin*, Feb. 2, 1959; interview, Bishop, Jan. 15, 1991; ADR, Oct. 12, Dec. 27, 1990.

13. *PI*, Jan. 26, 1959.

14. *PI*, Mar. 3, 1959.

15. Spokane *Spokesman-Review*, Mar. 9, 1959; *Daily Olympian*, Mar. 11, 1959.

16. Spokane *Chronicle*, Mar. 13, 1959; Longview *Daily News*, Mar. 16, 1959; *Daily Olympian*, Mar. 13, 1959.

17. *Tribune*, Mar. 28, 1959; ADR, May 9, 1994, July 22, 1995; Spokane *Spokesman-Review*, Apr. 1, 1959.

18. *Times*, Dec. 19, 20, 21, 22, 23, 1958.

19. *Ibid.*; interview, Ed Guthman, July 18, 1994.

20. Charles Hodde, *Oral History Project*, 1986, vol. 2, pp. 323–24; *Times*, Mar. 4, 1959; *PI*, Mar. 19, 1959.

21. *Times*, Dec. 23, 1958; ADR, Dec. 20, 1990, May 9, 1994; *PI*, Feb. 13, 1959; Hodde, *Oral History Project*.

22. *Times*, Apr. 12, 13, 14, 1960; *PI*, Apr. 13, 1960.

23. *Eastsider*, Apr. 13, 1960; *Argus*, Apr. 22, 1960.

24. ADR, Dec. 27, 1990, May 1, 1995; *Times*, Apr. 15, 1960.

25. ADR, Dec. 27, 1990, May 1, 1995; *Times*, Apr. 15, 1960.

26. *Eastsider*, Apr. 20, 1960; *Argus*, Apr. 22, 1960; interview, Guthman, July 18, 1994; ADR, radio talk script, *ca.* October 1960 (Rosellini Papers, Box 2R-3–06B).

27. *PI*, Feb. 9, 1960; Washington TBA, minutes, July 3, 1957 (Rosellini Papers, Box 2R-1–032).

28. *PI*, Feb. 9, 1960; Washington TBA, minutes, July 3, 1957.

29. *Times*, Feb. 16, 1960; *PI*, Feb. 9, 12, 1960; Vancouver *Columbian*, Mar. 9, 1961.

30. *Times*, Aug. 25, 1960.

31. ADR, Oct. 14, 1994; *Eastsider*, Aug. 3, 1960.

32. *Times*, Jan. 31, 1960; *PI*, Apr. 3, 1960; Portland *Oregonian*, Apr. 18, 1960.

33. *Times*, Jan. 31, 1960; *PI*, Apr. 3, 1960.

34. *PI*, Apr. 3, 1960.

35. Port Angeles *News*, Sept. 10, 1960;

gus, Jan. 17, Apr. 24, 1964; ADR, Dec. 27, 1990, Sept. 6, 1995; Day, address to state Junior Chamber of Commerce government affairs forum, Jan. 18, 1964; Spokane *Chronicle*, May 11, 1964.

28. *Argus*, Aug. 30, 1963.

29. Spokane *Chronicle*, May 11, 1964; ADR, Dec. 27, 1990, June 20, 1995.

30. *Tribune*, Jan. 23, 1964; *PI*, Sept. 17, 1964; *Argus*, Aug. 30, 1964; Spokane *Spokesman-Review*, July 7, 1964.

31. Spokane *Spokesman-Review*, July 7, 1964; *Argus*, Aug. 30, 1964.

32. Spokane *Spokesman-Review*, July 7, 1964; *Argus*, Aug. 30, 1964.

33. Dan Evans, Joseph Gandy, and Richard Christianson, "Where I Stand on Education," statements to the Washington Education Association, May 1964 (Rosellini Papers, Box 2R-3–009); *PI*, Apr. 9, Sept. 5, 18, 1964; Skagit Valley *Herald*, Sept. 12, 1964; Issaquah *Press*, Oct. 8, 1964; *Times*, Sept. 8, 1964; *Tribune*, Mar. 4, June 30, 1964; *Argus*, Sept. 18, 1964.

34. Evans, Gandy, and Christianson, "Where I Stand on Education," May 1964; *PI*, Apr. 9, Sept. 5, 18, 1964; Skagit Valley *Herald*, Sept. 12, 1964; Issaquah *Press*, Oct. 8, 1964; *Times*, Sept. 8, 1964; *Tribune*, Mar. 4, June 30, 1964; *Argus*, Sept. 18, 1964.

35. *PI*, Sept. 17, 1964; *Argus*, Sept. 18, 1964; Raymond *Herald and Advertiser*, Sept. 10, 1964; ADR, Dec. 27, 1990; Sept. 6, 1995.

36. *Tribune*, Sept. 20, 1964; "Dan Evans Voting Record and Goldwater," *ca.* Oct. 1, 1964 (Rosellini Papers, Box 2R-1–318); "Republican Issues" (Rosellini

Papers, Box 2R-3–010); "Barry's Word, Evans Deed—Identical," ADR campaign organizer handout (Rosellini Papers, Box 2R-3–010); *PI*, May 14, Sept. 9, 1964; "An Open Letter to Democrats," paid advertisement, Oct. 18, 1964 (Rosellini Papers, Box 2R-1–318); Evans campaign brochure, Aug. 6, 1964 (Rosellini Papers, Box 2R-1–318); *Washington Teamster*, Oct. 2, 1964; ADR, Sept. 5, 1995; Edmonds *Tribune Review*, Oct. 15, 1964; *Times*, Oct. 4, 14, 1964; Highline *Times*, Oct. 14, 1964; Bellingham *Herald*, Oct. 8, 1964; Bremerton *Sun*, Oct. 12, 1964.

37. *Tribune*, Sept. 20, 1964; "Dan Evans Voting Record and Goldwater," *ca.* Oct. 1, 1964; "Republican Issues"; "Barry's Word, Evans Deed—Identical"; *PI*, May 14, Sept. 9, 1964; "An Open Letter to Democrats," Oct. 18, 1964; Evans campaign brochure, Aug. 6, 1964; *Washington Teamster*, Oct. 2, 1964; ADR, Sept. 5, 1995; Edmonds *Tribune Review*, Oct. 15, 1964; *Times*, Oct. 4, 14, 1964; Highline *Times*, Oct. 14, 1964; Bellingham *Herald*, Oct. 8, 1964; Bremerton *Sun*, Oct. 12, 1964.

38. Skagit Valley *Herald*, Sept. 12, 1964; *PI*, Sept. 27, 1964; Cheney *Free Press*, Oct. 16, 1964; Bremerton *Sun*, Sept. 8, 1964; Tri-City *Herald*, Sept. 13, 1964; *Times*, Oct. 14, 1964.

39. Information for major Democratic speakers, October 1964 (Rosellini Papers, Box 2R-1–318, Box 2R-3–010); Clarence Dill, "Will the Real Dan Evans Please Stand UP," Aug. 25, 1964 (Rosellini Papers, Box 2R-1–318).

40. *PI*, Oct. 1, 1964; Seattle *Observer*, Sept. 23, 1964; *Times*, Sept. 27, 1964;

Bremerton *Sun*, Oct. 27, 1964; *Tribune*, Sept. 9, 1964; Issaquah *Press*, Sept. 9, 1964.

41. *Times*, Oct. 4, 21, 1964; *Tribune*, Oct. 7, 1964; University of Washington *Daily*, Nov. 3, 1964.

42. *Times*, Nov. 4, 1964; interview, Ida Bachechi, Nov. 28, 1992.

43. ADR, Message to the Thirty-ninth Legislature, Jan. 12, 1965 (Rosellini Papers, Box 2R-3-067).

Chapter 16. Campaigns of 1969 and 1972

1. ADR, Sept. 14, 1995; Bremerton *Sun*, July 19, 1966.

2. William R. Conte, *Is Prison Reform Possible? The Washington State Experience in the Sixties* (Tacoma, Wash.: Unique Press, 1990), pp. 100–102 *passim*; Conte to Payton Smith, March 25, 1996.

3. *PI*, Apr. 5, 1966.

4. *Times*, Oct. 27, 1965; *PI*, Feb. 8, 1966.

5. Interviews, Scott Wallace, Mar. 2, 1995, Apr. 8, 1996; *DeLaney v. Superior Court* 69 Washington (2) 519 (1966).

6. *PI*, Feb. 24, Nov. 10, 1966.

7. *PI*, Apr. 5, Sept. 19, 1966; *Times*, Sept. 16, 1966.

8. ADR, Feb. 14, 1996; press release, Feb. 18, 1969 (private collection of David G. Wood).

9. Press release (private collection of David G. Wood).

10. *PI*, Feb. 16, 1969; letter, David G. Wood to Harry Prior, Feb. 9, 1969 (private collection of David G. Wood).

11. Western Informational Services Survey, Feb. 27-Mar. 4, 1969 (private collection of David G. Wood).

12. Interview, Wallace, Apr. 6, 1996; *Sunday Olympian*, Apr. 11, 1971.

13. *Times*, Sept. 17, 1972.

14. ADR, Feb. 14, 1996; Bremerton *Sun*, Dec. 9, 1981.

15. *Daily Olympian*, Aug. 29, 1972; *Times*, Apr. 30, 1967, May 6, 1971, Mar. 27, 1972.

16. *State v. Sponburgh et al.*, 84 Washington (2) 203 (1973); Rosellini campaign literature press article, 1972 (private collection of Scott Wallace).

17. Interview, Wallace, Apr. 6, 1996; ADR, Apr. 19, 1996.

18. *Daily Olympian*, Aug. 29, 1972; press release, June 19, 1972 (Wallace collection).

19. *Times*, Sept. 18, 1972; ADR, Apr. 19, 1996.

20. ADR, Apr. 19, 1996; *Daily Olympian*, Aug. 29, 1972.

21. *Times*, Sept. 20, 21, 24, 1972; *Argus*, Sept. 29, 1972.

22. Rosellini and Evans campaign materials, 1972 (Wallace collection).

23. Rosellini advertising materials, *Times* article (Wallace collection).

24. ADR, April 6, 1996; *Times*, Oct. 18, 1972.

25. *PI*, Oct. 21, 1972.

26. *Times*, Oct. 26, 30, 31, Nov. 1, 2, 3, 1972; interview, Lou Guzzo, Nov. 25, 1995; KING television transcript, Nov. 10, 1972.

27. KING transcript, Nov. 10, 1972; ADR, Apr. 6, 1996; Dick Larsen, *Times*, Nov. 12, 1972; interviews: Shelby Scates; Lou Guzzo; Scott Wallace; Henry Seidel; Gerald Hoeck.

Chapter 17. Epilogue and Conclusion

1. Interview, Duane Berentson, Apr. 2, 1996.

2. Interview, Charles Odegaard, Jan. 5, 1991.

3. *Times*, Mar. 21, 1996.

4. *Argus*, Dec. 18, 1959.

Index

Abel, Don G., 80, 101
Aberdeen, WA, 50, 53, 159
Agriculture, Department of, 101
Ahlen, Erika, 16
Alaska, 11, 145
Alioto, Joseph, 213
Allison, Dan, 16
Almira *Herald*, 192
"America First," 63
American Marietta, 144
American Medical Association, 129
American Psychiatric Association, 85, 126, 129
American Rose Society, 90
Americans for Democratic Action (ADA), 62–63, 64, 65
Anderson, Emmett, 74, 77, 78, 91–93, 94, 105, 194
Andrews, Lloyd, 157, 208, 209; 1960 campaign, 65, 124, 137, 185, 186–89, 190–94
Angeloff, Sam, 52
Angelo's Cafe, 14
Ann Thompson's Place, 52
Anti-Communists, 40–41, 63, 64, 88
Anti-Saloon League of Washington, 18
Arboretum Foundation, 165
Arnold, Lawrence M., 143
Ashe, James, 16
Asotin, WA, 41
Association of Washington Business, 220

Association of Washington Industries, 154
Astoria-Megler Bridge, 159
Atkinson, Guy F., Company, 173
Auburn, WA, 144, 159
Auditor, State, 112, 113
Australia, 150

Bailey, Phil, 7, 148, 204
Bar Association, State, 36
Bargreen, Howard, 81, 87
Bates, L. H., 137
Belknap, Ray, 120
Bellevue, WA, 164, 174
Bellingham, WA, 56, 132, 155
Berentson, Duane, 227
Bergman, Ingrid, 90
Bertil, Prince of Sweden, 183
Bethlehem Steel, 144
Betlach, Roy, 101
Beverage Dispensers Association, 18
Bickelton, WA, 41
Biggs, John A., 101, 104
Bishop, Warren, 103, 104, 122, 133, 134, 141; chief of staff, 99–101; budget director, 108–14 *passim*, 203
Black, Donald, 33
Block, Robert J., 147
"Blueprint for Progress," 93, 209, 210, 224. *See also* Evans, Daniel J.
Boeing, Company, 17, 29, 98, 137, 141, 221

Evans, Daniel J., 93, 112, 113, 157, 196, 212, 214–15, 230; 1972 campaign, 7, 218–26; opposition to Evergreen Point site, 166, 172; proponent of private power, 197–99; leader of 1963 coalition, 199–200, 201, 203–4; 1964 campaign, 205, 206–11; 1968 campaign, 213
Everest, H. P. "Dick," 99
Everett, WA, 56, 159
Everett Junior College, 137
Evergreen Point Bridge, 106, 159, 163–74, 186, 195, 215, 229–30
Exchange Club (Spokane), 57

Fair-trade laws, 27, 29
Ferguson, Adele, 212
Fircrest School (Seattle), 130
Firland Sanatorium (Seattle), 130
Fisheries, Department of, 101
Fluent, Russell, 68
Folsom, Morrill, 198
Fornaciari, John, 70
Fort Worden, WA, 126, 131
Foster, Stanberry, 16
Frances Haddan Morgan Center (Bremerton), 131
Franco, John, 16
Frayn, Mort, 80, 87
Frederick and Nelson (Seattle), 146
French, C. Clement, 137

Gallagher, Michael, 25, 58, 86, 87, 95, 125, 203
Gambling, 8, 13, 50–51, 52, 54, 94, 193, 213
Game, Department of, 101
Ganders, Stanton, 41
Gandy, Joseph, 146, 150, 157, 206–8
Gardner, Booth, 227, 228, 230
"Garlic Gulch" (Seattle), 7, 21
Garrett, Avery, 198

Gasperetti, Fine, 12
Gasperetti's Restaurant (Union Gap), 12–13
Gazetta Italiano, La, 22
General Administration, Department of, 101, 103, 182–83
General Electric, 157
Georgetown Hospital (Seattle), 68
Geraghty, Patrick A., 16
Gibson, Harold, 143, 144
Giles, Frederick T., 137
Gillespie, John, 53
Giovan, Peter, 101, 110
Gissberg, William, 25, 87, 221
"Godfather" movies, 225
Goldendale Bridge, 159
Goldwater, Barry, 209
Goodloe, William, 54, 55, 119–20, 146, 147, 148, 187, 193, 194
Gorton, Slade, 7, 172, 207, 215, 225, 226
Governor's Advisory Commission on Alcohol (1933), 20
Graham, Luke, 221
Grand Coulee Dam, 28
Grandi, Louie, 14
Grand Mound Training School for Girls, 39, 42
Grange, Washington State, 26, 31, 58, 98
Grant County Journal, 193
Grays Harbor County, 28
Green, Paul, 24
Green Hill School (Chehalis), 42, 83, 104, 125, 126
Gregoire, Christine, 228
Grieve, Bob, 87
Guthman, Ed, 181, 182, 183, 185
Guzzo, Lou, 225, 226

Hagan, Jerry, 101
Hall, Tom, 42

Hallauer, Wilbur "Web," 25
Hanford, 157
Hannula, Don, 230
Hansen, Julia Butler, 25, 112, 155, 165, 166, 171, 227
Happy Valley Grange Hall, 170
Harborview Hospital (Seattle), 31, 68–69
Harriman, Averill, 140, 228
Harris, Thomas A., 84, 85, 86, 87
Harrison Memorial Hospital (Bremerton), 131
Hawaii, 145, 225
Hayner, Norman S., 79, 81, 83
Henderson, Leon, 62
Henry, Edward, 104, 142
Heyns, Garrett, 103, 116, 120–22, 125–28, 130–31, 213, 214
Highway 18, 159
Highway Commission, State, 227
Highways, Department of, 101, 163, 166, 167
Hill, Matthew D., 105
Hockett, Dr. A. J., 68–69
Hodde, Charles W., 37–38, 50; candidate for governor, 58, 59, 61, 62, 65; advisor to ADR, 99–101, 104, 108, 110; and Department of General Administration, 103, 182–83
Hoeck, Gerald A., 7, 8
Hoff, Irv, 143
Hoff, Neil, 77, 78, 79, 81, 82, 121
Hong Kong, 150
Hood Canal Bridge, 159, 185–86, 187, 191, 229
Hoover, Herbert, 14
Houghton, WA, 174
Humphrey, Hubert, 62, 213
Hunt, Les, 27
Hunts Point, WA, 174
Hurley, Maggie, 197

Idaho, 179
India, 150
Indonesia, 150
Industrial Development Council of Seattle and King County, 141
Industrial Workers of the World, 6
Initiative 198 (right-to-work), 91, 93, 96, 98
Institutions, Department of: under Langlie, 76–86; riots, 77, 80, 120–21; director of, 102–3; under ADR, 115–31; discretionary fund, 115, 126, 127, 128; federal grants, 117; civil service for employees, 118–24; mental health division, 127–30; under Evans, 213–14, 219, 221–22
Insurance Commissioner, State, 47
Intalco Aluminum, 144
Internal Revenue Service, U.S., 103
Interstate Expositions, Bureau of, 148, 150
Issaquah, WA, 174
Italians, 4–8, 27, 30, 231

Jackson, Henry M., 7, 59, 143, 148, 190, 208, 211, 226
James, Frank, 87
Japan, 144, 145, 150, 230
John Birch Society, 210
Johns, C. J., 113, 207
Johnson, Lyndon B., 189, 190, 209, 211, 212–13
Johnson, Montgomery, 214
Jones, Elton P., 16
Jones, Gorilla, 14
Jones, R. DeWitt, 51
Joy Manufacturing, 144
Judge, Tom, 48
Juvenile facilities: King County, 34, 35; legislative subcommittee on, 35–37
Juvenile justice system, 34–36

Juvenile protection bill (1949), 37–38, 40, 76. *See also* Youth Protection Act

Kadish, Maurice, 16
Kahin, George, 48
Keefe, James, 41
Kefauver, Estes, 48, 50, 57
Kennedy, John F., 7, 65, 189, 190, 194, 209
Kennedy, Robert, 212, 217
Kennewick, WA, 50, 56
Kerr, James, 52
King County, 141, 163, 170–71, 172, 174; commissioners, 17, 20, 167, 169, 171, 173, 214, 215–16; sheriff, 17; prosecuting attorney, 17, 215; liquor regulations, 18; Democratic party, 23, 60, 217; juvenile facilities, 34, 35; Republican party, 120; planning commission, 163; planning director, 172; home-rule charter movement, 214; executive, 214–18; courthouse, 215; reform, 215–16
King County Beer and Wine Vendors Association, 18
King County Hospital Board, 68, 71
King County Metro, 99
KING-TV, 49, 52, 55, 104, 225
Kink, Dick, 196, 197
Kinnear, George, 92
Kirkland, WA, 174
Kitsap County, 36
Kittitas Valley, 99
Klickitat, WA, 36
Knoblauch , Reuben, 39, 202
Korea, 144
Korean War, 132
Kreager, H. DeWayne, 67, 102, 143–45, 149, 151–52, 152–57
Kuen, Harold J., 16

Labor and Industries, Department of, 101
Labor Council, State, 100, 123. *See also* Davis, Joe
Lacey V. Murrow Bridge, 161–62, 164, 165, 168, 169, 171
Lakeland Village, 130, 131
Lake Washington, 159–74 *passim*, 186
Lake Washington Good Roads Association, 164
Lake Washington Planning Association, 165
Langlie, Arthur B., 33, 98, 99, 100, 106, 119, 120, 141, 143, 146, 175, 184, 185, 187, 205, 207; 1940–44 term, 28, 30, 31, 32; 1948–52 term, 37, 38, 39, 42, 44–46, 47, 48; and institutions, 45, 76–86, 102, 115, 202; 1952 campaign, 59, 61–65; 1952–56 term, 74–75; and Evergreen Point site, 163–64
Laos, 150
Larsen, Dick, 223
Las Vegas, NV, 50, 213
Lawrence, Joseph, 120
Lawrence, Wilbur, Jr., 16
League of Women Voters, 69, 87, 214, 216
Legislative council, 38, 46, 47; investigations, 39, 43, 48–57, 77, 78, 79, 80–82, 199–200, 202, 203–5; funding, 39, 49–50, 200–201, 202, 203
Lehman, Herbert, 62
Lelli, Sarafin, 17, 67
Lewis County, 198
Licenses, Department of, 101
Lindsay, Roderick, 41, 44, 88, 93, 143
Liquor: Italian attitudes toward, 8; ADR legal representation, 17–18, 20–21, 52, 53, 54, 66, 67, 68, 69–70; investigations, 71–72, 73, 202, 203–5;

political connections, 94, 155–56, 193, 207; and Langlie, 184. *See also* Bottle clubs; Liquor Control Board; Prohibition; Sunday closing case
Liquor Control Board, 20, 71–72, 101, 187, 203, 220
Litchman, Mark, 198
"Literary Racket" case, 16
Little, Stanley M., 137
"Little Hoover" committee, 43, 46, 47, 48, 61, 82, 118; report, 47
"Little Kefauver" committee, 51. *See also* Crime committee
Loney, Milton R., 56
Long, Harold B., 53
Long, Huey, 120
Long, William G., 34, 76
Los Angeles, CA, 145
Luther Burbank School (Mercer Island), 126, 127
Lynch, John S., Jr., 16

McCarthy, Eugene, 212, 217
McCarthy, Joseph, 50, 51. *See also* McCarthyism
McCarthyism, 63–64, 88, 139
McDermott, James, 219, 222
McKay, Clarence, 51
McLaughlin, Frank, 26
McLean, Dean, 170, 171
McNeil, John, 16
McNeil Island Penitentiary, 14
McVay, Alfred, 143
Mafia, 6, 225–26
Magnuson, Don, 88
Magnuson, Warren G., 7, 59, 100, 102, 105, 143, 190–91, 207, 209; King County prosecutor, 23; 1956 campaign, 88–89, 93, 96; support for Seattle World's Fair, 148, 149, 150
Malaya, 150

Maple Lane School for Girls (Centralia), 125, 126
Maple Leaf Club, 24
Marconi Wine, Spirits and Grocery Store (Tacoma), 12
Martha Washington School (Seattle), 126, 127
Martin, Clarence, 25, 28
Martin, Harry J., 34
Martin, Tom, 58, 62, 203
Maxwell, Earl, 25, 26, 28
Mayberry, Charles, 74
Medina, WA, 174
Memorial Stadium (Seattle), 147
Menninger, Karl, 85
Mental hospitals. *See* Eastern State Hospital; Institutions, Department of; Northern State Hospital; Western State Hospital
Mercer Island, WA, 162, 164, 171
Mexico, 14
Meyers, Victor, 23, 38, 69
Michigan Department of Corrections, Probation and Parole, 103
Miller, Floyd, 171
Miller, W. N., 24
Mitchell, Hugh, 58, 59, 60, 74, 189; 1952 primary, 62–65, 88
Monroe Reformatory, 38, 39; 1953 riots, 77–79, 115; superintendent, 116, 120
Montesano *Gazette*, 201
Moore, Milo, 101
Motor Vehicles, Department of, 211
Mountaineers Club, 165
Munro, Ed, 86, 104, 110, 169, 172, 215, 216
Murphy, Tiger Jim, 23, 24
Murray, Patty, 228
Murrow, Lacey V., 102, 162
Mussolini, Benito, 30

National Security Resources Board, 102

Natural Resources, Department of, 117
Neill, Marshall, 110
Nelson, Lloyd, 101, 103, 182
Nelson, Stub, 38, 41, 49
Nepal, 150
Ness, Henry, 81–82, 83
New Deal, 23, 24, 25, 41, 64, 190, 232
New York *Times*, 18, 107
New Zealand, 150
Nicolai, Max, 142
Nixon, Richard M., 193, 213
Norselander Hall (Seattle), 89
North Bend, WA, 159
North Borneo, 150
North Cascades Highway, 159
Northern Life Tower (Seattle), 16
Northern State Hospital, 128, 129, 222
Nuclear Development, Office of, 211

O'Brien, John L., 24, 35, 105, 110, 155, 196–99
O'Brien, Johnny, 216
O'Connell, John, 147, 203, 205, 208, 213
Odegaard, Charles, 133, 134, 136–37, 138–39, 229
Odell, Howie, 169, 172
Olmstead, Roy, 18
Olson, Ray, 146, 147, 148, 169
Olympia, WA, 12, 96, 159, 184
Olympia-Aberdeen freeway, 159
Olympian, 221, 222, 226
Olympia *News*, 113
Olympic Hotel (Seattle), 184, 188
Omak, WA, 56
Oregon, 179
Oregon Portland Cement, 144
Ott, Richard, 75
Our Lady of Mt. Virgin Church, 17
Owen, Henry B., 143
Owen, Mrs. Henry B., 137
Owens-Corning Fiberglass, 144

Pacific County, 28
Pacific Rim economies, 144, 150, 151
Pagni, Annunziata, 11
Pagni, Pietro, 11
Pakistan, 150
Parent-Teachers Association (PTA), State, 72, 76
Parks and recreation, 101
Parole Board. *See* Prison Terms and Parole, Board of
Pasco, WA, 50, 56
Payne, Ancil, 63
Pearson, Francis, 86, 87, 104
Pebbles, Harold A., 16
Pellegrini, Angelo, 7, 12, 100
Penberthy Instrument, 144
Penitentiary, Washington State (Walla Walla): under Langlie, 76, 78, 79, 80, 81–82, 83, 84; legislative council hearings, 80–82; riots (1953), 79–80, 115–16; reforms, 117–18
Pennock, William J., 40, 41
Perry, Robert, 196, 202, 203, 204, 205
Personnel Board, State, 100, 120
Phi Alpha Delta, 15
Philippines, 150
Pierce County, 12
Pike Place Market, 17
Pilotage Commission Bill, 15
Planning Council, State, 102, 141
Pomeroy, Alan, 54, 58, 147
Port Angeles, WA, 50, 87
Port of Seattle, 141, 145
Port Townsend, WA, 126
Prescott, George, 145
Prison Terms and Parole, Board of, 79, 81, 82, 83, 122
Pritchard, Joel, 187, 207
Probation and Parole, National Association of, 34, 103, 122
Progress Commission, State, 102, 141

Progressive Citizens of America, 62
Prohibition, 6, 8, 13, 14, 18, 19, 54; repeal, 66, 67–68
Property assessment, 179
Public Service Commission, 104
Public Utility Districts (PUDs), 26, 30, 196, 197, 198
Public vs. private power, 26, 28, 30, 31, 196–99
Puget Sound, 161, 185–86, 229
Puget Sound Industrial Development Council, 141, 142
Puget Sound Power and Light, 26, 196
Purchasing Department, State, 181–83, 211
Puyallup, WA, 41

"Question Before the House," 87

Rabbitt, Thomas C., 40, 41
Rainier Club (Seattle), 67
Rainier *Reporter*, 37
Rainier School (Buckley), 39, 42, 76, 130, 131
Ralls, Charles, 58, 62, 64
Ramm, Mrs. Aubrey, 69–70, 71, 72
Ray, Dixy Lee, 227, 230
Redmond, WA, 174
Red Wing Dinner Resort, 17
Reed, William G., 143
Renton, WA, 174, 192, 218
Renton *Town Talk*, 192
"Republicans for Rosellini," 93
Rhay, B. J., 116
Richland, WA, 50
"Right-to-work" initiative, 91, 93, 96, 98
Riley, Ed, 41
Ritzville, WA, 102
Rivers, Jack, 60
Roberts, Eddie, 13–14
Roberts, Weter and Shefelman, 15
Rochester, Al, 146

Rogers, Jack, 40, 41, 44
Roma Cafe, 12
Roosevelt, Eleanor, 62
Roosevelt, Franklin D., 24, 28, 60, 206
Roosevelt, Franklin D., Jr., 206
Rose, Robert E., 157
Rose Bowl, 90
Rosellini, Albert Dean:
—early life and education, 8–15
—legal career, 15–17, 23–24, 225; and liquor interests, 17–18, 20, 66, 67, 69, 71, 72; political law practice, 66, 71, 72; as assistant attorney general, 70–71
—legislator: campaigns, 23, 24; tax issues, 29, 44, 45, 46, 91; juvenile issues, 34, 35, 37, 38, 40, 77; institutions, 39, 77, 78, 82, 85, 93; participation in hearings, 48–57, 71–72, 73, 78, 81
—1952 campaign, 58–65, 175
—governor, 1956–60: decision to run, 74–75; campaign, 86–94; advisors, 99, 100; appointments, 99, 101, 102–3; inauguration, 104–6; budget reorganization, 108–14; institutions, 115–31; higher education, 132–39; economic development, 140–58; bridges, 159–73; taxes, 175–81
—governor, 1960–64; campaign, 188–94; legislative coalitions, 196–205
—1964 campaign, 207–11
—1969 campaign, 214, 216–18
—1972 campaign, 218–26
—status in Democratic party: vis-à-vis liberals, 64–65, 217–18; vis-à-vis Kennedy-Stevenson, 189–90; discussed, 231–32
—allegations of corruption, 8–9, 52–53, 54, 69–70, 72–73, 93–95, 181–85,

187, 188, 191, 193, 195, 199–200, 201–5, 207–8, 209, 210–11, 217, 225–26
—combative personal style, 62, 72, 78, 93, 182–83, 184–85, 192, 200, 201, 210, 224
—Italian heritage, 7–8, 11, 22, 30, 64, 66–67, 95, 225–26
—public service, 30, 68–69, 227–28
Rosellini, Albert Dean, Jr., 25, 105
Rosellini, Annunziata, 11, 14, 105
Rosellini, Argie, 11
Rosellini, Cecceo, 12
Rosellini, Erma, 13
Rosellini, Ethel, 16–17, 25, 105, 106–7, 190
Rosellini, Giovanni, 10–15 *passim*, 59, 64, 90, 105, 211
Rosellini, Hugh, 7, 12, 15, 16, 75, 87, 99, 100
Rosellini, Ida, 11, 211
Rosellini, Janey Katherine (Campbell), 25, 105
Rosellini, John Michael, 25, 105
Rosellini, Leo, 7, 12, 13, 31, 87, 99, 100
Rosellini, Lynn Christine, 25, 105
Rosellini, Primo, 12, 14
Rosellini, Rena, 11, 14, 15
Rosellini, Sue Ann (Stiller), 25, 105
Rosellini, Victor, 7, 12, 13, 87, 99, 100
Rosellini, Vittorio, 12, 13
Rosellini "rose," 90
Rossellini, Roberto, 90
Roup, Howard, 41

Sacco and Vanzetti trial, 6
Saint Leo's Catholic Church, 11
Salter, John, 143
Sand, Ed, 172
Sandritter, G. Lee, 101
San Francisco, CA, 14, 16, 17, 18, 145, 150, 151, 173

Sapp, Jess, 87
Sarawak, 150
Sawyer, Len, 196
Scandinavian immigrants, 5
Scarengi, Carlos, 24, 26
Schmitz, Henry, 133
Schram, Lloyd, 99
Schroeder, Ted, 41, 74
Schulman, Bob, 104
Schulman, Lee, 49, 52, 55, 104
Schumacher, William, 103
Scott, George, 76, 83
Scudder, Kenyon J., 38
Seattle, WA, 12, 16, 18, 19, 28, 35, 41, 49, 50, 54, 87, 96, 130, 141, 144, 149, 150, 161–71, 188, 193, 206; 33rd legislative district, 22, 24, 35
Seattle *Argus*, 7, 19, 148, 184, 185, 201, 204, 206, 223, 231
Seattle Chamber of Commerce, 141, 165
Seattle City Council, 146, 165
Seattle Coliseum, 149
Seattle Garden Club, 165
Seattle Historical Society, 165
Seattle Municipal League, 71, 164, 165, 214, 216
Seattle Planning Commission, 163
Seattle *Post-Intelligencer* (*PI*), 14, 23, 30, 37, 38, 41, 49, 52, 53, 58, 61, 63, 69, 72, 183–84, 204, 215, 225
Seattle School Board, 137
Seattle *Star*, 24, 27
Seattle Tennis Club, 67
Seattle *Times*, 7, 8, 16, 41, 45, 47, 55, 61, 63, 66, 89, 91, 94–95, 102, 103, 109, 118, 123, 124, 162, 167–68, 173, 181–87, 193, 201, 204, 220, 223, 224, 230, 231; antagonism toward ADR, 65; investigations, 181–85; support of

Evans, 210–11. *See also* Cunningham, Ross; Guthman, Ed
Seattle World's Fair, 98, 106, 146–49, 151, 195, 206, 230. *See also* World's Fair Commission
Seattle Yacht Club, 17
Seidel, Henry, 170, 171, 172
Selah Hospital, 130
Shefelman, Harold, 15, 46, 47, 61, 99, 100, 113, 147, 173, 176. *See also* "Little Hoover" committee
Shelton, WA, 117
Shermer, Jack, 23
Shipman, George, 110
Shorett, Lloyd, 23, 35, 67, 70
Shrag, Clarence, 84
Sick's Rainier Brewing, 144
Sideboard Tavern (Seattle), 14
Singapore, 144, 150
Skamania County, 42
Smith, Albert, 14
Smith, Dwight, 77
Snoqualmie, WA, 127
Snoqualmie Pass, 161
Snoqualmie Valley, 170
Social and Health Services, Department of (DSHS), 213–14, 219, 221
Social Security, 29, 30, 134
Sons of Italy, 24
Soviet Union, 132
Spellman, John, 215–19 *passim*, 227, 230
Spokane, WA, 36, 41, 50, 57, 87, 130, 187, 188, 193, 206
Spokane *Chronicle*, 80
"Sputnik," 132, 135
Squire, Paul, 77, 78, 79
State Employees, Washington Federation of, 122, 123
Steele, Freddie, 14
Steele Act, 19
Stevenson, Adlai, 63, 74, 189

Strauss, Alfred, 31
Street, William, 146
Sumner, WA, 39
Sunday-closing case, 17–18, 19–21, 66, 67
Superintendent of Public Instruction, State, 47, 137, 187
Superior Court Judges Association, 36
Supreme Court, State, 12, 54, 113, 172, 173, 174
Supreme Court, U.S., 27
Sweden, 183

Tacoma, WA, 11, 12, 13, 14, 50, 51, 52, 53, 126, 137, 161
Tacoma *News Tribune*, 16, 51
Taft, Robert, 89
Taft-Hartley Labor Relations Act, 98
Tau Kappa Epsilon fraternity, 10
Tavern Owners' Association, 17, 59, 67, 68
Tax Commission, State, 101, 103, 184–85
Taylor, Jack, 31, 47, 74
Taylor, Louise S., 101
Temperance Association, Washington State, 71
Tennant, Mel, 170
Thailand, 150
Thiery, Paul, 149
Thirty-third District Democratic Club, 24, 27
Thompson, Al, 203, 205
Thurston County, 53, 113
Timpani, Ernest, 116, 120
Tisch, Marie, 87, 90
Toll Bridge Authority (TBA), 163–67 *passim*, 169, 172, 173, 174, 185, 186, 187
Transportation, Department of, 112, 164
Transportation Commission, State, 174, 227

Troy, Smith, 29, 70
Truman, Harry S., 32, 37, 48, 62, 63, 64, 88, 102
Turnbold, Will, 103
Tuscano Restaurant (Tacoma), 12
Tyee Construction Co., 196

Un-American Activities Committee, U.S. House, 40, 50. *See also* McCarthyism
Unified Budget and Accounting Act, 108
Union Gap, WA, 12–13
United Airlines, 146
United Kingdom, 150
United Mine Workers, 6
United Nations, 188
U.S. Bureau of the Budget, 149
U.S. Olympic Committee, 227–28
U.S. State Department, 150
University of Puget Sound (Tacoma), 12
University of Washington, 10, 15, 99, 132–33, 229; Dental School, 31, 33, 34, 91, 228; Medical School, 31, 33, 34, 60, 91, 131, 228; and Canwell Committee, 63–64; School of Social Work, 85; 1960 Rose Bowl, 90; Asian Law Program, 138; Middle East Institute, 138; School of Governmental Affairs, 138; *Daily*, 210–11. *See also* Odegaard, Charles
"Untouchables, The," 211

Vancouver, WA, 49–53 *passim*, 179
Vancouver *Sun*, 49
Vander Ende, Gerrit, 143
Vanderzicht, John, 101, 104
VanEaton, Harold, 38, 76, 77, 79, 81, 82–83
Vashon Island, WA, 185
Veterans of Foreign Wars, 58
Vietnam, 150, 212, 213, 219

Volpe, Paul A., 143
Volpentest, Sam, 143
Volstead Act, 18, 19
Voorhees, Melvin, 206, 231

Wallace, Henry, 62
Wallace, Scott, 170, 171, 172, 173, 214–16, 217, 221
Walla Walla, WA. *See* Penitentiary, Washington State
Walla Walla County, 56
Wallgren, Mon C., 12, 32, 33, 34, 71, 72, 76, 105
Washington, D.C., 150
Washington Monument, 150
Washington Pension Union, 40
Washington State Committee on State Finance, 47. *See also* "Little Hoover" committee
Washington State Patrol, 101
Washington State University, 132, 134, 137
Washington Trade and Convention Center, 227
Washington Water Power, 196
Watson, Emmett, 146
Welch, Doug, 23
Western Governors' Conference, 177
Western International Hotels, 146
Western Interstate Commission for Higher Education, 85
Western State Hospital (Steilacoom), 128, 129
Weston, Ed, 155
White Center *News*, 192
Wilkie, Wendell, 28
Williams, Miles, 16
Williams, G. Mennen "Soapy," 103
Williams, Walter L., 187–88
Wilson, James B., 62
Wilson, Woodrow, 14
Winthrop, WA, 93

Women's Clubs, State Federation of, 76
Wood, David G., 105, 217, 218
Woodall, Perry, 224
Woods, Wilfred R., 144
Works Progress Administration (WPA), 162
World's Fair Commission, 149, 151–52, 157
World War I, 13
World War II, 29–35 *passim*, 97, 132, 141
Wright, Charles T., 53

Wright, Willard J., 94, 193

Yakima, WA, 50
Yakima *Herald*, 40, 41
Yakima Valley School, 130
Yarrow Point, WA, 174
Yelle, Cliff, 113, 171–72, 173
Young Men's Democratic Club, 22
Youth Protection Act, 37, 41, 42, 43, 60, 77, 91

Zatkovich, Tony, 52
Zent, Harry, 36